laughing
FEMINISM

Humor in Life and Letters Series

A complete listing of the books in this series can be found at the back of this volume.

laughing FEMINISM

Subversive Comedy in Frances Burney, Maria Edgeworth, and Jane Austen

AUDREY BILGER

 Wayne State University Press   Detroit

06 05 04 03 02   5 4 3 2

Library of Congress Cataloging-in-Publication Data

Bilger, Audrey, 1960–
   Laughing feminism : subversive comedy in Frances Burney, Maria
Edgeworth, and Jane Austen / Audrey Bilger.
      p.   cm. — (Humor in life and letters series)
   Includes bibliographical references and index.
   ISBN 0-8143-2722-2 (alk. paper)
   1. English fiction—18th century—History and criticism.
   2. Feminism and literature—Great Britain—History—18th century.
   3. Feminism and literature—Great Britain—History—19th century.
   4. English fiction—Women authors—History and criticism.
   5. English fiction—19th century—History and criticism.
   6. Humorous stories, English—History and criticism.   7. Women and
literature—Great Britain—History.   8. Burney, Fanny, 1752–1840—
Humor.   9. Edgeworth, Maria, 1767–1849—Humor.   10. Austen, Jane,
1775–1817—Humor.   I. Title.   II. Series: Humor in life and letters.
PR858.F45B55   1998
823′.60917′082—DC21   98-10828

   ISBN 0-8143-3054-1 (pbk. : alk. paper)

Grateful acknowledgment is made for permission to reprint the following
material:

An earlier version of Chapter 5 appeared as "Mocking the Lords of Creation:
Comic Male Characters in Frances Burney, Maria Edgeworth, and Jane
Austen," in Women's Writing: The Elizabethan to Victorian Period 1.1 (1994).

An earlier version of Chapter 7 appeared as "Goblin Laughter: Violent Come-
dy and the Condition of Women in Frances Burney and Jane Austen" in
Women's Studies 24 (1995). © 1995 OPA (Overseas Publishers Association)
Amsterdam B.V. Reprinted by permission of Gordon and Breach Publishers.

Book design by ARCdesign

For Martin

Contents

Preface

> No doubt the desire and the capacity to criticise the other sex
> had its share in deciding women to write novels, for indeed
> that particular vein of comedy has been but slightly
> worked, and promises great richness.
>
> —Virginia Woolf ("Women Novelists" 26–27)

This study focuses on three important early women novelists in order to investigate the intersection of feminism and comedy in the eighteenth century. Frances Burney, Maria Edgeworth, and Jane Austen each found acclaim as a leading novelist of her day, and although they met with vastly different fates in the late nineteenth century and beyond—Burney and Edgeworth being situated far below Austen in literary prominence—all three authors should rightly be viewed as innovators of the genre. As comic novelists, they form a mini-tradition of their own: Burney was a role model for Edgeworth, and Austen consciously benefited from both Burney's and Edgeworth's efforts.[1] Writing comic novels allowed these women to contribute to the ongoing debate about women's proper place in society by criticizing, among other things, eighteenth-century gender politics. As I will show, the critical "vein of comedy" that Virginia Woolf refers to appealed to Burney, Edgeworth, and Austen; and contrary to Woolf's opinion, they worked this vein deeply.

By focusing on gender politics in women's comic writing, I emphasize the radical and subversive ends of comedy. However, it is important to recognize that comedy can also be enlisted for conservative ends, to preserve order and to uphold the status quo, and that even within particular works, rebellious humor can stand alongside conservative tendencies. Radicalism is not inherent in comic expression, but comedy can serve as an excellent vehicle for making radical ideas palatable to an audience that might otherwise be offended by them. As Frances Gray puts it, "Laughter, like nuclear energy, has no opinions, positive or negative, about the *status quo*. What it does have, like nuclear energy, is power, to which we can relate in a number of ways" (33). My aim throughout is to bring to light the ways in which Burney, Edgeworth, and Austen enlisted the power of comedy in the service of feminism and in so doing participated in one of the most important ideological movements of the last three hundred years.

Even though the term "feminism" did not exist when these women were writing, the guiding principles of modern feminism did, as studies such as Alice Browne's *The Eighteenth-Century Feminist Mind* and Katharine Rogers's *Feminism in Eighteenth-Century England* have shown.[2] In examining Austen's feminism, Gary Kelly makes the important point that "feminism is always socially and historically particular, advancing the rights and claims of women within specific historical, social, and cultural conditions" (19).[3]

What I identify as Enlightenment feminist humor is based upon the eighteenth-century feminist tenet that women are rational creatures who should be treated as such. As a characteristic gesture, Enlightenment feminists subject prejudices against women to rational scrutiny in order to expose the absurdity and encourage readers to laugh at the folly of sexist views.

Recent theories of feminist humor emphasize how humor can serve both as a psychological survival skill and an emancipatory strategy for women in a sexist society. Regina Barreca sees women's laughter as essentially feminist: "anytime a woman breaks through a barrier set by society, she's making a feminist gesture of a sort, and every time a woman laughs, she's breaking through a barrier" (*Snow White* 182). Gloria Kaufman argues that the "persistent attitude that underlies feminist humor is the attitude of social revolution—that is, we are ridiculing a social system that can be, that must be changed" (*Pulling* 13). Some feminist critics have suggested that women's humor may provide a foundation for women's political solidarity. Alice Sheppard, for instance, urges social psychologists to explore women's comic writing at a given historical time in order to reconstruct a "lost perspective" on feminist resistance, in which "[h]umor, an instrument of social correction and subversion, reinforced women's shared perceptions, strengthened social bonds, and itself facilitated social change" (167). Feminist humor demands that its audience share an awareness of women's oppression and a desire to reform an unjust system.

I provide a context for understanding feminist comedy in the novels of Burney, Edgeworth, and Austen by drawing on current feminist criticism, comic theory, and the methodologies of literary history. To do justice to the historical specificity of this comedy I refer to a number of eighteenth-century sources, including feminist polemics, conduct literature, letters, and diaries. Throughout this study, I use the term "comedy" to designate a mode of writing, speech, or behavior that plays with cultural conventions either to affirm them or reveal their inadequacies. Feminist comedy, to be sure, tends toward the latter, even if it recognizes particular conventions as laudable. I will also use, from time to time, terms conventional to eighteenth-century writers in their discussions of comedy and laughter.[4] Each of the writers makes use of a full arsenal of comic weapons—satire, burlesque, parody, among others—to combat patriarchal nonsense. Although these authors seldom offer direct feminist polemics, they make comedy out of the discrepancies between the myths surrounding "woman" and the lives of real women.

The last two decades have witnessed a lively debate over the degree to which the "mothers of the novel" participated in eighteenth-century feminist discourse, particularly in the cases of Burney, Edgeworth, and Austen, whose writing careers did not damage their standing as "proper" middle-class ladies. Important recent studies have furthered our understanding of the complex ideological tensions in the works of these three authors.[5] *Laughing Feminism* will add to the ongoing discussion by recuperating Burney's and Edgeworth's reputations for comedy, reconfirming Austen's, and showing that all three enlisted humor in the service of feminism. At a time when overt feminist statements could ruin a woman's reputation, comedy furnished them with a means for smuggling feminism into their novels.

Acknowledgments

As is appropriate for a study of comedy, this book has benefited from the assistance of many generous and witty souls. I wish to thank Patricia Meyer Spacks and Susan Fraiman for their critical support of the book in its earliest stages. I am grateful as well to the University of Virginia Women's Center and to Sharon Davies and Ann Lane for teaching me a great deal about feminist solidarity.

During my stay at Oberlin College, I was able to share drafts with the illustrious Flaming Bitches (Ann Cooper Albright, Sibelan Forrester, Wendy Hesford, and Wendy Kozol) and to share my enthusiasm for eighteenth-century literature with a talented and inspiring group of students. My wits were sharpened at John Sitter's National Endowment for the Humanities summer seminar on eighteenth-century satire at Emory College in 1993 (in the company of a delightful group of fellow scholars), and I am particularly appreciative of his trenchant and helpful comments on the manuscript. I am also indebted to Sarah Blacher Cohen's and Regina Barreca's extensive work on women's comedy and their enthusiasm for this project.

At the Claremont Colleges, the Women Academic Reading group has provided invaluable support and assistance: thanks, Stephanie Bower, Stacey Freeman, Karen Goldman, Cynthia Humes, Claudia Klaver, Yoon Sun Lee, and Lora Wildenthal. Financial support in the final stages of the project came from Claremont McKenna College. Within the literature department at Claremont McKenna, John Farrell and Nicholas Warner provided helpful feedback on the manuscript as a whole, and Robert Faggen offered much encouragement and useful advice. The students in my "Women and Comedy" classes gave me a wonderful sense of a continuing audience for early women's comic writing. And the Claremont College's Intercollegiate Women's Studies program, Sue Mansfield in particular, welcomed me into a supportive community.

Friends have helped me in more ways than I can count. With their festive hospitality, Lisa and John Barclay erased many of the lines between work and pleasure. Eberle Umbach has been an ongoing and magical source of strength. Cee Harrelson and Irene Vasquez showed me how to find a way to laughter out of the blues. Unbounded thanks go to Martin Bilger, whose effort and attention made this book possible. And likewise to Cheryl Pawelski, for everything.

1

Women and Comedy in
Eighteenth-Century England

Make the doors upon a woman's wit, and it will out the
casement; shut that and 'twill out the keyhole; stop that,
'twill fly with the smoke out at the chimney.

—Rosalind in *As You Like It* (IV.i.161–64)

[T]he natural free spirits of ingenious men, if imprisoned and controlled, will find out other ways of motion to relieve themselves in
their constraint; and whether it be in burlesque, mimicry, or buffoonery, they will be glad at any rate to vent themselves,
and be revenged on their constrainers.

—Shaftesbury (50)

WOMEN AND COMEDY WERE CONTROVERSIAL TOPICS in
eighteenth-century England. The debates revolved around
questions of morality and control: Would women's freedom lead
to promiscuous behavior? Would unchecked comedy ridicule improper targets? Although not necessarily linked in the public
imagination, women and comedy were both seen as potentially
disruptive to the social order, and many pens combined to forestall any riotousness. But, as Shakespeare and Shaftesbury suggest
in the epigraphs, wit and humor seek out ways of escaping from
confinement, of breaking down barriers, and of turning the tables
on those who attempt to suppress them. Thus, when we find prohibitions against women's wit and humor cropping up in eighteenth-
century writings, we should pay attention to the boundaries being
put in place and ask whether closed doors, shut casements, and
stopped keyholes were able to contain women's laughing spirits.

In order to understand more fully the rebelliousness inherent in the comic writings of Burney, Edgeworth, and Austen, we need to consider the cultural milieu in which they wrote, in particular those views and values that exerted ideological pressure on women's self-expression. Unless we recognize the efforts that were made to control women's behavior, we are apt to misunderstand the specific forms their comedy takes and thus overlook some of their most trenchant social criticism.

In this chapter, I will first examine eighteenth-century comic theorists' appeal to gender categories in their attempts to make humor more acceptable to middle-class domestic values. Next, I will look at the literature designed to instruct middle-class women on proper femininity, focusing on these conduct-book writers' efforts to suppress women's laughter and humor. I will then consider how shifts in comic taste and domestic ideology affected women novelists, particularly those who disagreed with basic assumptions about gender that comic theorists and conduct-book authors wanted their readers to take for granted.

At the center of eighteenth-century controversies over comedy were anxieties about the nature of laughter and of women. Laughter's impolite qualities set it at odds with the norms of eighteenth-century manners. Furthermore, its capacity for breaking down hierarchies tended to have an irritating effect on members of the dominant classes.[1] Once laughter constituted an identifiable threat to the social order, female laughter came to be seen as a menace to society's very foundations.

Laughter's dubious reputation in the early eighteenth century may be traced back to Thomas Hobbes's definition of laughter as a "sudden glory" at the sight of another's inferiority. Like so much in his thought, this definition disturbed many eighteenth-century writers, and it added a sense of urgency to comic theory of the period, which literary critic Ronald Paulson describes as "the history of one attempt after another to refute Hobbes" (18). A notable champion of laughter, Shaftesbury, countered the Hobbesian view when he argued that shared laughter was evidence of a social impulse in mankind. However, even he recognized its possible hazards and recommended that the enjoyment of laughter be tempered, encouraging gentlemen to laugh within their own groups and to refrain from laughing at others.[2]

Essayist Joseph Addison, in an attempt to purge the comic spirit of its negative tendencies, found it necessary to mark off two categories—"humour" and "false humour"—in order to deposit all dangerous expression, such as raucous laughter, into the second category. Addison's *Spectator* essay on this topic (No. 35) sheds light not only on eighteenth-century ambivalence toward comedy but also on the century's view of women and its reliance on femininity as a necessary component of middle-class stability. In order to describe the opposition between true and false humor, Addison personifies both qualities and delineates their separate genealogies in an extended allegory. He uses women in his allegory as moral indicators, on the one hand condemning false humor with figures of disorderly femininity, and on the other hand expressing approbation of true humor by qualifying its patriarchal lineage with one chaste female figure.

"False Humour" is an "impostor," a "counterfeit," the illegitimate descendant of an unruly matriarch: "The Impostor of whom I am speaking, descends Originally from FALSEHOOD, who was the Mother of NONSENSE, who was brought to Bed of a Son called FRENZY, who Married one of the Daughters of FOLLY, commonly known by the Name of LAUGHTER, on whom he begot that Monstrous Infant of which I have been here speaking." Sexuality and individual women figure prominently in this genealogy: "Falsehood," "Nonsense," and "Laughter" are all females, as, by implication, is "Folly." The sole figure clearly identified as male, "Frenzy," represents a state of being rather than a concept and serves only as a stimulus to the propagation of rampant female traits. We can imagine, for example, the union of False Humour's parents as one of "frenzied laughter." Furthermore, we are told, False Humour displays his mother's stamp with his "loud and excessive Laughter."

In contrast to False Humour's matriarchal lineage, Humour's lineage is almost entirely of father figures. He is a felicitous blending of mostly masculine traits with one lighter, feminine quality:

> TRUTH was the Founder of the Family, and the
> Father of GOOD SENSE. GOOD SENSE was the Father

of WIT, who married a Lady of a Collateral Line
called MIRTH, by whom he had Issue HUMOUR.
HUMOUR therefore being the youngest of this
Illustrious Family, and descended from Parents of
such different Dispositions, is very various and
unequal in his Temper; sometimes you see him
putting on grave Looks and a solemn Habit,
sometimes airy in his Behaviour, and fantastick
in his Dress: Insomuch that at different times he
appears as serious as a Judge, and as jocular as a
Merry-Andrew. But as he has a great deal of the
Mother in his Constitution, whatever Mood he
is in, he never fails to make his Company laugh.

Although Addison emphasizes Humour's complementary gender
traits and assigns his particular talent for sociability to the mother's
influence, he nevertheless envisions the more substantial roles as
male. Masculine "Truth," "Good Sense," and "Wit" exercise a high
degree of control over the creation of Humour. It is even unclear
whether "Mirth" refers to the "Lady" or to the line she descends
from; her significance may not be personal. Whereas the genealogy of False Humour emphasizes the sexuality of individual women,
as suggested by the phrases "brought to Bed" and "on whom he
begot," the genealogy of Humour emphasizes the propriety of father and son relations; the "Lady" is merely the vehicle "by whom
[Wit] had Issue."

In the gender politics of Addison's comic theory, False
Humour is largely the offspring of powerful, uncontrollable women
and (true) Humour but partly the offspring of a gentle, subordinate woman. "Feminine" attributes merely serve to qualify true
(masculine) humor, tempering violence with a solicitude for others that precludes hostile laughter. In the story, Humour makes
people laugh unself-consciously instead of laughing at another's
expense, as False Humour does. Addison underscores his strict
hierarchy of gender traits by denying reciprocal relations between
male and female roles. Whereas his allegory reveals how a gentleman's character may benefit from a touch of femininity, Addison
gives no indication that women would gain from acquiring mas-

culine qualities. In fact, by constructing his virtuous family in opposition to one in which females are aggressive and sexually active, he places the blame for false humor on women's appropriation of a "masculine" mode of behavior. His ideal humorist is a
sensitive man, not a woman.

Addison's use of the family romance to valorize a domestic
brand of humor is evidence of an important eighteenth-century
phenomenon that critic Terry Eagleton has termed the "feminization of discourse." According to Eagleton, this "feminization"
served as a crucial strategy for evading actual class and gender
conflicts: "The 'feminization of discourse' witnessed by the eighteenth century was not a sexual revolution. It was imperative to
mollify ruling-class barbarism with the milk of middle-class kindness, but not, naturally, to the point where virility itself came
under threat. Male hegemony was to be sweetened but not undermined; women were to be exalted but not emancipated" (95).
In part as a result of the efforts of authors such as Joseph Addison
and, later, novelist Samuel Richardson, cultural authority shifted
in the course of the eighteenth century from the aristocracy to
the middle classes, which recognized a different set of values and
required a different sort of comedy. By the end of the century,
what literary historian Stuart Tave has called "amiable humor"
emerged as the fashionable and critically favored mode of comedy. Carrying the burden of the new agenda was the then also new
domestic woman, a granddaughter of Addison's "Lady," and from
her comedy took its increasingly gentle, nondisruptive traits.[3]

Feminist scholar Janet Todd has argued that there was a
great deal of ambivalence during the last third of the eighteenth
century about the feminization of discourse: "To many in Britain
the cult of sensibility seemed to have feminized the nation, given
women undue prominence, and emasculated men" (*Sensibility*
133). But even though the domestic brand of comedy had its opponents, its cultural influence was indisputable. In 1773, when
playwright and novelist Oliver Goldsmith perceived a battle raging between "laughing" and "sentimental" comedy, he saw his favorite losing.

Sentimental comedy, which Goldsmith abhorred, is a descendant of Addison's Humour: "a new species of Dramatic

Composition . . . in which the virtues of Private Life are exhibited, rather than the Vices exposed; and the Distresses rather than
the Faults of Mankind, make our interest in the piece" (188).[4]
Although Goldsmith does not discuss comedy in terms of "masculine" or "feminine" features as does Addison, by the end of the
century those distinctions were generally understood: "virtues of
private life," "sentiment," and "feeling" were all perceived as "feminine" traits. Worrying that sentimental comedy would have a so-
porific effect on the public, Goldsmith argued in favor of a critical comedy, one that would "excite our laughter by ridiculously
exhibiting . . . Follies" (187). He directed his attack as much
against the prevailing taste as at specific works, urging audiences
to save laughter before it was too late.

Goldsmith might not have been correct in his stated views
on the condition of the theater,[5] but he appears to have been accurate in his suggestion that people's ability to appreciate critical
forms of comedy had been hindered by the emphasis on a sentimental domesticity. In the shift in the national taste in comedy,
Shakespeare replaced the less assimilable Ben Jonson as the representative English playwright, Falstaff was reinterpreted as an
amiable figure, and Don Quixote came to be seen as a starry-eyed
dreamer whose delusions deserved sympathy rather than mockery.[6] The prevailing taste for domesticated humor[7] reflected and
helped produce bourgeois social solidarity; as a public entertainment, an indulgent, genial comedy could promote the consolida-
tion of class interests and assuage hostilities.[8] Moreover, as clamor
for political reform began toward the end of the century, the standard targets of "laughing" comedy (lower-class bumpkins and
upper-class hypocrites) became too politically loaded to treat in a
critical manner.

By the Victorian period, "wit" and "humor" were viewed as
manifestations of the head/heart dichotomy, with a preference accorded to the more genial faculty.[9] As one writer put it, Wit "elic-
its only the silent smile of the intellect. . . . I have no great regard
for wit, for I love to laugh with all my heart and none of my head"
(qtd. in Martin 35). According to this commonly held view, intellectual wit yielded only an isolated pleasure, whereas heartfelt
laughter testified to that sympathetic organ which bound to-

gether the human community. Jovial laughter became a prized manifestation of sentiment in the English gentleman.

Domesticated humor contributed to social concord by diffusing the family unit's affectionate atmosphere into the world at large. In 1847, an anonymous reviewer of Leigh Hunt's *Wit and Humour, Selected from the English Poets* could write of humor as a feminized, almost maternal, wit: "Wit, sweetened by a kind, loving expression, becomes Humour" ("Wit and Humour" 25). Hunt himself recalls Addison when he asserts that wit and humor function best in their wedded state, with humor providing the moral influence: "their richest effect is produced by the combination. Wit, apart from Humour, generally speaking, is but an element for professors to sport with. In combination with Humour it runs into the richest utility, and helps to humanize the world" (13).[10] This conception of humor's moral mission drew upon the trope of the new domestic couple, who combined head and heart in a single social unit.[11]

Because the preference for sentimental comedy relied so heavily on images of domestic order and because domestic order required that women be subordinate to men, social fears of noncompliance and disruption made it difficult for a writer to be comic, critical, and female. To quell such fears, numerous conduct books of the period defined proper feminine behavior for middle-class women largely in terms antithetical to the critical spirit of comedy. The conduct writers contributed to what literary theorist Mary Poovey calls the "naturalization of the feminine ideal"; that is, they constructed an ideal of femininity and then redefined female nature in terms of that ideal (15). Unlike earlier views of women as disobedient and seductive daughters of Eve, the late eighteenth-century ideal of the domestic woman wrote resistance out of the female character. Historian Marlene LeGates explains that during the eighteenth century, the "image of the disorderly woman is replaced by the image of the chaste maiden and obedient wife" (23). By the beginning of the nineteenth century, a rebellious female came to be seen as a contradiction in terms.

From the late eighteenth century onward, the expressive possibilities of women were increasingly hampered by culturally mandated ties of affection and solicitude to fathers, brothers, husbands, and other figures of male authority. According to Susan Moller Okin's historical account, the new domestic order soon took on a life of its own that depended upon women's complicity for its survival: "this special sphere of life was held to depend for its health on the total dedication of women. . . . Thus anyone who wished to register objections to the subordinate position of women had now to take considerable care not to be branded as an enemy of that newly hallowed institution—the sentimental family" (88).[12]

The establishment of this institution changed not only the character of relations within the family, but also of potential family members. In terms that illustrate what men expected of women, one of the most popular eighteenth-century conduct writers, James Fordyce, tells his female readers that if they want to get husbands, they must not be witty: "[W]hen I speak on this subject, need I tell you, that men of the best sense have been usually averse to the thought of marrying a witty female? . . . Men who understand the science of domestic happiness, know that its very first principle is ease. . . . But we cannot be easy, where we are not safe. We are never safe in the company of a critic; and almost every wit is a critic by profession" (191). He expresses compassion for the man who weds a witty woman: "He sought a soft friend; he expected to be happy in a reasonable companion. He has found a perpetual satirist; or a self-sufficient prattler" (193). Fordyce's ploy for male protection and his portrait of the disabused husband serve to prevent, through emotional blackmail, the appearance of that enemy of the sentimental family, the critical woman. Another well-known conduct writer, Thomas Gisborne, describes the incompatibility of critical humor and domestic tranquility in similar terms: "If wit be continually exercised in ridicule and satire . . . is it wonderful that the husband should regret that it had been granted to his associate?" (267).

Taken at face value, neither Fordyce's nor Gisborne's remarks seem unreasonable—a constant critic would indeed make an unpleasant companion. When we take into account, however, that middle-class women had few outside forums in which to register their discontent with their place within the domestic sphere, the remarks of the conduct writers can be read as protective of all masculine interests. Insofar as both writers offered a program for female activity that upheld male superiority, their prohibition against domestic satire aimed to forestall any criticism of the entire system. Their depictions of the domestic unhappiness brought about by witty women suggest that all men, not just husbands, are improper targets for humor.

Because the suggestiveness of female laughter threatened the stability of domestic relations, Fordyce recommends that women cultivate a sorrowful demeanor in order to please men: "With the character of a Christian Woman, nothing, methinks, can better correspond than a propensity to melt into affectionate sorrow. . . . The sigh of compassion stealing from a female breast, on the mention of calamity, would be rather more musical in their [men's] ears than the loud bursts of unmeaning laughter, with which they are often entertained" (185). The implied contrast between women who engage a man's sympathy and women who laugh with men has sexual connotations that Fordyce more explicitly formulates in relation to marriage: "there is still all the difference in the world between the entertainer of an evening, and a partner for life" (193–94). Faced with the moral cast of these choices, very few women would deliberately choose to become an evening's entertainment.

Suspicions regarding laughter's sexuality led John Gregory, in his extremely popular conduct book, to advise that young women beware of getting carried away by group laughter: "Sometimes a girl laughs with all the simplicity of unsuspecting innocence, for no other reason but being infected with other people's laughing: she is then believed to know more than she should do" (59). Whether the laughing young woman actually "knows" anything about sex is beside the point; laughter reveals an active understanding that belies innocence.

Such restrictions on female laughter would have made it difficult for an eighteenth-century woman to exercise comic talents in public when, even in private, she was urged to be self-conscious about her wit and humor. With the installation of the nuclear family as a cultural icon, to which female virtue served as handmaiden, female laughter came to represent a threat to the domestic order, an abandonment to pleasure that had revolutionary overtones. Laughter calls attention to itself in an aggressive, forceful manner, and, within the confines of decorum, it suggests an insubordination in proportion to its volume.

According to conduct-book writers such as Gregory, Fordyce, and Gisborne, domestic harmony required that a woman govern her sense of humor and her sexuality. Either feature, if not curbed, could compromise the safety of the domestic realm, one with insurrection, the other with illegitimate offspring. The fear of women's sexual powers was assuaged in the course of the eighteenth century by a reconstruction of femininity as virtually asexual. As feminist literary critic Ruth Perry summarizes, "by the eighteenth century, decent women were no longer expected to enjoy their sexuality" (151). What was once only imagined would become an article of faith: the ideal domestic woman promoted by eighteenth-century conduct literature took her place as an archetypal Victorian institution, the "angel in the house."

The definition of the feminine ideal excised, along with sexuality, a sense of humor from female nature so effectively that by the end of the nineteenth century a common refrain held that women had no sense of humor at all.[13] Thus, a writer for the *Saturday Review* begins his article on "Feminine Humour" (1871) with a received witticism: "The humour of women, it is said, resembles the snakes in Iceland [*sic*]. In other words it does not exist." His confidence on this account would not have been possible in the previous century when writers focused on controlling women's humor and laughter.

The *Saturday Review* writer refers to ideal femininity in order to account for women's alleged humorlessness: "women are too good to be humorists." He claims that women never succeeded as comic writers because "they are too pure and saintlike and enthusiastic to understand masculine cynicism, and they hate to be told that any cause to which they have given their affections has after all a tinge of absurdity." Alluding to the connection between humor and sexuality, he declares women exempt from the bawdy: "our lofty standard of feminine decorum" ensures that "a very large province of the humorous is absolutely interdicted to women."

He also considers women too selfless and dependent to be critical. "They are naturally hero-worshippers," he reports, and their heroes, in his view, are men. His language reveals both imperialistic intentions and anxiety. His insistence on decorum and hero worship, a conditioned mode of behavior and an authoritarian mode of behavior, suggests the complexity and insistence of the antifeminist denial of women's capacity for humor.

Although such rationalizing acknowledged women's power, the overt cultural pressure on women to promote male interests restricted their efforts to improve, or even evaluate, their own situations. Poovey explains how the belief in female influence actually served to disempower women: "as women accepted a definition of 'female nature' that was derived from a social role, they found it increasingly difficult to acknowledge or to integrate into their self-perceptions desires that did not support this stereotype. And, by the same token, they found it increasingly difficult to recognize that the stereotype was prescription, not description, and thus to renounce it" (15). This circle of oppressive ideology bribed women into accepting male domination as the natural order of things. Among other impositions, it curbed their sense of humor. Considering that the potency of female laughter made conduct writers condemn it as unfeminine and that a sense of humor was denied the ideal domestic woman, it follows that if we can catch women laughing, we will hear echoes of a defiance of this rule and of a reclamation of their right to humor.

Even though sentimental, domesticated comedy and its audience did not urge women into the field or take full account of their achievements, the emergence of the novel as the major vehicle for comedy did provide unprecedented opportunities for respectable middle-class women to engage in comic writing. In fact, the careers of the three novelists addressed in this study mark a key period for women's comedy.

By the end of the eighteenth century, a number of middle-class Englishwomen had attained a prominent position in the world of letters. Although writing was itself a rebellious act— requiring that women reject the ideal of passive womanhood that had arisen during the eighteenth century[14]—self-conscious, critical female writers could both seek shelter in and manipulate socially sanctioned domestic plots. And, if the writing of critical comedy involved elements of aggression and overt self-assertion, careful women writers learned to disguise such unfeminine behavior with otherwise conventional characterizations and scenes.

In general, the rise of the middle-class domestic woman as a repository for cultural values gave women increased access to the literary world by marking out a privileged territory—the domestic realm—in and about which women could actually claim authority. That authority, however, had its share of restrictions. Most significantly, domestic influence had to begin in the domestic realm; entering a public space like the theater could involve women in a risky exposure. The sexual nature of the risk becomes clear when one considers, for instance, the long-standing association of actresses and female playwrights with prostitutes.

An incident early in Frances Burney's career illustrates how the dividing line between the domestic realm and the public theater could prove to be an insurmountable obstacle for an aspiring middle-class female playwright. Following the enormous success of *Evelina* (1778), two famous men, painter Sir Joshua Reynolds and playwright Richard Sheridan, strongly advised Burney to write a comedy for the stage, a suggestion she recorded in her journal with pride and consternation:

> Mr. Sheridan. "I think, and say, she should write a comedy."
>
> Sir Joshua. "I am sure I think so; and hope she will."
>
> I could only answer by incredulous exclamations.
>
> "Consider," continued Sir Joshua, "you have already had all the applause and fame you can have given you in the closet; but the acclamation of a theatre will be new to you." And then he put down his trumpet, and began a violent clapping of his hands.
>
> I actually shook from head to foot! I felt myself already in Drury Lane, amidst the hubbub

of a first night. "Oh, no!" cried I, "there may be a
noise, but it will be just the reverse." And I returned his salute with a hissing. Mr. Sheridan
joined Sir Joshua very warmly. "Oh, sir!" cried
I, "you should not run on so—you don't know
what mischief you may do!" (*Diary and Letters*
1.158–59)

Even though Burney responds with physical terror at the
idea of public exposure, she initially accepted the men's endorsement as permission for her to step forth from her "closet" without
apology: "if I should attempt the stage, I think I may be fairly ac-
quitted of presumption" (*Diary and Letters* 1.159). She even progressed so far as to compose a comedy. But her public declaration
of independence still required private masculine approval. She
submitted *The Witlings* to two men more intimately connected to
her than Reynolds and Sheridan, who would stand as the final ar-
biters. They dissuaded her from going public. Her two "dad-
dies"—Samuel Crisp (a close friend of the family) and Dr. Burney—reminded her that her reputation as a woman and her
family's honor would be publicly damaged by an unfavorable reception. Burney's contradictory reaction to Reynolds and Sheridan's encouragement found justification in Crisp and Dr. Burney's
conservative response to her work. They urged her to stick to
novel writing as a more private forum for her comedy. Their assumption here is an interesting one: that a stage production would
more literally embody the woman writer and subject her and her
family to potential public disgrace.

Crisp had already warned Burney of the difficulties that
comic writing would entail for a proper lady:

A great deal of management and dexterity will
certainly be requisite to preserve spirit and salt,
and yet keep up delicacy; but it may be done, and
you can do it if anybody. Do you remember, about
a dozen years ago, how you used to dance Nancy
Dawson on the grass-plot, with your cap on the
ground, and your long hair streaming down your

back, one shoe off, and throwing about your head
like a mad thing? Now, you are to dance Nancy
Dawson with fetters on; there is the difference.
(*Diary and Letters* 1.137–38)

The difference proved to be too great, not for Burney herself, who
repeatedly declared herself ready to risk failure, but for her male
"protectors," who were not willing to share that risk with her.[15]
Her acceptance of their authority exemplifies the moral straits—
metaphorically depicted by Crisp as "fetters"—in which even the
most promising female writer found herself.

If paternalistic fears did not utterly stifle Burney's comic
spirit, it is largely because the domestic novel had emerged to
provide an acceptable vehicle of female expression. Unlike the
theater, the novel created the illusion of a private relation between the author and her audience. The successful *Evelina,* in
particular, paved the way for more women to follow in the path
of comic novel writing. If, as Sir Joshua Reynolds indicated to
Burney, a novelist's success allowed her to remain in the "closet,"
she was able to laugh with some freedom behind its closed door.
As long as women dutifully limited the action of their novels to
the domestic realm, they appeared to respect the confines of domesticated humor. As long as they supplied the obligatory love
interest and some kind of domestic fulfillment in the conclusions
of their novels, they could hope to receive the patriarchal stamp
of approval.

In exploring the domestication of comedy in the eighteenth century, my aim has been to elucidate what Burney, Edgeworth, and
Austen were working *against:* in their own day, a kind of censor-
ship, and afterwards, a reductive critical evaluation and appreciation of their works. Once we note the eighteenth-century shift
in perspective toward sentimental comedy, which relied heavily
upon the trope of the domestic family for its model of social concord, we can better appreciate the boldness of women writers who
adopted the more critical comic style.

The eighteenth-century spokesperson for critical comedy in
the novel was Henry Fielding, who saw the novel as an essentially

comic genre that provided a vehicle for lively social criticism. Like Goldsmith, Fielding was more concerned with the criticism of folly than the indulgence of sentiment. He argued that by exposing "affectation," the "only source of the true ridiculous," the comic novel could reveal underlying vanities and hypocrisies, and thereby promote social change (*Joseph Andrews* 28).

Burney, Edgeworth, and Austen each might have taken Fielding's statement that "Life every where furnishes an accurate observer with the ridiculous" (26) as her manifesto for comic writing; all three combined an insistence on realism with a decided taste for the ridiculous. However, because of the historical convergence of sentimental comedy, domestic angels, and the nuclear family, these writers' shared penchant for critical and feminist comedy has gone largely unrecognized. A review of the history of Austen's reception will reveal one female comic writer's treatment at the hands of readers who came to promote the domestic aspects of her novels at the expense of her humor.

Poet and novelist Sir Walter Scott recognized the radicalism inherent in Austen's gender politics and chastised her for it in politically charged terms. Reviewing *Emma,* he calls attention to her ungenerous treatment of the "powerful divinity": "Cupid, king of gods and men, who in these times of revolution, has been assailed, even in his own kingdom of romance, by the authors who were formerly his devoted priests." Scott sees Austen's departure from romantic values as a species of treason. He argues that women have a responsibility to preserve young men's illusions about love and ideal femininity because loving a woman is supposed to contribute to the ennoblement of male character. "Who is it," he queries, "that in his youth has felt a virtuous attachment, however romantic or however unfortunate, but can trace back to its influence much that his character may possess of what is honourable, dignified, and disinterested?" (qtd. in Southam 68).

After Austen's death, her brother Henry wrote the "Biographical Notice" that would influence her reputation throughout the Victorian period. He specifically addresses the possible incompatibility of comedy and femininity by portraying his sister's comic talents in the employment of domestic stability:

> If there be an opinion current in the world, that
> perfect placidity of temper is not reconcileable to
> the most lively imagination, and the keenest rel-
> ish for wit, such an opinion will be rejected for
> ever by those who have had the happiness of
> knowing the authoress of the following works.
> Though the frailties, foibles, and follies of others
> could not escape her immediate detection, yet
> even on their vices did she never trust herself to
> comment with unkindness. . . . Faultless herself,
> as nearly as human nature can be, she always
> sought, in the faults of others, something to ex-
> cuse, to forgive or forget. Where extenuation was
> impossible, she had a sure refuge in silence. (5–6)

Henry Austen reinterprets his sister's wit for her audience and ef-
faces her critical spirit by making use of the terms of the debate I
have detailed above; he attempts to "reconcile" the "keenest relish for wit" with the demands of ideal femininity. Declaring her
to be nearly "faultless," he emphasizes her passive virtues: her
"perfect placidity of temper," her reluctance to "trust herself to
comment with unkindness," her silence in the face of intransi-
gence.

Victorian readers seemed to accept the biographical sketch's
account of the author since they write about her humor as basically harmless. For example, essayist George Henry Lewes describes Austen's comic characters as foolish but amiable creatures:
"What incomparable noodles she exhibits for our astonishment
and laughter! What silly, good-natured women! What softly-
selfish men! What lively-amiable, honest men and women, whom
one would rejoice to have known!" (qtd. in Southam 157). In a
more ambivalent vein, Margaret Oliphant, herself a prolific novelist and critic, struggles to reconcile the humor with the woman
by placing Austen outside her own creations as a somewhat bemused maternal figure:

> She stands by and looks on, and gives a soft half-
> smile, and tells the story with an exquisite sense

> of its ridiculous side, and fine stinging yet soft-
> voiced contempt for the actors in it. . . . The po-
> sition of mind is essentially feminine . . . a sense
> that nothing is to be done but to look on, to say
> perhaps now and then a softening word, to make
> the best of it practically and theoretically, to
> smile and hold up one's hands and wonder why
> human creatures should be such fools. (qtd. in
> Southam 216)

Oliphant carefully compensates for the critical side of Austen's humor by stressing her ineffectuality and passivity. Although she refers to Austen's "feminine cynicism," she then defines away the hostile implications of the term: "It includes a great deal that is amiable, and is full of toleration and patience, and that habit of making allowance for others which lies at the bottom of human charity" (217). By the beginning of the twentieth century, the tendency to regard Austen as a good-natured family member became so pronounced that it merited novelist Henry James's sarcasm: "their 'dear,' our dear, everybody's dear, Jane" (62). The more intimacy Austen's readers felt toward her, the less able they were to recognize the critical bent of her humor.

Literary critic D. W. Harding, in his landmark essay "Regulated Hatred" (1940), summarized the prevailing view toward Austen's humor in the early twentieth century: "I was given to understand that her scope was of course extremely restricted, but that within her limits she succeeded admirably in expressing the gentler virtues of a civilised social order. . . . Chiefly, so I gathered, she was a delicate satirist, revealing with inimitable lightness of touch the comic foibles and amiable weaknesses of the people whom she lived amongst and liked" (346–47). However, having aligned her with domesticated humor, he proceeds to tear away the gauze that kept Austen in soft-focus. Harding shocked his contemporaries by pronouncing that "her books are, as she meant them to be, read and enjoyed by precisely the sort of people whom she disliked; she is a literary classic of the society which attitudes like hers, held widely enough, would undermine" (347). Although Harding did not recognize Austen's feminism, he challenged the accepted reading of her novels and correctly noted their subversive tendencies. In so doing, he calls attention to the way that ideological presuppositions affect what one sees in a text, a key factor in the invisibility of traditions of feminist humor.[16]

The history of Austen's reception reveals the particular complexities affecting readers of women's comedy. The same readers who enthused over "dear Jane" were denying women a sense of humor altogether. I have focused on Austen's critical reception because it is much more visible than either Burney's or Edgeworth's. The latter two did not share Austen's popularity with the Victorians; Burney's journals and Edgeworth's letters were widely read, but their fiction fell in critical estimation.[17]

In spite of the cultural pressures at work to suppress women's comedy, Burney, Edgeworth, and Austen began their careers during a period that was not unfavorable to women writers as a group. By the end of the eighteenth century, when women were the major novel-writers and novel-readers, this genre constituted an unprecedented public forum for female views.[18] According to literary scholar Joyce Tompkins, women banded together to invade the world of letters: "There is a remarkable solidarity about the attack of the women on the literary world, and the old rubbed military metaphors, that run almost unconsciously from the historian's pen, have at least this justification, that the women marched shoulder to shoulder" (123).

This background of female solidarity played an important role in these three authors' careers. Burney participated in the Bluestocking circles, having contact there with the leading literary women of her day. One of Edgeworth's characters lists only women novelists ("Miss Burney—Mrs. Opie—Mrs. Inchbald") in a defense of the novel (*Patronage* [1814] 58). In her own famous defense of the novel in *Northanger Abbey* (1818), Austen names works by Burney and Edgeworth ("Cecilia, or Camilla, or Belinda") as examples "in which the greatest powers of the mind are displayed, in which the most thorough knowledge of human nature, the happiest delineation of its varieties, the liveliest effusions of wit and humour are conveyed in the best chosen language" (38). Austen's confidence owed much to having inherited a female tradition in the novel. She made no apology for her gender as so many critics even now feel compelled to do; she also denied the relevance of limitations imposed on women's writing. Significantly for this study, her recipe for the perfect novel includes a good measure of lively wit and humor.

Feminist comic theorists agree that a shared awareness of sexist oppression within and among groups of women forms a necessary component for the development of feminist comedy. Nancy Walker applies Nina Auerbach's idea of "codes" existing within communities of women to elucidate how female solidarity might contribute to feminist humor: "The rules or 'codes' by which the dominant culture operates are announced, articulated —whereas those of the community of women are whispered and subversive, like those of the racial or minority group, who maintain a more or less invisible subculture within or alongside the larger society. . . . Humor is one of the expressions of the codes by which a group operates" (105). Feminist humor, then, encodes an important message about women's relation to the dominant ideology. Even if the rules for proper female behavior required a modest submission to masculine authority, women who could come to see themselves as an "injured body," as Austen terms novelists in *Northanger Abbey* (37), might also learn to laugh as a group at the impositions of male power.

We know that in their daily lives Burney, Edgeworth, and Austen did not allow themselves to be silenced by prohibitions against female laugher. In journals and letters, we can almost hear them laughing as they highlight the ludicrous aspects of acquaintances, construct witty anecdotes, and find in almost every aspect of life something ridiculous that can be offered up for the amusement of their readers. Their penchants for humor amounted to a comic perspective on life: each author used comedy not only as an entertainment, but also as a strategy for coping with life's difficulties.

Burney's early journal entries reveal her high spirits. On one occasion, she registers "a violent fit of laughter"; at another point, she declares herself "ready to die with laughter" (*Early Journals* 9, 40). In many of her laughing fits, she wrestles with female decorum: "[he] made me laugh to so immoderate a degree that I was quite ashamed"; "for the life of me I could not forbear laughing"; "I could not help myself bursting into laughter" (54–55, 128, 191). But decorum seldom conquers her irrepressible urges to laugh: "stand I did, as well as I could, for laughter"; "I was almost in convulsions with excessive laughter" (162, 197). Time and again, Burney records her own merriment, her boundless love of laughter. Through writing, she seems to recapture the pleasure of the moment and at the same time to mourn its passing: "[we] laughed till we were quite fatigued. Would to Heaven I was but often *so* fatigued" (214).

Edgeworth, too, demonstrates a predilection for life's comic side. She jokingly devises a scale of laughter by which to measure her happiness in a letter to a cousin as she looks back on a particularly enjoyable visit: "Write to me Dear Sophy for since Richard's departure I have not been the merriest of mortals—not above nine laughs & a $^1/_2$ per day, and none, such as you & my good kind aunt used to hear when I attended her happy Levee" (qtd. in Butler 126). Edgeworth's playful exactitude (the extra "$^1/_2$" laugh) illustrates both her appetite for and her capacity to arouse the laughter she values. Not even physical pain could prevent her from giving vent to her glee: "I had a most violent headache, so that I was forced to hold my head on both sides whilst I laughed, yet I could not refrain" (qtd. in Hare 1.147–48). In one letter, Edgeworth records a testimony to her ability to combine seriousness and mirth: "Mr. Hammond once, when piqued by my raillery, declared that he never in his life saw, or could have conceived, till he saw me, that a *philosopher* could laugh so much and so heartily" (1.162). To entertain her correspondents, she filled her letters with comic sketches and anecdotes; even during the Irish disruptions, "her letters habitually see the comic side of the disturbances" (Butler 114).

Like Burney and Edgeworth, Austen attests to a love of laughter in her private writings. She evaluates Cassandra's epistolary talents on comic grounds: "The letter which I have this moment received from you has diverted me beyond moderation. I could die of laughter at it, as they used to say at school" (*Letters* 8). In response to James Stanier Clarke's suggestion that she write "an historical romance founded on the House of Saxe Cobourg," Austen begs off by claiming to be compulsively comic: "I could no more write a romance than an epic poem. I could not sit seriously down to write a serious romance under any other motive than to save my life; and if it were indispensable for me to keep it up and never relax into laughing at myself or other people, I am sure I should be hung before I had finished the first chapter" (452). By repeating the offending word "serious," Austen pokes fun at Clarke for presuming to recommend a pompous (and boring) topic. Even when she coins a studious proverb, Austen cannot refrain from putting a laugh in edgewise: "Wisdom is better than Wit, & in the long run will certainly have the laugh on her side" (410).

Hester Chapone, in her 1773 conduct book for young ladies, speaks of an appropriate kind of female laughter: "You will wonder, perhaps, when I tell you that there are some characters in the world, which I would freely allow you to laugh at, though not in their presence. Extravagant vanity, and affectation, are the natural subjects of ridicule, which is their proper punishment" (134). In terms that bear an affinity to Fielding's statements about comic targets, Chapone advocates laughter for "unfeminine" ends, namely "ridicule" and "punishment." She makes it clear that young women may only exercise this freedom in private and warns that "whispering and laughing" with female friends in the midst of a group of adults will "give them cause to suspect, what is too often true, that they themselves are the subjects of your mirth" (132). Chapone's conduct rules, which emphasize "the improvement of the mind," present laughter as an important tool for social criticism, as long as it does not impinge upon actual social ease.

I wish to summon up an image, then, of late-eighteenth-century women in their "closets," or behind their walls and hedge-rows, laughing at the follies of a society that tried to contain them. One of Austen's nieces, recounting her aunt's visits, depicts such a scene: "she used to bring the MS of whatever novel she was writing with her, and would shut herself up with my elder sisters in one of the bedrooms to read them aloud. I and the younger ones used to hear peals of laughter through the door, and thought it very hard that we should be shut out" (qtd. in Honan 325). In the chapters that follow, I strive to allow us not only to hear this type of laughter but to participate in the joke, to understand and decipher the codes, and thereby to uncover a new passage in the history of British women's resistance to sexism.

2

Defiant Laughter:
Mary Wollstonecraft
and Feminist Humor

> For Custom has usurpt such an unaccountable Authority, that she
> who would endeavour to put a stop to its arbitrary sway, and reduce
> it to Reason, is in a fair way to render herself the Butt for all
> the Fops in town to shoot their impertinent censures at.
> And tho' a wise woman will not value their censure,
> yet she cares not to be the subject of their Discourse.
>
> —Mary Astell (rptd. in *First English Feminist* 162)

WRITING ALMOST ONE HUNDRED YEARS before Mary Wollstonecraft, Mary Astell, in her *Serious Proposal to the Ladies*
(1696), concluded that for women to escape from the tyranny of
Custom, "The only way . . . is to retire from the World" (rptd. in
First English Feminist 162). A staunch Tory, Astell did not advocate the overthrow of established male authority; instead, she advised women to refrain from entering into marriage contracts
with men and proposed to form an alternative community of
women, a Protestant convent in which women would be free to
pursue learning without fear of male derision. Because she recognized the unchecked power men wielded in society and believed
that many would ridicule women who tried to shift the balance of
power, she strove to sidestep confrontation and avoid being "the
subject of their Discourse."

Astell and other seventeenth-century feminists realized that
in order to improve the position of women in society, the customs

that framed reality for men and women of the time needed to be changed and recast along more rational lines. Specifically, they saw a need to alter the terms of the debate in order to be able to function as subjects in their own right rather than as the objects of male discourse. Whether women were lauded as angels or satirized as lustful beasts, patriarchal discourse, especially in writing, exercised control over their behavior. In her study of seventeenth-century feminists, Hilda Smith identifies a faith in women's rationality as the central feature that sets them apart from earlier writers on women. According to Smith, pre-seventeenth-century defenders of women (frequently male writers) responded to a long tradition of misogynist satire with its lists of wicked women by supplying competing lists of "women worthies" (xiii). What made this type of response ineffective in the struggle for improving women's condition was its emphasis on exceptional figures. Whereas misogynist satirists, whose catalogues often began with the archetypal temptress Eve, employed examples to support their contempt for women in general, women's defenders supplied lists of exemplary females whose extraordinary actions allegedly set them apart from their sex. Seventeenth-century feminists shifted the emphasis away from individual women and focused instead on rationality as a gender-neutral aspect of human nature.[1]

In the quoted passage, Astell's invocation of reason as the opponent of oppressive custom connects her not only to her seventeenth-century predecessors and contemporaries, but to the entire history of modern Western feminism. Her separatist solution and stated belief in the necessity of male domination in society would not appeal to the late-twentieth-century feminist; nonetheless, with her faith in women's equal rational capacities and her attacks on the system of keeping women in ignorance, Astell set the tone for subsequent discussions about women.

Although educational opportunities for women increased during the eighteenth century, women who wanted to learn and be educated still had to fly in the face of custom. Astell comments on the controlling force of mockery in preventing women from improving their minds: "Laughter and Ridicule that never-failing Scare-Crow is set up to drive them from the Tree of Knowledge" (rptd. in *First English Feminist* 85). Rather than appealing to catalogues of historical figures in order to mock women's attempts at improvement, antifeminist satirists after the seventeenth century began to work from stereotypes that highlighted women's vulnerable social status. Along with other comic types, such as the spinster, the prude, and the coquette, the learned lady appeared as a stock comic character throughout the eighteenth century.[2]

One important aspect of women's entry into the literary world, however, was that women began to laugh back. As Jo Anna Isaak has argued, laughter can be viewed as a "metaphor for transformation, for thinking about cultural change. . . . [L]aughter can also provide an analytic for understanding the relationships between the social and the symbolic while allowing us to imagine these relationships differently" (5). By inciting critical laughter at assumptions about female limitations and male superiority, feminist writers both expose the frame that defines the status quo and indicate that it can be changed. From the late seventeenth century on, appeals to reason bolstered women writers' challenges to male hegemony; laughing at the irrationalities of arguments for male supremacy became a feminist pastime.

Critics have paid little attention to early feminist laughter, perhaps because of two common and related misconceptions: first, the notion that humor cannot be used for serious ends, and second, the widespread belief that feminists lack a sense of humor.[3] However, the history of women's comic expression reveals a tradition of feminist humor that disproves such misconceptions. An examination of how Enlightenment feminist writers made use of comic strategies will enable us to see how Burney, Edgeworth, and Austen built upon a tradition of feminist laughter. In particular, by exploring Mary Wollstonecraft's role within this tradition, we can become familiar with the rhetoric and lexicon of laughing feminism in the political tracts of the period and thus be able to recognize it when it appears in fictional works.

The new reliance on reason to fight women's battles achieved at least one victory by the latter half of the eighteenth century—the death of misogynist satire in its traditional form. In England, the period stretching from the Restoration to the mid-eighteenth century has been identified as the heyday of misogynist satire, the culmination and conclusion of a tradition that dates back to Juvenal. Rather than attempting to correct or reform, misogynist satire merely reifies the status quo: "men on the one hand describe women as inherently giddy and unstable, while on the other they create an ideal woman, the mirror of their highest expectations, who is to establish order in the domestic sphere" (Nussbaum 5). At the height of this satirical period, Edward Young expressed a common joke: "The Sex we honour, tho' their faults we blame; / Nay thank their faults for such a *fruitful* theme" (83). Along with other misogynist satirists, Young willfully disregarded women's honorable qualities in order to participate in what Alison Sulloway has termed "the national sport of chastising women" (15).

In key Enlightenment feminist texts, we can trace women's resentment against misogynist satire in their growing tendency to mock the mockers. In fact, we can gauge the state of the feminist reprisal by the ease and the various means with which female polemicists summoned up laughter to combat male hegemony. At the end of the seventeenth century, Judith Drake hazarded a "defence" of her sex and laid out a program for turning the tables on misogynists; by mid-eighteenth century, "Sophia" confidently ridiculed men as frauds; at century's end the tradition of feminist laughter reached its height in Wollstonecraft's *Vindication of the Rights of Woman* and, due to the backlash of the French Revolution, went undercover after her death. Whatever their degree of caution or confidence, however, early feminists spared no ink in exposing sexist nonsense and shared a penchant for deriding male superiority.

Drake responded to misogynist satirists by declaring war on ridicule:

> We have a sort of ungenerous Adversaries, that deal more in Scandal than Argument, and when they can't hurt us with their Weapons, endeavour to annoy us with Stink Pots. Let us see therefore . . . whether we can't beat them from their Ammunition, and turn their own Artillery upon them; for I firmly believe there is nothing which

> they charge upon us, but may with more Justice be
> retorted upon themselves. . . . They tax us with a
> long list of Faults, and Imperfections, and seem to
> have taken a Catalogue of their own Follies and
> Vices, not with a design to correct them, but to
> shift of the Imputation to us. (64–65)

Drake proceeds to list male characters who deserve to be ridiculed—the beau, the fop poet, the coffee-house politician, the city militiaman, the virtuoso, and the city critic—and devotes twenty pages of her tract to giving these types their due. She distinguishes between natural and studied impertinence, declaring that the former "is not worth Laughing at." Drake stresses that chosen folly is more laughable than ignorance; however, by indicting "*Systems* of impertinence" (96), she implies what later feminists would declare—that the belief in male superiority as the organizing principle of society is a foolish choice, and anyone who goes along with it deserves to be ridiculed.

More assured of the injustice of the system than was Drake, "Sophia" directed her raillery at all men, not just particularly bad examples, in the influential pamphlet *Woman Not Inferior to Man* (1739).[4] Sophia heaps scorn upon the notion of male superiority by proclaiming that men—"those lordly creatures, as they modestly stile themselves"—do not even attempt to raise themselves above "Brutes" (1, 2). "How many things do these mighty wise creatures hold for undoubted truths, without being able to assign a reason for any one of their opinions!" she jeers. "What mighty superiority of reason then have these over-grown boys over lesser children?" (3, 4). Unlike Drake, who draws up a limited list of foolish male types, Sophia holds male folly to be varied and pervasive: "I should never have done, was I to reckon up the many absurd notions the *Men* are led into by *custom:* Tho' there is none more absurd, than that of the great *difference* they make between their own sex and ours. Yet it must be own'd that there is not any vulgar error more antient or universal. For the learned and illiterate alike are prepossest with the opinion that *Men* are really superior to *Women*" (6). By scoffing at men's "tyrannical usurpation of authority," Sophia attempted to shame them into a sense of justice and a recognition of women as equals. In the sequel to this pamphlet, she went one step further and openly claimed what her sarcasm implied, *Woman's Superior Excellence Over Man* (1740).

In *A Vindication of the Rights of Woman* (1792), Wollstonecraft reflects the political situation of the early 1790s by calling for "a revolution in female manners" (45). She declares that a "state of warfare" exists between the sexes (126), and she scorns the euphemisms that mask women's oppression. A central part of Wollstonecraft's revolutionary program involves laughter.[5] She parodies the most extreme prejudices against women and encourages her readers to laugh at the folly of such irrational views. George Meredith's evaluation of Molière applies equally well to Wollstonecraft: "The source of his wit is clear reason; it is a fountain of that soil, and it springs to vindicate reason, common sense, rightness, and justice" (17). Because reason and common sense tell Wollstonecraft that the oppression of women relies on convention and prejudice, she strives to mock these prejudices out of existence.

Some of these prejudices take up where traditional misogynist satire left off in their use of mockery to keep women in line. Wollstonecraft identifies such prejudices, exposes their hidden danger, and attacks them with her own overt ridicule. In *A Vindication of the Rights of Woman*, various kinds of antifeminist laughter and smiling serve as foils for Wollstonecraft's defiant laughter. One sort of laughter especially stirs Wollstonecraft's anger: the "sneer" male satirists direct against women, which usually mocks them for flaws resulting from women's limited opportunities for growth. She wants to silence this laughter by drawing attention to its sinister quality. The poets who compare women to angels and valorize women's weakness should, in her view, "drop the sneer" (52) and consider the hardships of women's lot. Wollstonecraft voices indignation at the injustice of such laughter: "To laugh at [women] . . . or to satirize the follies of a being who is never to be allowed to act freely from the light of her own reason, is as absurd as cruel" (187). According to Wollstonecraft, any man who upholds artificial views about women's nature probably sneers at women behind their backs.

A smile that angers Wollstonecraft almost as much as the male sneer appears in women who go along with the system—the smile of complacency. "They will smile,—yes they will smile," Wollstonecraft writes of the women who credulously receive excessive male praise, "But the adoration comes first, and the scorn is not anticipated" (56). Male sneers and submissive women's smiles fortify one another: men laugh as they heap compliments upon women; women accept such flattery with smiles. What Wollstonecraft makes clear, however, is that even the most obtuse women should see through the contradictory treatment they receive. Men may claim to be enslaved by women's charms, but in reality, women are the slaves. She characterizes the dependent woman's smile as "smiling under the lash at which it dare not snarl" (33).[6]

It would be a mistake to disregard Wollstonecraft's use of ridicule as an antidote to contemporary prejudices against women, especially since ridicule was a factor that helped to maintain these prejudices. She sees that women's restricted opportunities contribute to misogynist satire: women receive no education, yet are scorned for their ignorance; they depend upon and must attract male protectors, yet are derided for their attention to appearance; they cannot engage in politics, yet are scoffed at for their limited sphere of interests. She refuses to be duped by the system and laughs to steal power away from the oppressors.

Male sneers and slavish female smiles represent the falsity of the present system; one arises from an unjust tyranny, the other participates in degradation. In contrast to these expressions of bad faith, Wollstonecraft engages in the laughter of defiance. In a delightfully explosive textual moment, Wollstonecraft registers both her impatience with sexist folly and her utopian longings. This moment appears during a discussion of the attentions that women receive from men who chivalrously pretend to act in the service of female rule, "when, in fact, they are insultingly supporting their own superiority. . . . So ludicrous, in fact, do these ceremonies appear to me, that I scarcely am able to govern my muscles, when I see a man start with eager, and serious solicitude, to lift a handkerchief, or shut a door, when the *lady* could have done it herself, had she only moved a pace or two." Wollstonecraft suppresses her laughter at the foolish ceremonies, but her emphasis on the word *lady* indicates a pressure point, and the remembrance of her past suppressions leads to a more violent response: "A wild wish has just flown from my heart to my head, and I will not stifle it though it may excite a horse-laugh.—I do earnestly wish to see the distinction of sex confounded in society" (57). Here she unleashes the "governed" muscles that prevented her from mocking the handkerchief incident and gives voice to the reason for her amusement. Her desire for the eradication of gender distinctions is as revolutionary as coarse laughter is indecorous: by engaging raucousness she promotes the triumph of reason.

Wollstonecraft's treatise displays her talent for reading with critical laughter, particularly through the use of what Mikhail Bakhtin calls "parodic stylization"[7]—that is, she brings antifeminist voices into her text in order to expose their self-interest and to drown their authoritative pronouncements in female laughter. She excerpts passages from the conduct literature of Jean-Jacques Rousseau, James Fordyce, and John Gregory in order to subject them to ridicule. To a large degree, she relies on sarcasm, reproducing the language of oppression with glosses that emphasize its absurdities. Her exclamation marks register her sarcastic tone and frequently stand in for the twice-uttered phrase "What nonsense!" (26, 78). Her technique might be read as simple anger rather than as a complex blend of confidence and rebellion that comprise laughter, if Wollstonecraft did not provide a model for us to follow in reading her text. Before we can fully understand her comic treatment of conduct literature, we need to look at this model.

Wollstonecraft condemns texts that foster a romantic sensibility in women and thereby contribute to their subjection. Specifically, she denounces "stupid novelists, who, knowing little of human nature, work up stale tales, and describe meretricious scenes, all retailed in a sentimental jargon, which equally tend to corrupt the taste, and draw the heart aside from its daily duties" (183). Like the conduct literature of writers such as Rousseau, Fordyce, and Gregory, the novels she opposes promote a false picture of female existence and offer illusions instead of knowledge.

The strategy she proposes to dispel these illusions appears throughout the *Vindication*.

> The best method, I believe, that can be adopted to correct a fondness for novels is to ridicule them: not indiscriminately, for then it would have little effect; but, if a judicious person, with some turn for humour, would read several to a young girl, and point out both by tones, and apt comparisons with pathetic incidents and heroic characters in history, how foolishly and ridiculously they caricatured human nature, just opinions might be substituted instead of romantic sentiments. (185)

This method of using ridicule to combat delusion plays an important part in Wollstonecraft's work as a whole. Herself the "judicious person, with some turn for humour," she "reads" antifeminist texts for her own audience and expects her readers to acknowledge the folly of sexist dogma. By subjecting these texts to mockery and laughter, she strives to dissolve their power.

Wollstonecraft's method involves both sarcastic readings of the offending texts and translations into the language of common sense to lay bare the skeleton of tyranny beneath the honeyed tones. For instance, she quotes from *Paradise Lost* and claims to be unable to understand Milton's view that women are "formed for softness and sweet attractive grace" (19). To his claim that women should unquestioningly accept male authority because men know what is best for them, she responds, "These are exactly the arguments that I have used to children" (20). In Judith Fetterley's terms, Wollstonecraft operates as a "resisting reader": she insists upon calling things by their right names and ridicules the highflown disguises that the language of oppression adopts. She exposes the myths that constrain female development and deconstructs the "ridiculous jargon" (44) these myths promote.

In turning her attention to the literature designed to teach women how to be "proper" ladies, Wollstonecraft finds much to arouse her critical laughter. By bringing Gregory, Fordyce, and

Rousseau into her text and mocking them, she discredits antifeminist ploys to maintain authority. She describes the experience of listening to men like Rousseau and Gregory who assert that a fondness for dress is natural to women: "If they told us that in a pre-existent state the soul was fond of dress, and brought this inclination with it into a new body, I should listen to them with a half smile, as I often do when I hear a rant about innate elegance" (28). Her half-smile, unlike the complaisant smile of the submissive female, has an air of resistance about it, a conscious superiority. By pointing out the incongruity of a fondness for dress residing in the soul, she uncovers the absurdity of making pronouncements about women's nature based upon their behavior in a sexist society.

Gregory's *A Father's Legacy to His Daughters* purports to offer advice to his female offspring, who have been deprived of their mother's influence, but as a published work, it actually seeks to advise a wider audience of female readers about proper feminine behavior. Wollstonecraft underscores the irony of Gregory's assertion to his daughters at the beginning of *A Father's Legacy* "that they will hear, at least once in their lives, the genuine sentiments of a man who has no interest in deceiving them" (97). "Hapless woman!" retorts Wollstonecraft, "what can be expected from thee when the beings on whom thou art said naturally to depend for reason and support, have all an interest in deceiving thee!" (97). Although she praises Gregory's "paternal solicitude" and "the melancholy tenderness which his respect for the memory of a beloved wife . . . diffuses through the whole work" (96), she casts doubts upon his motives, hinting that he writes for fame rather than for family: "there is a degree of concise elegance conspicuous in many passages that disturbs the sympathy; and we pop on the author, when we only expected to meet the—father" (96–97). Perhaps because she accepts the emotional ploy (the dead wife), she cannot quite bring herself to expose "the father" as a tyrant in his own right, but she strives to separate the sentimental context of Gregory's *Legacy* from its political force as a widely circulated book, referring to his gallantry as "lip-service" and his notion of female decorum as a "system of dissimulation" (97, 99).

Like Gregory, Rousseau exerted a strong influence on

eighteenth-century views of female education, and Wollstonecraft similarly discredits him by ridiculing his ideas about women.
In a passage from *Émile* that Wollstonecraft quotes in a footnote,
Rousseau discusses a little girl he knew who wrote only the letter
"O," until one day, upon seeing her contorted face in the mirror
while she made her Os, she decided to give up writing altogether.
Rousseau employs this anecdote as an illustration of women's natural vanity. Wollstonecraft derides this and other examples: "His
ridiculous stories, which tend to prove that girls are *naturally* attentive to their persons, without laying any stress on daily example, are below contempt.—And that a little miss should have
such a correct taste as to neglect the pleasing amusement of making O's, merely because she perceived that it was an ungraceful attitude, should be selected with the anecdotes of the learned pig"
(43). In other words, what nonsense! Her emphasis on the word
"naturally" mimics Rousseau's use of the word in order to call attention to its lack of substance. She insinuates that his stories do
more than distort women's "nature"—they fabricate it.

Nevertheless, Wollstonecraft's treatment of Gregory and
Rousseau sounds tame next to her mockery of Fordyce, author of
Sermons to Young Women. She declares that he would be beneath
her contempt if it were not for his enormous popularity (96).
Because of the influence he wields, she turns the full gale of her
laughter upon him. Damning epithets abound: his "affected style"
and "sentimental rant" (93) are the products of his "little vain
mind" (94). "Florid appeals are made to heaven," she scoffs, "and
to the *beauteous innocents*, the fairest images of heaven here
below, whilst sober sense is left far behind" (94). She particularly
dislikes "the lover-like phrases of pumped up passion, which are
everywhere interspersed . . . the lullaby strains of condescending
endearment!" (94). Challenging the propriety of his sentimental
tones, she asks, "should a grave preacher interlard his discourses
with such fooleries?" (95).

In one excerpt, Fordyce chastises women whose husbands
seek entertainment outside the home; he assures them that husbands would stay at home if wives treated them with utter defer-
ence, anticipated their desires, and accepted harsh words without
demur. Wollstonecraft introduces this passage with the caption

"Is not the following portrait—the portrait of a house slave?" (95). To Fordyce's assurance that the submissive, accommodating woman can ensure "domestic bliss," Wollstonecraft jeers, "Such a woman ought to be an angel—or she is an ass—for I discern not a trace of the human character, neither reason nor passion in this domestic drudge, whose being is absorbed in that of a tyrant's" (96). Her juxtaposition of incongruous alternatives—angel or ass—tears the veil away from Fordyce's domestic figure and reveals the tyranny that such "domestic bliss" imposes.

Wollstonecraft's confidence in the self-evident foolishness of all three writers explains the long quotations she includes in her text. She gives us Rousseau's view of women "in his own words, interspersing comments and reflections" (77). "He shall speak for himself," she states about Fordyce: "I will use the preacher's own words" (93, 95). She adds emphasis and exclamation marks, and she even inserts her views into the middle of quotations with footnotes. For example, she footnotes the following sentence by Fordyce on men's duty to female virtue: "Can you find in your hearts [*] to despoil the gentle, trusting creatures of their treasure, or do any thing to strip them of their native robe of virtue?" (93). Wollstonecraft's note (indicated by the asterisk) parodies his assumption of male paternalism: "Can you?—Can you? would be the most emphatical comment, were it drawled out in a whining voice." She turns the words of Rousseau, Gregory, and Fordyce against them and fuels her own argument with laughter at their expense.

Wollstonecraft applies sense and reason to the systems of female education set forth by these writers and finds their ideal woman lacking in both attributes. This woman is a product of ideological abuse, the result of being told to use manipulative strategies to compensate for the power that society denies her, to define her activities as instrumental to men's well-being, and to adapt to this system gracefully. In Wollstonecraft's eyes, such systems of education lay themselves wide open to satire: "It does not require a lively pencil, or the discriminating outline of a caricature, to sketch the domestic miseries and petty vices which such a mistress of a family diffuses" (49). She regards feminist satire as the natural response to the conduct-book writers' prescriptions.

One final passage will demonstrate the power that Wollstonecraft assigns to laughter. She believes in reason's capacity to sweep aside the fictions that maintain female oppression: "Tyrants would have cause to tremble if reason were to become the rule of duty in any of the relations of life, for the light might spread till perfect day appeared. And when it did appear, how men would smile at the sight of the bugbears at which they started during the night of ignorance, or the twilight of timid inquiry" (150). In her utopian world, all "men would smile" at the tactics that constrain women.

As it is, Wollstonecraft sees "bugbears" everywhere. For example, she declares that "the word masculine is only a bugbear" used to prevent women from breaking out of the limitations of their gender role (11). According to the *Oxford English Dictionary*, a bugbear is "a sort of hobgoblin . . . supposed to devour naughty children; hence, generally, any imaginary being invoked by nurses to frighten children." Wollstonecraft's laughter demystifies the bugbears used to frighten women. When she delves into the social structures that restrict women's behavior, she finds only self-interested males who want to make women believe that patriarchy is natural. With reason on her side, Wollstonecraft defies the system that keeps women in a perpetual state of childhood and the men who then make fun of women's enforced childishness. She turns the laugh against the tyrants and encourages "high treason" (27) by setting an example with her own revolutionary text.

A Vindication of the Rights of Woman marks a high point in feminist confidence. In the hysteria that followed the French Revolution, when conservatives were prone to exaggerate even moderately feminist claims, laughing at male authority figures was tantamount to treason. Feminist polemicists began to exercise more caution. Following in Wollstonecraft's footsteps, Mary Hays challenged the principle at the base of contemporary society in her *Appeal to the Men of Great Britain in Behalf of Women* (1798). According to Hays, the notion of male superiority is "beyond a doubt, not the opinion only, of the generality of men;—but the leading principle upon which the laws by which we are governed are founded,—the grand pivot upon which social and domestic politicks turn." She calls this principle the "essence, nay the very quintessence, of prepossession, of arrogance, and of absurdity!" (*Appeal* 96). By scoffing at masculinist authority as the foundation for society, Hays hoped to topple the entire system. Once the principle of male superiority disappeared, social and domestic politics could perhaps be rebuilt upon an equitable foundation.

Like Wollstonecraft, Hays argues that the absurdly unbalanced system of the day is inherently faulty and dangerous to people of either sex:

> Of all the systems,—if indeed a bundle of contradictions and absurdities may be called a system, —which human nature in its moments of intoxication has produced; that which men have contrived with a view to forming the minds, and regulating the conduct of women, is perhaps the most completely absurd. And, though the consequences are often very serious to both sexes, yet if one could for a moment forget these, and consider it only as a system, it would rather be found a subject of mirth and ridicule than serious anger. (47)

What women at the end of the eighteenth century had to "forget" in order to find "mirth and ridicule" in the "system"—namely, the reality of life in a repressive society—inevitably curtailed Hays's ability to laugh at male supremacy. It was a dangerous time to be an egalitarian in England; her tract was therefore not a call to arms but an "appeal." She restrained her laughter accordingly and sought to mask its angry source.

When Horace Walpole called Wollstonecraft "that hyena in petticoats" (quoted in Janes 299), he certainly did not intend it as a compliment; her radical politics so offended him that he associated her with a beast known for its maniacal laughter.[8] Walpole's characterization of Wollstonecraft, unflattering though it may be, calls our attention to the subversive position of the laughing woman and indicates that female laughter and revolutionary politics might go hand in hand. The hyena in petticoats may well be a fitting image for a laughing feminist.

In its most radical function, Wollstonecraft's laughter attempts a destruction such as Hélène Cixous describes in "The Laugh of the Medusa": "A feminine text cannot fail to be more than subversive. It is volcanic; as it is written it brings about an upheaval of the old property crust, carrier of masculine investments. . . . [I]t's in order to smash everything, to shatter the framework of institutions, to blow up the law, to break up the 'truth' with laughter" (258). Wollstonecraft aims to "explode" the current system of female education (92) and replace "mistaken notions of female excellence" (11)—the myths about women as angels and so forth—with honest views of women as rational creatures. Her ultimate goal is to mock those myths out of existence.

When Wollstonecraft satirizes the manners that men and women adopt toward one another, for example, she shows that these manners are part of a social script that contributes to women's subjection; her laughter aims to eliminate the basis for much conventional behavior by attacking the norms that govern conventions. Judy Little argues that "when satire attacks the norm, the resulting comedy becomes distinctly political and the laughter is revolutionary":

> It is one thing to find "manners" amusing, to "scourge" vices—as the satirist claims to do—or to mock the follies of lovers; it is a much more radical act of the imagination, however, to mock the very norms against which traditional satire judges the manners, the vices, and the follies. As women writers come to perceive the ambiguous, even oppressive qualities of certain values and behaviors which society has respected and advocated for centuries, some of them are making comic fun of these norms. ("Satirizing" 39)

The norms that Little focuses on as targets for revolutionary laughter form the basis of traditional gender relations: males as questers, females as nurturers. Clearly, Wollstonecraft perceives the oppressive qualities of these gender roles, and she recognizes that the ceremonies of everyday life often highlight the imbalance of power (for example, her criticism of a man's picking up a woman's hand-kerchief is its implication that the woman is too frail to bend over and do it herself—his gesture may be an act of kindness, but it replicates the larger cultural pattern that opposes male strength to female weakness).[9]

Interestingly, Wollstonecraft claims, "Let it not be concluded that I wish to *invert* the order of things" (26, emphasis mine). Instead, she wants to redress the balance between the sexes ac-cording to the dictate of reason, not self-interest; she aims to es-tablish equality between the sexes, not to replace one system of domination with another. Thus, she refuses to return male satires against women with a female satire against men. Wollstonecraft attacks particular men and particular situations with an under-standing that there might be sensible men who would act differ-ently. In this regard, Wollstonecraft's reformist agenda becomes clear: to laugh at all men would only perpetuate a system based upon sexual difference; laughing at specific choices people make implies confidence that the system can be changed.[10]

Wollstonecraft's desire for equality rather than inversion is at the same time the most reasonable and the most radical of her aims. That Wollstonecraft does not simply put women on top in-dicates her wish for a more radical reshaping of society than the category of inversion would allow for. Because she emphasizes gender roles as socially constructed, not as essentialized features of male and female identity, Wollstonecraft refuses to see woman as the "inversion" of man: she advocates equality and an end to hierarchical or dichotomized paradigms.

Wollstonecraft's *Vindication* provides an example of how feminist humor can engage with and undermine the authority of patriarchal discourse. She attacks prejudices against women by appealing to reason and invites her readers to join with her in laughter directed against present injustices and follies. Her polit-ical goal is at least partly achieved when readers learn to recognize the foolishness of many of the traditions surrounding women. Burney, Edgeworth, and Austen share Wollstonecraft's sense of the absurdity of sexist mandates. Although they seldom offer di-rect feminist polemics, they make comedy out of the discrepan-cies between the myths surrounding "woman" and the lives of real women. Unlike the "stupid novelists" Wollstonecraft attacks for romanticizing women's oppression, these writers depict in their works rational women living in a sexist society. By stressing the value of women's activities, they criticize the workings of the present system that strictly limit the scope of those activities. By setting up marriages of mutual respect, they propose new possibilities for a society that values women as men's equals. In mocking the follies of characters who uphold sexist points of view, Burney, Edgeworth, and Austen display the same faith as Wollstonecraft in people's ability to make more rational choices. By drawing their audience into the circle of feminist laughter, they create fellowship among all who share their sense of women's potential.

Bergson tells us that "laughter is always the laughter of a group" (64). It makes a difference, however, whether that group is empowered or subordinate. When authors belonging to an empowered group employ comedy against a disenfranchised group, they draw upon the authority of the existing social structure. But when authors belonging to a subordinate group direct their comedy at those in power, they propose an overthrow of the present structure and a new distribution of power.[11] And if they get people to laugh with them rather than at them, the proposition may become a reality.

3

From Inside Jokes to
Published Comedy

Spirited, easy, full of fun, verging with freedom upon sheer
nonsense,—*Love and Freindship* [sic] is all that; but what is
this note which never merges in the rest, which sounds
distinctly and penetratingly all through the volume?
It is the sound of laughter. The girl of fifteen is
laughing, in her corner, at the world.

—Virginia Woolf ("Jane Austen" 136)

As Virginia Woolf notes, Austen's juvenilia resound with irreverent laughter. She laughs at everything imaginable—literary conventions, social mores, history, love, death—with a wild abandon that must have puzzled as well as delighted the relatives for whom she wrote. Viewed together, these early efforts reveal the training ground of Austen's comic talent. She signs herself "the Author," mimics the fawning tone of dedications to patrons, and exudes the confidence of one who knows that her audience will find her funny.

Family laughter formed part of the background for Burney and Edgeworth as well as for Austen. Each author had a gift for entertaining her family circle. Both Burney and Edgeworth amused relatives with their talents for mimicry; all three honed their writing skills by practicing on a familial audience. Burney kept a lifelong journal that she shared with her sister Susanna, other select family members, and close friends. Edgeworth entertained her schoolmates with tales (gauging her success by their wakefulness) and tested her stories on the many children in her family. By playing the author's role in intimate surroundings, Burney, Edgeworth, and Austen began establishing their authority to write for a wider audience.

The relative freedom Burney, Edgeworth, and Austen enjoyed within their homes can be viewed as one beneficial side effect of the eighteenth-century sentimental family. Historian Lawrence Stone has identified the period between 1670 to 1790 as one dominated by this new middle-class family type, "a family serving rather fewer practical functions, but carrying a much greater load of emotional . . . commitment." Features of the sentimental family included greater "ties of affection," a structure that was "more internally liberal," and a base of power "less patriarchal and authoritarian" than earlier models of the family (657). Although the sentimental family had methods of coercing young women to conform to the feminine ideal,[1] it offered women membership in a group in which they might exchange ideas—and share jokes—with others. A growing emphasis on the domestic realm as a haven from the hectic public sphere gave this membership a heightened prestige. The family replaced the coffeehouse as a club unto itself. Close friends could join, and within the family group there might be subgroups: women alone at work, men together after dinner, or siblings behind bedroom doors.

An appreciative audience contributes enormously to the development of a sense of humor. Because Burney, Edgeworth, and Austen laughed and joked in their youth, they had a distinct advantage over women who were forced at an early age to conform exclusively to the feminine ideal.[2] Under explicitly patriarchal roofs, women learn to repress outward displays of mirth. Within their family groups, however, these three budding authors enjoyed opportunities to laugh with others, opportunities which led them to take comic liberties in their writing. Participation in jovial family parties allowed Burney, Edgeworth, and Austen to engage in humor that was both public (an assembled group) and private (a family).

The preceding chapter addressed the defiant stance of eighteenth-century feminist laughter; in this chapter I will relate this defiance more directly to the comic writing of Burney, Edgeworth, and Austen. I shall look first at theories of how humor can evolve from an awareness of the contradictory position of women in a male-dominated society as a coping strategy and an outlet for revolt. Next, I will show how Burney, Edgeworth, and Austen used humor in their own lives to channel aggression and how they experimented with encoding techniques for directing humor to a sympathetic audience. And finally, I will reconstruct their comic theories based upon statements on comedy and laughter in their novels. Throughout this chapter, I aim to establish an affinity between Wollstonecraft's revolutionary laughter and the comic strategies that allowed Burney, Edgeworth, and Austen to express their own rebellion against sexism.

If Burney, Edgeworth, and Austen were products of their time with their strong family ties and convivial assemblies, they also participated in what literary critic Richard Simon has labeled "an important moment in the history of laughter." Simon contends that during the eighteenth century, the comic came to be seen as "a fundamental quality shared by everyone, an essential attribute of our consciousness, of the patterns of human thought" (17). Even though conduct-book writers discouraged women from laughing, shared laughter came to be viewed as an important component of social concord. Eighteenth-century essayist Francis Hutcheson's *Reflections Upon Laughter* (1750) articulates this view of laughter as a healthy state of mind: "Laughter, like many other dispositions of our mind, is necessarily pleasant to us, when it begins in the natural manner, from some perception in the mind of something ludicrous. . . . Every one is conscious that a state of Laughter is an easy and agreeable state, that the recurring or suggestion of ludicrous images tends to dispel fretfulness, anxiety, or sorrow, and to reduce the mind to an easy, happy state" (26–27). Laughter, according to this view, alleviates the mind's otherwise anxious, nervous state by distracting it with "ludicrous images." Of course, Hutcheson insists that the laughter must arise "in a natural manner," in keeping with the eighteenth-century preference for amiable humor, and the laughter that he prescribes is gentle and uncritical. Because of laughter's alleged healing powers, Hutcheson advocates the "implanting" of "a sense of the ridiculous, in our nature" as "an avenue to pleasure, and an easy remedy for discontent and sorrow." In addition to the immediate personal benefits, he attributes to laughter the ability to forge intersubjective links: "Laughter is none of the smallest bonds of common friendship" (27). Thus, for Hutcheson, laughter serves as a release of tension that might otherwise be experienced as sorrow or discontent, and it fosters shared alliances.

Freud would later extend the eighteenth-century argument about laughter's role in mental health by contending that jokes give vent to social criticism that might otherwise be repressed to the detriment of the individual's state of mind. He, too, characterizes joking as an essentially social activity, one that "aims at drawing pleasure from mental processes, whether intellectual or otherwise" (96). According to Freud, tendentious or hostile jokes can serve as an acceptable means of expressing aggression against social superiors: "jokes are especially favored in order to make aggressiveness or criticism possible against persons in exalted positions who claim to exercise authority. The joke then represents a rebellion against that authority, a liberation from its pressure" (105).[3] Because Freud sees jokes as originating in the unconscious, he argues that they exert a stronger influence over the mind of the listener than other persuasive strategies: "Where argument tries to draw the hearer's criticism over on to its side, the joke endeavours to push the criticism out of sight. There is no doubt that the joke has chosen the method which is psychologically the more effective" (133). Although he sees jokes as differing from humor and the comic—which are more controlled by the conscious mind—he indicates that the various modes of humorous expression are interconnected. What jokes contribute to the comic and humor is a potent form of criticism and a covert style of rebellion.

Because of their ability to mask aggressive intentions, to sidestep opposition, and to build solidarity, joking and other forms of comic expression make perfect tools of resistance for individuals who are discouraged from wielding power openly and from displaying hostility. One such group, eighteenth-century middle-class women, was encouraged by conduct-book writers like

John Gregory and James Fordyce to employ indirect, male-flattering tactics to get their way. To act the part of the proper lady, a woman had to conceal anger, aggression, and other "unfeminine" feelings; a ladylike demeanor involved much indirect, circuitous behavior and a great deal of repression and duplicity. Thus, the eighteenth-century woman who had independent views of selfhood was required to live a double life.

But this very doubleness could create the conditions for humor, as humor scholar Louis Cazamian explains: "humor thrives on mental complexities, . . . contrasts are its food, . . . a duality of mental planes is the law of its being" (111). Cazamian compares the historical situation of the Renaissance—when new learning advanced too quickly to be assimilated, and old ideas coexisted with new—to the life of an individual, in which the boundlessness of childhood gives way to the limitations of maturity, and an ironic separation develops between the self and its former illusions (112). Paradoxically, the more serious and self-conscious a person is, the greater potential he or she will have for recognizing and taking advantage of the humorous implications of this inner doubleness.

Cazamian's statements on the serious source of the comic temperament have an added force when applied to the situation of women. If human maturation in general contributes to ironic detachment, then traditional female maturation must lead to multiple levels of irony. Kristina Straub, writing on the double standard that Burney faced as a woman coming of age in the eighteenth century, sums up the situation: "Whereas middle-class young men are encouraged to look forward to their futures, to conceive of the shape of their lives on the model of progress, young women like Burney are told not to expect too much from their maturing process—indeed, are often told to expect the worst" (4).

The eighteenth-century poet Edward Young succinctly states one paradox of female existence: "Your sex's glory 'tis to shine *unknown*" (117). When conduct-book writers elaborate on this paradox, they tend to mask its misogyny by first granting women a level of equality with men as rational beings and then insisting that, for the sake of order, women be satisfied with a subordinate status. John Bennett, for example, concedes a "natural equality" between the sexes at the beginning of his strictures, yet he ends up urging women to accept subordination for their own good: "whenever they are tempted to repine at the appearance of insignificance and inferiority, it becomes them to remember that their greatest strength lies in their *weakness*" (99). William Duff makes a convincing case for the importance of improving female education, yet still believes that women's place lies in "the humble, but not inglorious walks of private life" (99–100).

If the authors of conduct books acknowledge the paradox behind their "separate-but-equal" arguments, they tend to fall back on a divine first cause to justify women's subordination rather than on rational argumentation. Bennett uses weak and circuitous logic to defend male supremacy: "Superiority, for the sake of order and protection must be lodged *somewhere*. And it seems *providentially* lodged in the *males*" (84). Thomas Gisborne views women's "otherness" as part of the divine plan: "Providence, designing from the beginning, that the manner of life to be adopted by women should in many respects ultimately depend, not so much on their own deliberate choice, as on the determination, or at least on the interest and convenience of the parent, of the husband, or of some near connection; has implanted in them a remarkable tendency to conform to the wishes and examples of those for whom they feel a warmth of regard" (116). Earlier in the century, Mary Astell railed against the difficulty of responding to the argument from divine causes and claimed that opponents only resorted to it in a pinch: "One does not wonder, indeed, that when an Adversary is drove to a Non-plus, and Reason declares against him, he flies to Authority, especially to Divine, which is infallible and therefore ought not to be disputed" (*Some Reflections* 103). Whether all readers of conduct books shared her skepticism or not, many must have noted the points where argumentation gave over to faith and women were allotted a contradictory status: equality in reason, subordination in fact.

Recent feminist critics have analyzed the way that women's sense of "doubleness" in society—their status as human beings in conflict with feminine roles—affects their identity. Rachel Brownstein calls this doubleness "the ironic self-awareness of a rational creature absurdly caught in a lady's place" (61). In the case of female writers, according to Katherine Pope, anger at the implacability of women's double lives may surface in conflicted protagonists who function as inside jokes: "The fictional woman, like her real life counterpart, often sees the dichotomy between the self and the public image as a private joke, which she may or may not share with other women. Much of women's humor is based on the incongruity between the inner and outer self, between reality as women perceive it and the myths of male superiority, for example. Women's humor also exposes the myths of ideal womanhood which require that a woman be different from, often less than, what she is" (23). Humor in fiction, then, can function as a way for an author to represent the contradictions of women's lives without risking the exposure of a feminist polemic. As Regina Barreca sums it up, "Comedy can effectively channel anger and rebellion by first making them appear to be acceptable and temporary phenomena, no doubt to be purged by laughter, and then by harnessing the released energies, rather than dispersing them" (*Untamed* 33).

By adopting a comic frame of mind early in life, Burney, Edgeworth, and Austen paved the way for their mature social criticism. Wordplay, jokes, and riddles taught them an essential subversive strategy—to carnivalize language, to "humor the sentence" (Little, "Humoring" 10).[4] As anthropologist Mary Douglas points out, "The joke . . . affords opportunity for realising that an accepted pattern has no necessity. Its excitement lies in the suggestion that any particular ordering of experience may be arbitrary and subjective" (96). Douglas argues that a joke is always potentially subversive: "Since its form consists of a victorious tilting of uncontrol against control, it is an image of the levelling of hierarchy, the triumph of intimacy over formality, of unofficial values over official ones" (98). Burney, Edgeworth, and Austen wielded the power of jokes and laughter as a means of self-assertion. As members of middle-class families, they identified with the laughter of a privileged group; but the confidence they gained by joking within this group enabled them to apply critical humor to their situation as females in a sexist society and thereby challenge the necessity of women's subordinate status. They used comedy as an outlet for aggression and as a means of social criticism in their lives.

In spite of the fact that Burney and Edgeworth enjoyed much laughter in their family circles, their home lives were not uniformly happy. Each author suffered, at a young age, from the death of her mother: Burney was ten, and Edgeworth only five. Both had intense and problematic relations with their fathers and even more difficult relations with their stepmothers. Burney despised her stepmother and vented hostility by making her the butt of many jokes. Edgeworth had to deal with a succession of stepmothers and with an ever-increasing contingent of stepsiblings. In keeping with the model of the sentimental family, Burney and Edgeworth did not perceive their fathers as authoritarian figures to obey out of fear; rather, they saw them as affectionate mentors toward whom they felt bonds of love. Longing for the approval of their fathers, both Burney and Edgeworth took part in their fathers' projects and to a certain extent followed in their fathers' footsteps by becoming writers. Moreover, each author learned to use humor to cope with her complicated circumstances.

Biographer Margaret Doody describes tensions in the Burney household that developed because of Charles Burney's disposition and social bearing. She reports that Charles Burney made his way in the world by manipulating important people through flattery and even self-abasement; he wrote excessively florid poems to patrons, praising their generosity while figuratively holding his hand out for more money. According to Doody, Charles Burney expected his family to live up to his example—to strive for success in the eyes of the world. He related his children's behavior to family honor in ways that inhibited Frances's writing. Because he viewed every Burney's actions as a reflection upon the honor of the family, he discouraged risk-taking and other exceptional or independent behavior. His concern for public opinion made Frances extremely self-conscious about her behavior: on the one hand, she wanted to please; on the other, she did not want to imitate her father's fawning tendencies. Charles Burney insisted that his family maintain an appearance of domestic tranquility so as not to interfere with his work. As a result of his prohibition on open disputes, the Burney children learned to conceal their negative emotions from their father, developing covert tactics to express anger and frustration to one another while keeping up appearances. This division between appearances and intentions contributed to Frances Burney's method of encoding her anger in a humor that would be accessible only to co-conspirators.

In the early part of her life, Frances kept secret from her father not only her anger, but also her humor. Among her siblings and peers she had a reputation for lively wit. Around her father and with strangers, however, Burney was so shy as a child that Charles nicknamed her "The Old Lady." Once the second Mrs. Burney joined the household, Frances had even more to conceal from her father since she and her siblings hated their stepmother—and not without reason, for she discouraged her stepdaughter's writing. Doody characterizes the strategic behavior of the Burney children: "Before outsiders they usually acted according to a forced decorum relieved by sly petulance and secret hostilities; those they trusted with the truth were enlisted as accomplices in their guerrilla games" (28). Among her siblings, Frances engaged in a good deal of laughter at her stepmother's expense. In what Doody calls "codes of hatred," the Burney children referred to their stepmother as "the *Lady*," "Precious," and "Madam" (29, 27). The adult Frances Burney purged all direct evidence of her hatred for her stepmother from her journals, but biographer Joyce Hemlow detected that she refers to her happiest times as those when her stepmother was absent (*History* 35–36).

The Burney children initiated family friend Samuel Crisp into their codes, and he joined them in ridiculing their stepmother. Rather than helping the children become reconciled with this woman, Crisp insulted her in their presence and mimicked her behind her back. The stepmother suspected that conspiracies surrounded her and accused the children of "sedition" and "treason," but her complaints never led to Charles Burney's intervention—possibly because she never found hard evidence to present to her husband and possibly because he preferred the illusion of domestic quietude to any revelation of personal tension or incompatibility. Hemlow reports on the Burney children's covert solidarity: "Sometimes they worried over the safety of letters 'full of Treason,' and sometimes when away they were not above solic-iting the Burney unhappy enough to be left at home for some 'pretty little bits of sedition'" (*History* 37). Making up jokes about their stepmother allowed the Burney children to channel their aggression in a way that made day-to-day life with the enemy pos-sible. They could appear in their father's eyes as happy family members without having to repress their hostility completely.

When Frances left the Burney household to enter court ser-vice as deputy keeper of the robes to Queen Charlotte, she en-gaged in the same kind of conspiratorial humor, this time aimed against the tyrannical Mrs. Schwellenberg, first keeper of the queen's robes, and even the queen herself. Her journal entries provide us with clearly documented accounts of her suffering at court in a position that required her to stand in attendance on the queen for hours on end. She also included samples of the "trea-sonous" sessions that she held with her fellow court-dependents. Hester Thrale reports that (according to her sources) Burney "takes off her Mistress," mimicking her behavior by pretending to "take Snuff like the Queen, & draw the White hand across the dirty Nose" (821). Although Burney herself did not leave a record of such graphic mockery, she did express the relief that laughing among companions afforded her.

An account from her court diaries illustrates Burney's al-most reflexive use of humor to mask discomfort. A "Mr. Turbu-lent" offered Burney sympathy for her servitude to Mrs. Schwel-lenberg, and she deflected the painful reflections that his sympathy aroused by instigating group laughter:

> He exclaimed, "This ma'am, is your colleague!—Who could ever have imagined it would have been Miss Burney's fate to be so coupled? Could you ever, ma'am, foresee, or suspect, or believe you should be linked to such a companion?"
>
> No, thought I, indeed did I not! But to re-cover myself from the train of thoughts to which so home a question led, I frankly narrated some small circumstances of a ludicrous and unimpor-

tant nature, which regarded this lady with some of her domestics.

They were almost in fits of laughter; and Mr. Turbulent's compassion so fleeted away from the diversion of this recital, that he now only lamented I had not also known the other original colleague, that she too might have lived in my memory. I thank him much! (*Diary* 3.335)

By joking about Mrs. Schwellenberg, Burney directed anger at her subservient position against her mistress and in the process got the upper hand. Nonetheless, the disparity between her thoughts and the entertaining narrative she provided to mask those thoughts reveals the degree of concealment that went into her humor. Mr. Turbulent's question—"so home a question"—was not new to Burney in the course of her five-year immurement at court. Yet she refused to indulge in public self-pity; to dispel Mr. Turbulent's compassion became a point of honor. His lament that she had not been there even longer marks her independence of his sympathy, but not without pain on her part for having done the job so well. Here we can see that Burney coped with an almost intolerable sense of oppression by establishing an alternative society of like-minded individuals who laughed to ease the strains of court life.[5] In the court as in her family, she concealed her dissatisfaction from those in power and found in humor and a chosen circle of conspirators a way to express hostility.[6]

Burney's awareness of her own satirical tactics can be seen in a letter to Samuel Crisp, in which she defends herself against the charge of inventing comic characters for her journal sketches: "The world, and especially the Great World, is so filled with absurdity of various sorts, now bursting forth in impertinence, now in pomposity, now giggling in silliness, and now yawning in dulness [sic], that there is no occasion for invention to draw what is striking in every possible species of the ridiculous" (qtd. in Hemlow, *History* 122). Burney took her cue here from Fielding's statements on social comedy in *Joseph Andrews*,[7] but she clearly found a comic perspective useful in life as well as in fiction. That she converted impertinence, pomposity, silliness, and dullness—annoying if not insulting modes of behavior—into topics for comic sketches indicates her tendency to use satire and humor as a means to rise above discomfort.

Because Edgeworth did not leave behind the kind of detailed record of her life that Burney produced in her diaries, it is more difficult to demonstrate her use of humor to channel aggression. Plenty of evidence exists, however, of her early hostile behavior. In the period following her mother's death, she committed a series of rebellious acts, including throwing tea in someone's face, climbing out of a garret window (causing a passerby to run inside and warn her maid), trampling on a set of newly glazed hotbed frames, and cutting the squares out of her aunt's checked sofa covers.[8] Biographer Marilyn Butler suggests that Edgeworth's aggressive acts sprang from her desire for attention and love: unable to attract the attention she desired by behaving with "proper" feminine passivity, the young Edgeworth took extreme measures. At boarding school, she found in scholarship a way to gain adult approval without resorting to aggression. She exhibited a willingness to learn and a talent to excel that pleased her teachers, who praised her accordingly. But since teachers' pets make unpopular peers, Edgeworth employed other talents to please her fellow students—she compensated for their jealousy by entertaining them with stories at bedtime.

Like Burney, Edgeworth presented one side of herself to authority figures and another to her peers. Both women had reputations for being painfully shy around strangers yet voluble and amusing among friends. By the time she was in her twenties, Edgeworth had established herself as the family comic: "She prided herself on being the only person who could always make her serious cousin Letty laugh, but more frequently her function was to amuse her aunt and Sophy" (Butler 126). In company, she delighted her relatives with imitations of Irish figures, accurately mimicking accents and mannerisms (the kind of playful mimicry that would serve her well in the Irish tales); privately, she recorded amusing anecdotes (from newspapers and hearsay) in notebooks and used them in her letters as well as in her fiction.

Once Burney and Edgeworth relaxed around people, they

were able to verbally unleash their comic spirits. In their writings, they extended the tactics they developed in intimate settings—mimicry, anecdotage, sarcasm, and in-group joking—into comic characterization, humorous sketches, irony, and double-sided or encoded comedy. Because their family difficulties are fairly well documented, we can gain insight into their comic worldviews from the tensions that surrounded their lives. Burney used humor as a channel for her aggression whereas Edgeworth learned to employ humor instead of aggression to obtain the attention she desired. Both chose humor as a method of expressing hostilities and establishing solidarity with others.

Compared to Burney's and Edgeworth's stormy youth, Austen's early years seem rather smooth. If she had tensions with her parents, they do not appear to have been of great magnitude. In fact, she had the benefit of a number of witty family members and relatives—her mother, her brother Henry, and her sister, Cassandra, to name those within her immediate family. In common with Burney and Edgeworth, however, Austen was shy in the company of strangers, reserving her wit almost exclusively for family members. Austen biographer Park Honan compares her experience at school with that of Edgeworth and unjustly faults Edgeworth for her diplomacy: "[Edgeworth] suppressed part of herself by learning to disguise her aggression as a pleasant 'improvisatrice' or teller of entertaining stories at the expense of her ability to observe women. She paid a high price for compliance: at Mrs. Latuffière's [school] she took small measure of her own needs, desires, impulses. But Jane Austen, however mousy and inconsequential she seemed, did not play false to herself, and her shyness was in some ways an advantage" (34). Whereas Honan faults Edgeworth's sociability and implies that she let her desire for popularity get the better of her judgment, he views Austen's shyness as a sign of the detachment that allowed her to be a keen observer of people. Instead of a contrast between her and Edgeworth, however, I see an affinity. In spite of Edgeworth's sociable storytelling abilities, she, like Austen, made no close friends at school; her stories functioned as a mode of interaction that permitted her to control the response of her peer audience while pursuing her scholarship.

Within her own family, Austen found ample opportunities

for exercising her critical sense of humor. In her early teens, she began to circulate burlesques, plays, and short novels among her family members. When her brother James started a periodical at Oxford in the *Spectator* style, Austen gained access to a wider sphere and a wider audience. The *Loiterer*, as the publication was called, engaged in lively political discourse and moral tales along Tory party lines. Honan attributes one *Loiterer* letter signed "Sophia Sentiment" to the thirteen-year-old Jane Austen. The letter stands as an early example of Austen's playfully aggressive style, a style that only slightly masks its hostile intent beneath a light tone.

"Sophia" opens with a statement of her credentials: "You know, Sir, I am a great reader, and not to mention some hundred volumes of Novels and Plays, have, in the two last summers, actually got through all the entertaining papers of our most celebrated periodical writers" (qtd. in Honan 60). Because of her experience with periodicals, she claims to have been at first delighted with the *Loiterer*. Her tone quickly changes, however, as she proceeds to attack the journal's male-centeredness: "You neglect the amusement of our sex, and have taken no more notice of us, than if you thought, like the Turks, we had no souls" (61). "Sophia" concludes with a devastating threat: if the paper does not print any stories for ladies soon, she menaces, "may your work be condemned to the pastry-cook's shop, and may you always continue a bachelor, and be plagued with a maiden sister to keep house for you" (61). The joking tone of the "Sophia Sentiment" letter did not hinder Austen's brother from taking it seriously. According to Honan, the *Loiterer* altered its focus and attempted to write more about love and marriage to satisfy its female readers.

Another interesting case of Austen's use of humor to counterbalance anger occurred later in her life when she attempted to ascertain the intentions of the Crosby publishing house toward her novel *Susan* (*Northanger Abbey*). Crosby & Co. purchased *Susan* in 1803 and even advertised it, but when the novel still had not appeared in print by 1809, Austen wrote a tactfully worded letter requesting information on its fate. In a straightforward, sober, and assertive manner, she informed Crosby & Co. that if they did not respond to her request she would attempt to publish the work elsewhere. What makes this letter remarkable is not so much the content as the signature: Austen adopts the pseudonym Mrs. Ashton Dennis, and signs the letter, "I am, Gentlemen, etc., etc., M. A. D." (*Letters* 263). The acronym bespeaks a hostility that diplomacy forbids her to express directly, implying as it does either derangement or anger. As Margaret Kirkham notes, "The correspondence about this shows quite clearly Jane Austen's urgent interest in achieving publication and, in the curious manner in which she signs her letter, a rising sense of persecution, only partially controlled by making a silly joke of it" (70). Encoding a joke into her otherwise serious letter must have provided Austen with a sense of control—the meaning of her "name" was her private jest.

In general Austen writes more openly aggressive humor than either Burney or Edgeworth. Her letters to family members are noteworthy for their acerbic wit; indeed, one twentieth-century reader has called them "a desert of trivialities punctuated by occasional oases of clever malice" (qtd. in *Letters* xlii). But rather than expressing malice or bitterness, Austen's epistolary wit exhibits a playful competitiveness. A sense of "neighborly" competition fuels many of her humorous quips:

> Mrs. Portman is not much admired in Dorsetshire; the good-natured world, as usual, extolled her beauty so highly, that all the neighbourhood have had the pleasure of being disappointed. (28)
> Charles Powlett gave a dance on Thursday, to the great disturbance of all his neighbors, of course, who, you know, take a most lively interest in the state of his finances, and live in hopes of his being soon ruined. (36)
> The Wylmots being robbed must be an amusing thing to their acquaintance, & I hope it is as much their pleasure as it seems their avocation to be subjects of general Entertainment. (114–15)

One senses from the letters that Austen's preference for "3 or 4 families in a country village" as material enough for a novel came from her appreciation of local gossip. Austen jokes about what the neighbors think of each other and what she thinks of the neighbors. She even jokes about what the neighbors might think of her: "Whenever I fall into misfortune, how many jokes it ought to furnish my acquaintance in general," she declares stoically, but quickly adds, "or I shall die dreadfully in their debt for entertainment" (57). Even though Austen comes out on top in this remark, she admits the possibility that the tables could be turned. Her epistolary remarks on neighborhood laughter mirror her published comments on humor in *Pride and Prejudice* (1813). Mr. Bennet's famous dictum—"For what do we live, but to make sport for our neighbours, and laugh at them in our turn?" (364)—could stand as an epigram for the humor exhibited in Austen's letters. According to Austen the letter writer, everyone must expect to give and receive her share of laughter in this world.

I have discussed the lives and letters of Burney, Edgeworth, and Austen in order to trace their individual development of a comic perspective that was both social and critical and to show how they encoded humor for insiders in their circles. In their letters to family and relations, these women were certainly less guarded than they had to be in their published works; however, even in their private letters they presented themselves as comic authors. Furthermore, because they used humor to channel aspects of their personality that clashed with traditional models of femininity, their comedy strikes a defiant posture that simultaneously acknowledges social stress and declares personal independence. Given a degree of license within their families to experiment with humor, Burney, Edgeworth, and Austen developed comic talents that allowed them to subvert the codes of feminine conduct.

We can extrapolate from the lives and letters of Burney, Edgeworth, and Austen a feminist rationale for their use of humor. Because they developed covert comic strategies in their lives, they were better equipped to mock sexism and restrictions upon women in their fiction. A significant aspect of their humor connects them to the feminists of their day: it derives from their views of an equality between men and women based upon rationality and a perception of the incongruity of women's lot. Frequently we can see behind their comic masks an anger that resembles that of Mary Wollstonecraft in *A Vindication of the Rights of Woman*, anger both at the restrictions upon women's behavior and the lack of choices available to them.

Burney, Edgeworth, and Austen each produced working theories of comedy that combine social criticism with sympathy. Burney's *The Wanderer* (1814) and Edgeworth's *Helen* (1834) contain extended passages on the subject of comedy; Austen scatters remarks on the subject throughout her most comic novel, *Pride and Prejudice*. These authors advocate a wide variety of comic strategies, including varying degrees of satire. Each shows a capacity for casting a cool eye on society's shortcomings, particularly on the limitations of women's situation, that aligns their writings more closely to satirical works than to so-called "amiable" humor. They satirize sexist values and those who uphold them while arousing our sympathy for female characters who must negotiate their destinies in a society that restricts their growth as human beings.

Containing more references to laughter than any of her other works, *Pride and Prejudice* gives us the clearest picture of Austen's theory of comedy. As literary scholar Patricia Meyer Spacks points out, this novel problematizes laughter. Spacks describes the various functions of laughter in the novel: "Laughter allows useful defensive transformations of pain into pleasure; it records the freedom and power of a kind of wit closely allied with intelligence. Its dangers are equally clear: it evades discrimination" (74). According to Spacks, *Pride and Prejudice* ultimately teaches the reader to laugh in moderation and to beware of indiscriminate laughter. Yet Austen's sense of moderation and decorum is not conventional, recognizing as it does the restraints on women imposed by conventional eighteenth-century morality. Austen laughs with the "freedom and power" of a lucid, rational feminist.

Although *Pride and Prejudice* puts us on our guard about laughter—we would be mistaken if we were to laugh too confidently at Darcy or with the wayward Lydia Bennet—the novel concludes with a strong statement about the role of laughter in marriage. The narrator reports that the hero's sister, Georgiana Darcy, at first "listened with an astonishment bordering on alarm"

71

to Elizabeth's "lively, sportive, manner of talking" with Darcy. "He, who had always inspired in herself a respect which almost overcame her affection, she now saw the object of open pleasantry. *Her mind received knowledge which had never fallen in her way. By Elizabeth's instructions she began to comprehend that a woman may take liberties with her husband*, which a brother will not always allow in a sister more than ten years younger than himself" (387–88, emphasis added). We know that immediately after Darcy proposes, Elizabeth has resolved to teach him an important lesson: "he had yet to learn to be laught at, and it was rather too early to begin" (371). From Georgiana's "alarm" we may deduce that Elizabeth carries out this plan; but Elizabeth carries her program of instructional laughter even further.

In addition to teaching Darcy to counter his pride with self-mockery—a valuable lesson for all human beings—she gives Georgiana a sound lesson in gender politics. Barreca suggests that, in looking for feminist humor, we pay attention to points in novels where older people tell younger people not to laugh, because such points will indicate an imminent transgression against the established order (*Last Laughs* 11). *Pride and Prejudice* offers more than imminent transgression; it calls into being a new order when the novel's heroine instructs a younger female character to take "liberties" with her husband, giving the young woman "knowledge" that had not previously fallen her way. Georgiana has hitherto viewed her brother with an awe that constrains even her affection for him; Elizabeth teaches her that while authority may be legitimately exercised by a brother/guardian over his much younger sister, the authority does not derive from masculinity but from experience.

A scene early in the novel elaborates on the gender concerns that underlie Austen's view of laughter as a necessary correlative of sexual equality. The scene takes place at Netherfield. Miss Bingley, who sees Elizabeth as a rival, has persuaded her to "take a turn" around the drawing room, ostensibly for exercise, but with the obvious intention of attracting Darcy's attention and showing her superiority to Elizabeth (56). When Darcy indicates that he knows what she is up to, Miss Bingley asks Elizabeth how they might "punish" him for teasing them:

"Nothing so easy, if you have but the inclination," said Elizabeth. "We can all plague and
punish one another. Teaze him—laugh at him.—
Intimate as you are, you must know how it is to
be done."

"But upon my honour I do *not*. I do assure you
that my intimacy has not yet taught me *that*. Teaze
calmness of temper and presence of mind! No,
no—I feel he may defy us there. And as to laughter, we will not expose ourselves, if you please, by
attempting to laugh without a subject." (57)

Clearly, Miss Bingley means to flatter Darcy, but she also invokes
the conduct-book rule that women who laugh at men will "expose" only themselves. By advising laughter, Elizabeth implies on
the one hand that Miss Bingley does not know Darcy quite so well
as she pretends, and on the other that intimacy involves a certain
amount of critical laughter. Moreover, she challenges Miss Bingley to act like a spirited, rational being.

After Miss Bingley's smug refusal to laugh, Elizabeth stages
her own assault on Darcy's authority: "Mr. Darcy is not to be
laughed at! . . . That is an uncommon advantage, and uncommon
I hope it will continue, for it would be a great loss to *me* to have
many such acquaintance. I dearly love a laugh" (57). We can hear
overtones of Austen's letters in Elizabeth's remarks; here, however, the comments are significantly directed at a male who has
been declared infallible.

The exchange that then takes place between Darcy and Elizabeth invokes the conduct-book restrictions on female laughter.
Darcy believes that a tendency to laugh can lead to mockery; the
dialogue that follows gives the witty female a chance to talk back:

"Miss Bingley," said he, "has given me credit for
more than can be. The wisest and the best of
men, nay, the wisest and best of their actions,
may be rendered ridiculous by a person whose
first object in life is a joke."

"Certainly," replied Elizabeth—"there are

> such people, but I hope I am not one of *them*. I
> hope I never ridicule what is wise or good. Follies
> and nonsense, whims and inconsistencies *do* di-
> vert me, I own, and I laugh at them whenever I
> can.—But these, I suppose, are precisely what
> you are without." (57)

In effect, Darcy accepts Miss Bingley's tribute to his infallibility when he claims that people might laugh at him in spite of his wisdom and perfection. Elizabeth defies his authority as one of "the best of men" in a manner that goes against Miss Bingley's exaggerated sense of decorum. The discussion does not end until Elizabeth obtains an explicit acknowledgment of what she knows must be true—that Darcy, too, has flaws. The chapter concludes with a comment from Darcy's point of view: "He began to feel the danger of paying Elizabeth too much attention" (58).

    The effects of the scene just described are far-reaching in the novel, and the layers of irony tell against Elizabeth and Darcy both. Elizabeth will learn to respect Darcy as a decent, if flawed, individual (as she does not at this point), and Darcy will learn to be more generous with people. In fact, this scene strengthens Darcy and Elizabeth's relationship: the "danger" he fears is one of attraction to a woman who challenges him. Once they are engaged, Elizabeth teases him about having admired her for her "impertinence" (380). Even though he identifies the engaging quality as "liveliness of mind," she insists upon her initial word choice and elaborates upon her own unconventionality: "You may as well call it impertinence at once. It was very little less. The fact is, that you were sick of civility, of deference, of officious attention. You were disgusted with the women who were always speaking and looking and thinking for *your* approbation alone. I roused, and interested you, because I was so unlike *them*. Had you not been really amiable you would have hated me for it" (380). The final part of Elizabeth's statement amounts to Shaftesbury's "ridicule as the test of truth" applied to courtship. Elizabeth gets rewarded for behaving in contradiction to the conduct-book regulations, and Darcy reveals his sterling character by admiring her strengths. She violates the conventions that guide gender relations, but her ability to do so frees her for the rewards of a true partnership—one that will, no doubt, involve its share of laughter.

The comic theory that underlies *Pride and Prejudice* involves a mixture of satire and sympathy. Elizabeth declares herself bound to laugh at "follies and nonsense, whims and inconsistencies," but she sees this laughter as an essential part of intimacy. In the end, Elizabeth achieves the conventional goal of the heroine in a comedy—she marries—but she continues to maintain her active, lively mind, vowing "to find occasions for teazing and quarrelling with [Darcy] as often as may be" (381).

Similarly, Edgeworth's *Helen* provides a theory of comedy as a potent source of female expression. The theory contrasts the "happy genius of Nonsense" with the "vulgar imp yclept Fun," and it appears two-thirds of the way through the book, directly after a debate about female power—whether it should be exerted directly or indirectly and in what sphere (249). A Frenchman expresses one extreme of the debate. He first compliments "English ladies" because they, unlike Frenchwomen, refrain from political activism, and then states his opinion that women should be "omnipotent" within the domestic sphere (248). Several participants in the debate express the other extreme and locate women's power in female influence (i.e., as indirect power) regardless of sphere or location. Neither position allows women much room for authentic behavior.

A fight between two of the disputants—Lady Masham and Lady Bearcroft—interrupts the debate and threatens to end in serious mischief. Fortunately, Lady Cecilia comes to the rescue with her diplomatic talents, and her peacemaking tactic involves comedy, or "the happy genius of Nonsense." The narrator inserts a commentary that merits quotation at length because of the light it sheds on Edgeworth's view of comedy's function. In its personification of Nonsense and Fun, Edgeworth's comic theory harkens back to Addison's *Spectator* genealogy of Humour and False Humour. Edgeworth's mixture of violent and whimsical imagery suggests the range of possibilities of her humor:

Lady Cecilia, at utmost need, summoned to her aid the happy genius of Nonsense—the genius of Nonsense, in whose elfin power even Love delights; on whom Reason herself condescends often to smile, even when Logic frowns, and chops him on his block: but, cut in twain, the ethereal spirit soon unites again, and lives, and laughs. But mark him well—this little happy genius of Nonsense; see that he be the true thing—the genuine spirit. You will know him for his well-bred air and tone, which none can counterfeit; and by his smile; for while most he makes others laugh, the arch little rogue seldom goes beyond a smile himself! Graceful in the midst of all his pranks, he never goes too far—though far enough he has been known to go: he has crept into the armour of the great hero, convulsed the senate in the wig of a chancellor, and becomingly, decorously, put on now and then the mitre of an archbishop . . . [A]t [Lady Cecilia's] utmost need, obedient to her call came this happy little genius, and brought with him song and dance, riddle and charade, and comic prints; and on a half-opened parcel of books Cecilia darted, and produced a *Comic Annual,* illustrated by him whom no risible muscles can resist. All smiled who understood, and mirth admitted of her crew all who smiled, and [political] party-spirit fled. But there were foreigners present. Foreigners cannot well understand our local allusions; our Cruikshank is to them unintelligible, and Hood's *Sorrows of Number One* is quite lost upon them. Then Lady Bearcroft thought she would do as much as Lady Cecilia, and more—that she would produce what these poor foreigners could comprehend. But not at her call came the genius of lively nonsense, he heard her not. In his stead came that counterfeit, who thinks it witty to be rude: "And placing raillery in railing, / Will tell aloud your greatest failing"—that vulgar imp yclept Fun—known by his broad grin, by his loud tone, and by his rude banter. Head foremost forcing himself in, came he, and brought with him a heap of coarse caricatures, and they were [political] party characters. (249)

Here we have a full-fledged comic theory that takes a straightforward stand in favor of "good-natured" as opposed to "ill-natured" humor. Lady Cecilia sets people at ease with her comic talents; Lady Bearcroft's raillery attacks her companions and makes them uncomfortable. Roughly speaking, Lady Cecilia's approach puts "heart" into humor as opposed to Lady Bearcroft's "Fun" that plunges in "head foremost." This does not mean, however, that Edgeworth simply agreed with the eighteenth-century's appreciation of amiable humor and denigration of critical comedy. In fact, her theory of comedy contains some strikingly subversive undertones.

The placement of the discussion of comedy—it comes after a debate about women's proper role in society—suggests that female advocacy is not and should not be either omnipotent or indirect: Lady Bearcroft divides people according to political parties and offends by loudly telling them their faults; Lady Cecilia works through diplomacy and moderation. Moreover, because both Lady Cecilia and Lady Bearcroft exercise "masculine" (active) powers, Edgeworth indicates that gender stereotypes are more a product of social definition than of biology. The difference between the two women lies neither in their femininity nor in the degree of "masculine" activity they display, but rather in the ends to which they exercise their powers. Lady Bearcroft delights in divisiveness; Lady Cecilia strives for social concord.

The most radical of the subversive inflections in this passage involves its veiled reference to the French Revolution. The fight breaks out shortly after the Frenchman has decried female politicians and exaggerated the role of female domestic power. Thus, the image of Reason, smiling while Logic chops Nonsense on his block, and of Nonsense, uniting again to live and laugh, becomes fraught with significance. First, the alliance between Reason and Nonsense here suggests that in spite of the violence in France (the implied guillotine), the revolutionaries spoke some truth. Second, this alliance—and subsequent truth—is feminist: Reason, personified as a goddess during the French Revolution, is associated with the unimposing, beguiling (masculine) Nonsense over against the aggressive, intrusive (masculine) Logic. If the behavior of Lady Cecilia and Lady Bearcroft depicts Edgeworth's criticism of essential, gender-specific qualities, the allegory of Reason, Logic, and Nonsense depicts Edgeworth's commitment to feminist psychology and politics.

The curious intermingling of public and domestic politics in the scene indicates one of the novel's central tensions. While the domestic realm undoubtedly privileges female presence and activity, neither it nor the political realm is self-contained— neither is safe from the other's influence. Lady Davenant's early absorption in political affairs made her a bad mother, whereas Lady Cecilia, a truly domestic female, allows her moral integrity to be compromised because of her distorted views about gender relations (she lies to her husband about his being her "first love"). On the whole, the novel advocates equality between the sexes in marriage and hints that women have the capacity to practice politics if only the world would accept them on equal terms with men in political spheres.[9] Edgeworth saw in comedy the potential for a diplomatic strategy with domestic applications.

In *Helen,* Edgeworth provides her most explicit statement about the function of comedy, aligning it implicitly with late-eighteenth-century feminism. Like Austen, she favors a mixture of satire and sympathy, and she values comedy's potential for fostering intimacy. Although the subversive implications of her discussion of "Nonsense" are subtle, she clearly sees comedy as an acceptable and powerful tool for feminism.

Burney's ideas about the rebelliousness of women's comedy are best expressed in her most political work, *The Wanderer; or, Female Difficulties*. Set against the backdrop of the French Revolution, *The Wanderer* questions hierarchies of gender, class, and race. Without attempting to do justice to this novel's political complexities, I want to focus on one point at which feminism and comedy intersect.[10] A discussion of the subversive potential of laughter that occurs midway through the novel sheds light on the feminist implications of eighteenth-century women's comedy. Burney portrays in the character of Mr. Scope conservative male anxieties about the danger of female laughter and leaves us to conclude that he may have some reason to worry.

Mr. Scope represents the traditional English gentleman, whom Burney satirizes both for his provincial perspective on revolutionary politics and for his limited view of women's capacities. His politics are mainly blind prejudices, and he thinks that women are deficient in reason and inferior to men in understanding. Mr. Scope's anxieties about female laughter reflect his conservative views and echo the sentiments of conduct-book writers who argue that laughter is not compatible with womanly virtue.

Mr. Scope describes the danger of laughter in terms of both gender and class:

> If one of those young milliners . . . should take the liberty to laugh at my expence, what, you might ask, could it signify that a young girl should laugh? Young persons, especially of the female gender, being naturally given to laughter, at very small provocatives, not to say sometimes without any whatsoever. Whereupon, persons of an ordinary judgment, may conclude such an action, by which I mean laughing, to be of no consequence. . . .
>
> Persons, I say, of deeper knowledge in the maxims and manners of the moral world, would look forward with watchfulness, on such an occasion, to its future effects; for one laugh breeds another, and another breeds another; for nothing is so catching as laughing; I mean among the vulgar; in which class I would be understood to include the main mass of a great nation. (396)

Young girls, lower-class people, working women, the "vulgar": Mr. Scope lumps the disempowered into one colossal source of social unrest. He clearly wants to protect his own interests as an empowered English gentleman. For Mr. Scope, general laughter leads to a disruption of the class structure that could cause an actual revolution.

He rephrases himself in legalistic terms, using the rhetoric of rationality to argue for a totalitarian state:

> My argument . . . is a short, but I hope, a clear one, for 'tis deduced from general principles and analogy. . . . [W]hat I mean, in two words, is that the laugh raised by Mr. Gooch, and those young milliners . . . may, in itself, perhaps, as only announcing incapacity, not be condemnable; but when it turns out that it promulgates false reports, and makes two worthy persons . . . appear to be fit subjects for ridicule; then, indeed the laugh is no longer innocent; and ought, in strict justice, to be punished, as seriously as any other mode of propagating false rumours. (397)

Mr. Scope announces his anxieties about gender and class by conflating laughter with stupidity and seditious slander. He bases his argument on the principle of social hierarchy; his analysis of subversive activities implicitly refers to the upheavals of the French Revolution. To protect his privileged status, he would like to punish those who laugh at their betters.

Like the laughing milliners, Burney subjects Mr. Scope to ridicule. The groups he wants to control and silence—women and the working classes—have voices that Burney wants to be heard.[11] Juliet, the novel's heroine, "wanders" into the lowest strata of English society, observing and commenting on problems in the social order. Characters like Mr. Scope and the wealthy individuals who plague Juliet with their whims and judgments become targets of Burney's satire precisely because they take advantage of gender and class privileges and ignore their social responsibilities. *The Wanderer* challenges the status quo in ways that should make men like Mr. Scope uneasy.

In their private letters and published works, Burney, Edgeworth, and Austen employed comic strategies both to entertain and to express anger. When they wrote for friends and families, their comic tactics yielded mainly personal pleasure, but when they included those strategies in their published works, they publicly registered a source of female power. The next four chapters of this study will explore various targets and angles of feminist comedy in the works of Burney, Edgeworth, and Austen. I will show that these authors made extensive use of comic tactics to criticize the established order and to cover their tracks: those who understood their humor would learn something about the absurdity of female subordination; those who missed the joke would be none the wiser. If, as Freud states, "Every joke calls for a public of its own" (151), then the public these writers evoke is one that values women.

4

Comedy in Manners: Making Fun of the Angel in the House

Women, in general, have a quicker perception of any oddity or singularity of character than men, and are more alive to every absurdity which arises from a violation of the rules of society, or a deviation from established custom. This partly arises from the restraints on their own behaviour, which turn their attention constantly on the subject.

—William Hazlitt (124)

I N HIS BRIEF TREATMENT OF BURNEY'S FICTION, essayist William Hazlitt calls attention to the "rules of society" as the basis of women's comic writing. Although he accords Burney a "distinguished place" among contemporary novelists (123), the statements about "women, in general," that he inserts into the discussion of her work effectively diminish that place. For example, Hazlitt honors Fielding and Smollett as comic writers, "the one as an observer of the characters of human life, the other as a describer of its various eccentricities" (117), but he denigrates Burney's comedy because her observations on human life are restricted to a woman's sphere. He suggests that her gender prevents her from rivaling the male novelists he has discussed (Cervantes, Fielding, Smollett, Richardson, and Sterne): "Madame D'Arblay is . . . a mere common observer of manners, and also a very woman. It is this last circumstance which forms the peculiarity of her writings, and distinguishes them from those masterpieces which I have before mentioned" (123).

Because Hazlitt faults an aspect of Burney's writing that I intend to explore in the works of all three of this study's novelists—namely, their attention to "manners" and the rules of conduct—I will quote his views at greater length. He sees Burney's female point of view as her greatest limitation:

> She is a quick, lively, and accurate observer of persons and things; but she always looks at them with a consciousness of her sex, and in that point of view in which it is the particular business and interest of women to observe them. There is little in her works of passion or character, or even manners, in the most extended sense of the word, as implying the sum-total of our habits and pursuits; her *forte* is in describing the absurdities and affectations of external behaviour, or *the manners of people in company*. (123)

Burney falls short in Hazlitt's estimation because her works do not address the "sum-total" of male habits and pursuits; what interests women holds little interest for him. His sweeping condemnation of Burney's plots reveals the extent of his disregard for women's lives: "The difficulties in which she involves her heroines are too much 'Female Difficulties' [the subtitle of Burney's *The Wanderer*]; they are difficulties created out of nothing" (124).

The specific "nothings" of female difficulties that offend Hazlitt involve issues of conduct. As the epigraph makes clear, he sees women as overly concerned with society's rules and "established custom." He shows some understanding of women's oppression, noting that the restrictions society places upon women might account for their attention to its rules. However, rather than examining women's comedy for a deeper understanding of their treatment of social restrictions, he assumes that there is nothing beneath the surface: "There is little other power in Miss Burney's novels, than that of immediate observation: her characters, whether of refinement or vulgarity, are equally superficial and confined" (124).[1]

In her attention to the rules of conduct, Burney reflects "one of the major preoccupations" of the age (Simons 28). The eighteenth century witnessed "an explosion of print all bent on telling people how to conduct themselves in the rituals of everyday life" (Armstrong 258). Beginning with Joyce Hemlow's groundbreaking essay "Fanny Burney and the Courtesy Books" (1950), critics have explored in depth what Hazlitt registered—the relation between rules of conduct and eighteenth-century women's fiction. One recent critic declares that "the line between the conduct books and the female novels of the period is often quite thin; the two genres virtually shade into one another" (Linda Hunt 9).

Much of the criticism that explores conduct literature focuses on its production of the ideal domestic woman.[2] Forerunner of the Victorian "angel in the house," this woman was an essentially passive creature; her power was not in action but in influence. Her virtues consisted primarily of negatives: she did not contradict or complain; she did not attract undue attention; and most of all, she did not make selfish demands.

Virginia Woolf's famous characterization pins down the salient features of the domestic angel: "She was intensely sympathetic. She was immensely charming. She was utterly unselfish. She excelled in the difficult arts of family life. She sacrificed herself daily. If there was chicken, she took the leg; if there was a draught, she sat in it—in short she was so constituted that she never had a mind or a wish of her own, but preferred to sympathize always with the minds and wishes of others" ("Professions" 237). It is well known that Woolf harbored murderous intentions toward this angel; less recognized is the fact that Woolf killed her with comedy. In order for Woolf the writer to live, the angel had to die, and to kill her, Woolf needed to adopt conduct most unladylike. Pausing only to bless the ancestors who gave her an independent income so that "it was not necessary for [her] to depend solely on charm for [her] living," Woolf grabbed the angel by the throat and presumably strangled her.

But angels do not die easily, Woolf discovered: "[W]henever I felt the shadow of her wing or the radiance of her halo upon my page, I took up the inkpot and flung it at her. She died hard. Her fictitious nature was of great assistance to her. It is far harder to kill a phantom than a reality. She was always creeping back when I thought I had dispatched her" (238). In both the description of the angel and the account of her murder, Woolf reduces the ideal woman to an object of mockery. In fact, she resurrects the angel in order to kill her again and again for the comic (and feminist) satisfaction of her audience.

Women writers of the eighteenth and nineteenth centuries shared Woolf's frustration with the feminine ideal. Feminist scholar Katharine Rogers argues that restrictions on female behavior extended into the realm of fiction: "the chastity, propriety, sense of duty, delicacy enjoined on women in real life were doubly enjoined on the fictitious woman who was not worthy to be a heroine if she could not serve as a model" ("Inhibitions" 65). Although many women writers created heroines who conformed to acceptable standards, they did not necessarily endorse the ideal itself.

The humor with which Woolf slays her nemesis appears in the works of Burney, Edgeworth, and Austen when they present comic characters in scenes that make fun of conduct rules for "proper" ladies. Whereas most critics who connect conduct literature to women's novels focus on virtuous heroines and see authors writing what Hemlow calls "courtesy novels"—that is, novels that teach women how to behave like proper ladies—I want to examine playful deviations from rules of conduct that comprise an important aspect of their comedy. These deviations celebrate insurrection and perform the act that Woolf sees as central to the woman writer's occupation—killing the angel in the house.

On one level, Burney, Edgeworth, and Austen sidestepped the requirement that women's heroines follow conduct-book guidelines by making their own heroines less than perfect—that is, virtuous, but error-prone. They achieved an even greater degree of liberation by satirizing the standards of female conduct and by creating characters who mock authority and gleefully reject traditional notions of decorum.

We know that Austen shared Woolf's revulsion at angel figures; she confided as much to her niece: "pictures of perfection as you know make me sick & wicked" (*Letters* 486–87). Edgeworth, too, disliked angels, as her reaction to the heroine of Elizabeth Inchbald's *A Simple Story* reveals. She compares her own Belinda to Miss Milner in an unfavorable light: "I really was so provoked with the cold tameness of that stick or stone Belinda, that I could have torn the pages to pieces; and really, I have not the heart or the patience to *correct* her" (qtd. in Hare 1.178). Edgeworth's emphasis on the word "correct" suggests that the correctness of Belinda's character irritated her when contrasted with the impetuosity of Miss Milner, who defies all rules of conduct.

Burney, too, expressed impatience with the angel figure in a journal entry concerning her less-than-angelic stepsister Maria Allen. The qualities that Burney admired in Allen—courage, candor, and wittiness—go against the conventions of ladylike behavior. Her remarks illustrate the young Burney's hesitation between propriety and license:

> [I]f it is possible, she is *too* sincere; she pays too little regard to the World, & indulges herself with too much freedom of raillery & pride of disdain, toward those whose vices or follies offend her. Were this a *general* rule of conduct, what real benefit might it bring to society! but being *particular*, it only hurts and provokes Individuals: but yet, I am unjust to my own opinion in censuring the first who shall venture, in a good cause, to break through the confinement of custom, & at least shew the way to a new & Open path;— I mean but to blame severity to *harmless* folly, which claims pity, & not scorn: though I cannot but acknowledge it to be infinitely tiresome, &, for any length of Time, even—or almost—disgustful. (*Early Journals* 166)[3]

Burney clearly suffered from the pressure to follow the "general rule of conduct" since it prevented her from reprimanding, mocking, or otherwise forthrightly expressing her displeasure with those who offended her, as Allen did. Even though Burney could not take her stepsister's path, however, she delighted in Allen's irreverence and probably based the characters of Mrs. Selwyn (*Evelina*), Lady Honoria Pemberton (*Cecilia* [1782]), Mrs. Arlbery (*Camilla* [1796]), and Elinor Joddrel (*The Wanderer*) upon her.

Burney, Edgeworth, and Austen, as intelligent women and as authors, had adequate motives for killing the angel figure, and, like Woolf, they employed comedy to do their dirty work. In my chapter on Wollstonecraft's humor, I discussed her strategy of bringing patriarchal discourse into her text in order to subject it to mockery. Similarly, as I will show, the novelists parody conduct-book platitudes by placing them in contexts that unmask their absurdity.

By emphasizing the absurdly narrow confines in which women were expected to comport themselves, Burney, Edgeworth, and Austen made comedy out of societal pressures on female behavior. Critic Zita Dresner's account of the development of mid-twentieth-century housewife humor could apply equally well to the humor of the early novelists:

> The domestic humor which emerged during the fifties and early sixties seems to have grown out of the anxiety and confusion many young women felt as they attempted to meet the conflicting demands of their prescribed role and to assimilate the endless barrage of often contradictory "expert" advice from the popular media on how to keep their houses spotless and attractive, their budgets balanced, their meals nutritious and exciting, their children physically and emotionally healthy, their husbands happy, and themselves radiantly attractive. (30)

Although the eighteenth-century woman faced a different set of demands, she was beset with advice on proper behavior that threw her into a similar state of confusion. In Burney's *Evelina*, the heroine's desire for a precise account of the "laws and customs à-la-mode" (83) arises from her experience of intricate, and often conflicting, rules governing social intercourse. Humor provided an antidote to an overdose of expectations. Even if respectable heroines had to walk the narrow path that propriety dictated, their authors could incite laughter at the steps along the way.

In their writings, Burney, Edgeworth, and Austen modify comedy's traditional weapons to suit feminist ends. Comic tactics that they use to make fun of restrictions on women include satirical commentary (or, in Burney's case, naive satirists) and the creation of female "trickster" characters. These strategies allow the authors to offer up conduct-book advice to the reader's laughter and thereby kill off the specter of the ideal woman. Edgeworth and Austen employ satirical commentary as a direct and witty way to criticize society's more absurd demands upon women. Burney tends to eschew direct commentary; she prefers to utilize "naive" characters who call attention to injustices against women by unwittingly violating social conventions. All three writers introduce secondary women characters who defy all rules of conduct, mocking male authority and laughing as they do so; these tricksters are the fictional representatives of eighteenth-century laughing feminists.

In my discussion of the comic approaches that Burney, Edgeworth, and Austen take to conduct-book advice, I will move from the most direct form—satirical commentary—to the indirect but more subversive form enacted by the female trickster character. The authors generally make their safer feminist statements directly, through commentary, and give voice to more radical views about the overthrow of sexism through the mouths of comic characters. Whichever mode they employ, they share the Wollstonecraftian goal of dispelling antifeminist bugbears by exposing them to the clear light of reason.

Edgeworth's *Essay on the Noble Science of Self-Justification* (1795) provides an excellent introduction to feminist satirical commentary.[4] Edgeworth's piece may be viewed as an anti-conduct book. Its comic force derives from the iconoclasm of its mock-heroic treatment of bad manners. By pushing bad behavior to extremes, her satire advocates humane standards of decency and fairness in the same way that Swift's "A Modest Proposal" does when he proposes baby-eating as a satirical argument for better treatment of the Irish poor. As an eighteenth-century woman, however, Edgeworth wrote satire from a different angle than male writers did; her ironies have gendered inflections. Whereas Swift and other male satirists appeal to humanity as comprised of all humans (even if they might only have men in mind), Edgeworth recognizes the point at which humanity bifurcates into genders.

Edgeworth represents incivilities in women as behavior that ought to be corrected, not in reference to the rules for female behavior, but rather in compliance with human standards of decency; at the same time, she criticizes restrictions on women's conduct. In a society that asked women to accept paradoxes such as separate-but-equal status and strength-in-weakness psychology, Edgeworth's satire offered female readers an opportunity to delight in transgression. Even as she sought to reform abuses of power, she provided consolation for female victims of an oppressive system.[5]

Edgeworth's *Essay on the Noble Science of Self-Justification* takes as its starting point the conduct writers' insistence that women exercise power by indirection. Halifax, for instance, perceives a balance of power between the sexes, in which female influence counters male might: "You have more strength in your looks, than wee have in our Lawes; and more power in your tears, than wee have by our Arguments" (370). John Bennett apotheosizes this widely held view of women's power influence: "Their greatest strength lies in their *weakness*, their commands in their tears, . . . their softness has frequently disarmed the rage of emporor's [sic] and tyrants, . . . [their] charms have worked *miracles* in every age and nation, and brought about the most important revolutions of the world" (99–100). Such exaggerations of women's paradoxical condition provided grist for Edgeworth's satirical talents.

In Edgeworth's essay, women reign supreme in their separate sphere and good manners count for nothing; the basic maxim alone must be rigidly enforced: "That a lady can do no wrong" (2). Adopting the didactic tone of conduct literature, the essay shamelessly encourages selfish behavior. Edgeworth tells her readers not to be intimidated by her maxim of infallibility; they need not live up to it by actually doing no wrong. "Instead then of a belief in your infallibility," the author counsels, "endeavour to enforce implicit submission to your authority. This will give you infinitely less trouble, and will answer your purpose as well" (4). Right and wrong, according to the essay, have little to do with maintaining power; in fact, the writer urges her readers to "chuse the wrong side of an argument to defend; whilst you are young in the science, it will afford the best exercise, and as you improve, the best display of your talents" (18).

Edgeworth takes arms against the double standard by satirizing marriage as a battle zone and repeatedly referring to the husband as "the enemy." Whereas conduct writers instructed women to tolerate their husband's shortcomings, she turns the tables and places women in the infallible position. Halifax bluntly states that infidelity in a husband must be pardoned, drunkenness must be tolerated, and anger, jealousy, and stinginess must be borne with in the best possible manner.[6] Even in extreme cases, he advises his daughter to be content with the power of influence rather than seek open control.

Edgeworth has a field day with the notion that female influence can triumph over male power. She informs her readers that if a woman appeals to her husband's generosity, he will yield every trifle to the being "who is in his power; who is weak, and who loves him" (8). She warns young women to remain alert to the shifts in power that take place early in a marriage and not to be lulled into a false sense of security by superior treatment: "Timid brides, you have, probably, hitherto been addressed as angels— Prepare for the time when you shall again become mortal. Take the alarm at the first approach of blame, at the first hint of a discovery that you are less than infallible. Contradict, debate, justify, recriminate, rage, weep, swoon, do any thing but yield to conviction" (6). Edgeworth's tract derives a good deal of its humor from juxtaposing such "Timid . . . angels" with descriptions of the melodramatic poses they must enact in order to retain their bridal power.

Like the conduct writers who advocate female influence, Edgeworth discounts rational argument. Instead, she promotes noise in the service of self-justification: "are you voluble enough to drown all sense in a torrent of words? Can you be loud enough to overpower the voice of all who shall attempt to interrupt or contradict you? Are you mistress of the petulant, the peevish, and the sullen tones?" (6–7). This and more will be required, she assures them, if their power is to be maintained. Whereas Mary Hays labeled the condition of women "a state of PERPETUAL BABYISM" (*Appeal* 97), Edgeworth ostensibly encourages her readers to play their baby-like roles with a vengeance.

The keynote of the essay—that a lady can do no wrong—takes an essentially passive attribute of the ideal woman in a chivalrous relationship and turns it into an active force to be reckoned with in the details of everyday life. The primary difference between the sexes being the unspoken premise of male selfishness, Edgeworth counsels the female reader to compensate for social liabilities by establishing herself, verbally and physically, as a powerful arbiter in her own right. The true self-justifier awaits no cue, according to the essayist: "Who is there amongst you who cannot or will not justify when they are accused. Vulgar talent! the sublime of our science, is to justify before we are accused" (32). In a brilliant stroke, Edgeworth parodies the biblical injunction to love one's enemy, linking it to that bane of womanhood, the serpent, and prepares the reader for a twist on the age-old comparison between women and flowers: "The sensitive plant is too vulgar an allusion; but if the truth of modern naturalists may be depended upon, there is a plant which instead of receding timidly, like the sensitive plant, from the intrusive touch, angrily protrudes its venomous juices upon all who presume to meddle with it: don't you think this plant would be your fittest emblem" (33). Not a fragile rosebud but a lethal serpent-plant constitutes the emblem for Edgeworth's self-justifying female. Her humor does not prevent her from including her own note of self-justification, however—the sensitive plant, as she sees it, must suffer "the intrusive touch." Her followers should get the jump on their tormenters by striking first. Even though Edgeworth's essay clearly does not advocate violence as an acceptable outlet for women's frustration, it relentlessly calls attention to the abuses inherent in a system that pretends to favor women as angelic beings—as ladies who can do no wrong—while denying them access to direct methods of exerting power or authority.

Edgeworth's essay stands out as one of the most thoroughly satirical instances of feminist writing in the eighteenth century. It appeared in the same volume as her popular *Letters for Literary Ladies* (1795), an epistolary exchange that defends women's education. Echoes of feminist satire recur throughout Edgeworth's fiction, particularly in her commentaries on fashionable life. A similarly satirical voice pervades Austen's parodic *Northanger Abbey*, a work that she began several years after the appearance of Edgeworth's *Letters*.

Numerous studies have examined Austen's parody of literary conventions in *Northanger Abbey*.[7] Less remarked upon is the feminist satire encoded in her mockery of conventional female behavior. In addition to satirizing conventions of romance literature, Austen derides the features that make up the ideal heroine of conduct literature. Her satire runs counter to John Gregory's warning in *A Father's Legacy to His Daughters* that young ladies should live up to the vision of perfection men see in them, lest they lose their influential status: "The power of a fine woman over the hearts of men, of men of the finest parts, is even beyond what she conceives. They are sensible of the pleasing illusion, but they cannot, nor do they wish to dissolve it. But if she is determined to dispel the charm, it certainly is in her power: she may soon reduce the angel to a very ordinary girl" (42–43). In *Northanger Abbey*, Austen rejects all "pictures of perfection" and exposes the folly of a system that values illusory angels more than real women.

The narrator of *Northanger Abbey* takes great pains to let her readers know that Catherine Morland is, above all, an ordinary girl, unusual only in her refusal to adhere to gender stereotypes as a child. Catherine, we are told, "was fond of all boys' plays, and greatly preferred cricket not merely to dolls, but to the more heroic enjoyments of infancy, nursing a dormouse, feeding a canary-bird, or watering a rose-bush" (13). If this summary does not dispel any illusions about innate femininity, the narrator confides that "she was moreover noisy and wild, hated confinement and cleanliness, and loved nothing so well in the world as rolling down the green slope at the back of the house" (14). A brief excerpt from Rousseau's *Émile* discloses the gender stereotypes that Austen wants to dismantle: "Boys seek movement and noise: drums, boots, little carriages. Girls prefer what presents itself to sight and is useful for ornamentation: mirrors, jewels, dresses, particularly dolls. The doll is the special entertainment of this sex. This is evidently its taste, determined by its purpose" (367). Austen's humorous characterization of Catherine Morland re-futes the restrictive ideas about femininity that accompany Rous-seau's notion of a fondness for dolls and ornamentation as a "def-inite primary taste" in little girls (367). Although the narrator jokingly refers to Catherine as "a strange, unaccountable charac-ter" (14), she clearly asks us to value her heroine's eccentricity.

In one instance of satirical commentary, Austen attacks a prejudice against female learning best expressed in Gregory's con-duct book: "if you happen to have any learning, keep it a pro-found secret, especially from the men, who generally look with a jealous and malignant eye on a woman of great parts, and a culti-vated understanding" (31–32). During the scene in which Henry Tilney instructs Catherine on the picturesque, the narrator ironi-cally notes her heroine's "misplaced shame" at her ignorance of the subject: "Where people wish to attach, they should always be ignorant. To come with a well-informed mind, is to come with an inability of administering to the vanity of others, which a sensible person would always wish to avoid. A woman especially, if she have the misfortune of knowing any thing, should conceal it as well as she can" (110–11). Lest we miss the feminist implications of such satirical comments, the narrator drives her point home with a witty twist: "I will only add in justice to men, that though to the larger and more trifling part of the sex, imbecility in fe-males is a great enhancement of their personal charms, there is a portion of them too reasonable and well informed themselves to desire any thing more in woman than ignorance" (111). Woll-stonecraft herself might have penned this scathing indictment of the male-centered approach to female education that Gregory and others advocated. Along with the foolishness of romantic conventions in *Northanger Abbey*, the bugbear of ideal woman-hood evaporates when exposed to reasonable laughter. In no other work does Austen insert so much satirical commentary.

That Burney seldom resorts to direct satirical commentary gives evidence of her selective deployment of feminist humor. When Burney directly addresses feminist issues in her novels, she tends to take a moralizing stance (as in the "FEMALE DIFFICULTIES" passages in *The Wanderer*[8]). To unmask the more entrenched follies of a male-dominated society, she utilizes naive characters who question the system from a position outside its values and mores. Naive satirists are incapable of making fun of the standards of perfection for female behavior since they often do not know the rules; their naivete, coupled with a good dose of common sense, allows the author to reflect upon the contradictory status of women by exposing the difference between "proper" manners and rational conduct. For example, as an ingenuous girl, Evelina opens up a wide array of satirical targets for her author when she makes her entrance into the stratified social world. Her false steps and critical comments express her inexperience, but it is exactly this innocence that instructs the reader; it provides a screen behind which the author and reader can laugh together freely.

Significantly, one of Evelina's first public actions is an ill-timed laugh. Describing, in a letter to her guardian, the treatment of women at her debut ball, she observes: "The gentlemen, as they passed and repassed, looked as if they thought we were quite at their disposal, and only waiting for the honour of their commands" (28). Evelina explains that she had already made up her mind not to be treated with impertinence when a young man addressed her, bowing to the ground and behaving "with the greatest conceit." Rather than succumbing to his foppish gallantry, Evelina "could scarce forbear laughing." The man—Mr. Lovel—persists in his fawning attentions, and Evelina writes that she had to turn her head "to conceal [her] laughter" (29). Lovel's obsequiousness strikes her as irresistibly funny, and, at last, when he interrupts her conversation with Lord Orville "with a most ridiculous solemnity" (32), Evelina can control her laughter no longer: "I interrupted him—I blush for my folly,—with laughter" (33). If we recall Wollstonecraft's attempt to stifle her laughter when she watched a man stooping to pick up a "lady's" handkerchief (*Vindication* 57), the source of Evelina's laughter appears even more explicitly feminist.

Evelina's laugh proves that she, like Catherine Morland, is a rational, ordinary girl. She wonders that a gentleman would ask for the "honour" of her hand: "but these sort of expressions, I find, are used as words of course, without any distinction of persons, or study of propriety" (29). Her social criticism arises from her surprise at the conventions of social behavior: she did not know that men bow and scrape and profess their honor indiscriminately; she was ignorant of the conventions that exalt rank above merit; how could she have known that an unprotected beauty invites insolent male behavior? Such premises of naivete underlie and excuse Evelina's truth-telling propensity. More importantly, they provide the author with a safe outlet for feminist social criticism.

Because so many of her early readers saw Evelina as a portrait of the author, it would have been either demeaning or risky for Burney to attempt another suggestively satirical heroine. Burney's other heroines show more savoir faire than Evelina, and the naive satirist in her later novels is generally a minor character. One way to recognize the naive satirist at work is to gauge the degree of social embarrassment she or he causes by speaking plainly. Evelina's laughter at Mr. Lovel embarrasses the urbane Lord Orville, even though the reader must find her mirth wholly justified. In *Cecilia,* Mr. Briggs pains Cecilia when he publicly comments on the Harrels' expenditures and on Mr. Delvile's snobbishness; however, Briggs correctly identifies two sources of Cecilia's misfortunes. His vulgar statements about getting Cecilia married off and not trusting girls with money reflect badly upon the society that treats women as merchandise to be exchanged among men. In *Camilla,* Sir Hugh Tyrold's naivete consists in an inability to recognize social obstacles—he encourages his nieces to become scholars because he does not understand that learning can be a social liability for young women.

Giles Arbe, perhaps the most delightful of Burney's male naive satirists, always speaks "the plump truth" (*The Wanderer* 75) and continually pops up to embarrass those who mistreat the novel's heroine, Juliet. It is he who calls Juliet's position as companion to the irascible Mrs. Ireton by its vernacular name when he repeats a report that she has turned "toad-eater." That he does so in Mrs. Ireton's presence makes his frankness particularly gratifying to the reader, especially when he proceeds to define the term: "I asked them what they meant . . . for I never heard of any body's eating toads; though I am assured our neighbours on t'other bank, are so fond of frogs. But they made it out, that it only meant a person who would swallow any thing, bad or good; and do whatever he was bid, right or wrong; for the sake of a little pay" (496). Giles Arbe's outspokenness arouses Mrs. Ireton's displeasure and makes Juliet uncomfortable, but it offers the reader some relief to have Mrs. Ireton's brutality described in frank terms. His definition adequately represents the situation of unfortunate dependents like Juliet at a time when society offered scarcely any employment opportunities for an unmarried, well-bred woman.

Burney's naive satirists create awkward situations by drawing attention to the nonsense of sexist values. As Halifax, an early conduct-book writer, explains, a lady may recognize absurdities in her situation, but propriety demands that she remain silent: "An aversion to what is criminal, a contempt of what is ridiculous, are the inseparable companions of understanding and vertue; but the letting them goe further than our own thoughts, hath so much danger in it, that . . . it is necessary they should be kept under great restraint" (396). Naive satirists speak more frankly than the heroine can, especially when the heroines are trying to swallow their pride and submit to discomfort with good grace. Comic truth-tellers protect the heroine even as they air female grievances.

When Burney, Edgeworth, and Austen employ such comic features as satirical commentary and naive satirical characters, they call attention to foolish restrictions placed upon women. These women authors destabilize the authority of conduct rules by placing conduct-book platitudes in ludicrous contexts that expose their absurdity. Their comedy makes serious feminist points about the distance between the feminine ideal and real women's lives. Nowhere is this ridicule more evident than in their representation of female trickster characters.

I use the term "trickster" to identify a fictional female character who mocks and challenges male power. Tricksters in folk tales enact the revenge of the underdog: they employ cunning means to triumph over their enemies, subverting established powers by beating members of the ruling class at their own games. Folklorist Lawrence Levine explains that "one central feature of almost all trickster tales is their assault upon deeply ingrained and culturally sanctioned values" (104). Tricksters in the novels of Burney, Edgeworth, and Austen are women characters who challenge rules of conduct, mocking male authority and laughing as they do so. Like the folk-tale characters, female tricksters offer their audience a vicarious victory over restrictive forces. Umberto Eco explains the satisfaction that comic characters offer when they transgress social rules: "we in some way welcome the violation; we are, so to speak, revenged by the comic character who has challenged the repressive power of the rule (which involves no risk to us, since we commit the violation only vicariously)" (2). Female tricksters make fun of society's rules, celebrate transgression, and effectively slay the angel figure with their iconoclastic laughter.

The female trickster is the polar opposite of an angel: she is outspoken; she makes people uncomfortable; she willfully violates codes of female behavior; and above all, she laughs. She may be a satirist, like Mrs. Selwyn (*Evelina*), a prankster, like Mrs. Freke (*Belinda* [1801]) and Lady Honoria Pemberton (*Cecilia*), or possibly even a hedonist, like Lydia Bennet (*Pride and Prejudice*). What all trickster figures share is a propensity to flaunt their unconventional behavior and a capacity to get the last laugh on their male opponents. Tricksters draw attention to themselves and force the heroines and the reader to take a look at what all the fuss is about. They embody a potent threat to the status quo by providing a foil for the heroines' discreet conduct and by acting out the heroines' transgressive desires.

What distinguishes the female trickster from a naive satirist like Evelina is her self-conscious strength. She has her eyes open and knows what rules she violates. Since Burney, Edgeworth, and Austen all make use of such a character, we can assume that they enjoyed the comedy of transgression such characters make possible. All three authors keep a certain moral distance from their tricksters by having the heroines criticize aspects of their behavior. But that criticism does not fully dispel the energy of these unruly female figures; in none of the examples I mention above does the heroine completely condemn the female trickster. Instead, each heroine is simultaneously shocked and fascinated by the trickster's volatility. Before examining specific instances of trick-ster humor, I want to show how the tension between tricksters and heroines derives from issues about proper female behavior. Tricksters force the heroines to question the standards that govern their own behavior as women.

In some cases the heroine expresses her sense of the female trickster's worth and measures that worth against a standard evaluation. Evelina writes with mixed feelings about Mrs. Selwyn: "Mrs. Selwyn is very kind and attentive to me. She is extremely clever; her understanding, indeed, may be called *masculine;* but unfortunately, her manners deserve the same epithet; for in studying to acquire the knowledge of the other sex, she has lost all the softness of her own" (268–69). Evelina does not repress her approbation of Mrs. Selwyn's "masculine" understanding, despite her concern about "manners." Furthermore, Evelina's inquisitive mind leads her to question the necessity of feminine "softness": "I have never been personally hurt at her want of gentleness; a virtue which, nevertheless, seems so essential a part of the female character, that I find myself more awkward, and less at ease, with a woman who wants it, than I do with a man" (269). At the center of Evelina's evaluation lies a question about the construction of female character: If gentleness is an "essential" aspect of femininity, then how can any woman lack it? Even as she places gentleness in the realm of female virtues, Evelina relativizes the virtue by presenting it as a matter of social comfort—that is, she prizes it in both men and women.

Likewise, in Edgeworth's *Belinda,* Mrs. Freke's manners are measured in terms of gender roles: "there was no such thing as managing Mrs. Freke, who, though she had laid aside the modesty of her own sex, had not acquired the decency of the other" (38). Here again, gender-specific traits are not viewed as biologically determined, but rather as put on and cast off by individual choice. Nonetheless, Belinda begins to question her own acceptance of conventions of female behavior after Mrs. Freke "talk[s] treason" to her (207). Following an extended discussion of women's nature in which Mrs. Freke tells Belinda, "For my own part . . . I own I should like a strong devil better than a weak angel" (206), Belinda begins to search for a rational basis for social rules. "Good may be drawn from evil," the narrator tells us. "Mrs. Freke's conversation, though at the time it confounded Belinda, roused her, upon reflection, to examine by her reason the habits and principles which guided her conduct" (210). We know that Belinda is in need of such an arousal, since we have been told early in the novel that "Her mind had never been roused to much reflection; she had in general acted but as a puppet in the hands of others" (4). Ultimately, Belinda chooses a path of domesticity, but, because of her confrontation with Mrs. Freke, reason rather than gender dictates this choice.

Frequently the trickster figure's bold manners are represented in terms that contrast her freedom with the restrictions placed upon the conduct of the heroine. According to Burney's Mrs. Delvile, Lady Honoria Pemberton's fault lies in her selfish penchant for laughter: "how wild, how careless, how incorrigible she is. . . . Lately, indeed, she has come more into the world, but without even a desire of improvement, and with no view and no thought but to gratify her idle humour by laughing at whatever goes forward" (*Cecilia* 487). Lady Honoria's disregard for "improvement" makes her a model for other anti-conduct-book heroines. Another trickster whose abandoned behavior reveals her independence from conduct-book strictures is Lydia Bennet. The narrator of *Pride and Prejudice* describes Lydia Bennet after her marriage to Wickham as unaltered by the effects of her departure from conventions: "Lydia was Lydia still; untamed, unabashed, wild, noisy, and fearless" (315). Lydia's refusal to be domesticated even after her near fall has a provocative quality, as registered in the sheer strength of her features.

Plot, even more than personal attraction, binds Lady Honoria and Lydia to the central heroines of these novels. Each female trickster contributes to her novel's romance plot by breaking social rules. Lady Honoria kidnaps Mortimer Delvile's dog and sends it to Cecilia, an action that leads to the scene in which Mortimer overhears Cecilia's declaration of passion. When Lydia Bennet blurts out that Darcy was present at her wedding, Elizabeth stifles her own unladylike curiosity and actively seeks from her aunt the information that reveals Darcy's interest in her own affairs.

Mrs. Selwyn, Mrs. Freke, Lady Honoria Pemberton, and

Lydia Bennet all fly in the face of convention, breaking conduct rules and challenging society's views about women's nature. Their ties to the heroines give their iconoclasm an edge of urgency as well as immediacy. Conforming to the social structure, the more proper heroine cannot openly ridicule masculine authority, but the pain she endures as a result of it is alleviated by the trickster's antics. Because the heroine is endowed with rational faculties, she cannot help but acknowledge the follies of sexism when female tricksters urge her to laugh at them, and the female tricksters' major comic target—authoritarian males—gives their humor an undeniably feminist thrust.

Many of Mrs. Selwyn's witticisms target the notion that men possess superior intellects by virtue of their maleness. Rather than keeping her learning a "profound secret," as Gregory and other conduct-book writers advised women to do, Mrs. Selwyn flaunts her wit and understanding. She calls one group of men's learning into question by suggesting a competition to see who can recite the longest ode of Horace. "I am sure you cannot be afraid of a weak *woman*" (290), she teases when they fail to accept the challenge, implying that men, not "weak" women, are supposed to know the classics.

Mrs. Selwyn goes beyond innuendo in her indictment of the male monopoly on higher education; her interrogation of Mr. Lovel on the mysteries of a university education derives its comic force from exposing the ignorance of at least one product of the system. She begins by asking if Lovel studied classical literature at the university; his response only serves to encourage her probing wit:

> "At the university!" repeated he with an embarrassed look; "why, as to that, Ma'am,—no, I can't say I did; but then, what with riding,—and—and—and so forth,—really, one has not much time, even at the university, for mere reading."
>
> "But to be sure, Sir, you *have* read the classics?"
>
> "O dear, yes, Ma'am!—very often,—but not very—not very lately." (291)

Mr. Lovel's claim that he had no time for "mere reading" makes a university education sound rather foolish. When we take into account that his education was a privilege denied to women, the feminist message behind the humor becomes evident.

In another of Mrs. Selwyn's comic scenes, the males try to get the upper hand over her by praising female delicacy with phrases borrowed from the conduct literature, but in the process they expose their vested interests and allow her the last laugh. Lord Merton opens up the subject by declaring, "devil take me if ever I had the least passion for an Amazon." The other men take up the topic with a vengeance aimed at Mrs. Selwyn:

> "I have the honour to be quite of your Lordship's opinion," said Mr. Lovel, looking maliciously at Mrs. Selwyn, "for I have an insuperable aversion to strength, either of body or mind, in a female."
>
> "Faith, and so have I," said Mr. Coverley; "for egad I'd as soon see a woman chop wood, as hear her chop logic."
>
> "So would every man in his senses," said Lord Merton; "for a woman wants nothing to recommend her but beauty and good-nature; in every thing else she is either impertinent or unnatural. For my part, deuce take me if ever I wish to hear a word of sense from a woman as long as I live!" (361)

As the men repeat commonly held views about the nature of women, their self-interest stands out conspicuously. None of them wants women to engage in male pursuits, as Mrs. Selwyn does, because they are afraid of being shown up.

Mrs. Selwyn confirms their worst fears when she turns the laugh against them. She invokes the maxim from which the men derive their sense of superiority, only to flaunt its absurdity:

> "It has been always agreed," said Mrs. Selwyn, looking round her with the utmost contempt,

"that no man ought to be connected with a
woman whose understanding is superior to his
own. Now I very much fear, that to accommodate all this good company, according to such a
rule, would be utterly impracticable, unless we
should chuse subjects from Swift's hospital of
idiots." (361–62)

Naturally, the men in question find this speech less than polite.
Mrs. Selwyn's lack of concern for masculine approval and her
ability to sacrifice social comfort for comic conquests contribute
to her role as a trickster figure. Since in the course of the novel
Mrs. Selwyn's "victims" have all victimized the heroine, Evelina
(who transcribes these dialogues in her letters) vicariously participates in Mrs. Selwyn's triumphs and transgressions—as does
every reader who gets the point of her jokes.

Like Mrs. Selwyn, Mrs. Freke plays out her trickster role by
scoffing at masculine authority and reveling in unconventional-
ity. She delights in cross-dressing, employing this disguise to appropriate male privileges such as hearing speeches in the House of
Commons and walking alone at night. With "bold masculine
arms," an above-average height, and brash manners, Mrs. Freke
embodies a violation of female decorum. In a society that values
women according to their physical beauty, Mrs. Freke stands out
as a "freak."

In a chapter entitled "Rights of Woman" (an obvious allusion to Wollstonecraft's *Vindication*), Mrs. Freke battles with the
novel's male mentor, Mr. Percival, over the issue of female delicacy. Although Mrs. Freke does not achieve decisive victories, as
does Mrs. Selwyn, she casts aspersions on some damaging views
about female nature. Her pronouncements that "Your most delicate women are always the greatest hypocrites" and that "women
blush because they understand" (208) bespeak Belinda's situation
with regard to Clarence Hervey. Delicacy prevents Belinda from
openly avowing her feelings for Hervey and causes her to blush
when Mrs. Freke boldly asks, "[W]hy, when a woman likes a man,
does not she go and tell him so honestly?" (208). Mrs. Freke's indelicate question calls attention to the injustice of a system of

courtship that allows the woman only the power of silence or negation.

In their debate about female delicacy, Mrs. Freke and Mr. Percival disagree over terminology, with Mr. Percival employing conduct-book terms while Mrs. Freke makes use of the feminist vocabulary of Wollstonecraft's *Vindication*. Their battle digresses into a comic shouting match, culminating in the following condensed exchange with Mrs. Freke taking the lead:

> "Cunning!—cunning!—cunning!—the arms of the weakest."
>
> "Prudence! prudence!—the arms of the strongest." (209)

Each opines that the present state is one of warfare; but each holds to her or his terminology. Mr. Percival shares the conduct-book writers' view that women should strive for influence rather than direct power, while Mrs. Freke claims power by refusing to submit to his authority. It is no wonder that Mr. Percival labels Mrs. Freke a "female outlaw" (231).

Unlike Mrs. Selwyn, who overcomes male opposition with witty argument, Mrs. Freke conquers with physical comedy. When Mr. Percival alludes to "the decent drapery of life," Mrs. Freke takes him literally and retorts, "drapery, whether wet or dry, is the most confoundedly indecent thing in the world." She ends the debate by rising and "stretching herself so violently that some part of her habiliments gave way" (209) She bodies forth her position on female delicacy, delighting in the confusion she excites and "bursting into a horse laugh" to cap her point.[9]

Mrs. Freke admits to taking pleasure in shocking people: "I do of all things delight in hauling good people's opinions out of their musty drawers, and seeing how they look when they're all pulled to pieces before their faces!" (210). Her trickster function consists of forcing Belinda to examine her own "good opinions." As a result of this self-analysis, Belinda learns to be guided by reason rather than by received authority.

Lady Honoria Pemberton also exhibits the trickster's talent for ridiculing male authority figures. She has a more suitable target in Cecilia's future father-in-law than Mrs. Freke found in Mr. Percival. In the main a reasonable man, Mr. Percival maintains his dignity despite Mrs. Freke's assault on his views about women. By contrast, Mr. Delvile's character is inseparable from his patriarchal pride; he deserves every satirical attack Lady Honoria can launch against him.

Some of Lady Honoria's wittiest remarks concern the solicitude of the Delvile parents for their son and heir. She makes fun of how they coddle him, but also of his submissiveness: "Mortimer . . . is in the parlour, and the poor child is made so much of by its papa and mama, that I wish they don't half kill him by their ridiculous fondness. It is amazing to me he is so patient with them, for if they teased me half as much, I should be ready to jump up and shake them" (478–79). Cecilia does not comprehend how Lady Honoria can refer to this as a "comical scene" and asks, "what is there so comical in the anxiety of parents for an only son?" (479). Considering that the Delviles' parental fondness ends up driving both Cecilia and Mortimer to the brink of madness, their behavior does not seem as humorous as Lady Honoria makes it out to be; but she does recognize that they perpetrate emotional violence. Cecilia, however, is deaf to the sinister overtones of the relationship, and her interpretation of the Delviles's parental attentions as solely based on affection misses the mark.

As a sly dig at the Delviles' repressive authority, Lady Honoria jokes about turning the Delvile family mansion into a jail, inciting Mortimer's laughter and receiving a stern reproof from Mr. Delvile. He tells her that the word "gaol" is an improper word to use in connection with Delvile Castle: "Because it is a term that, in itself, from a young lady, has a sound peculiarly improper; and which, applied to any gentleman's ancient family seat,—a thing, Lady Honoria, always respectable, however lightly spoken of!— has an effect the least agreeable that can be devised; for it implies an idea that the family, or the mansion, is going into decay" (496). His interpretation of Lady Honoria's joke acknowledges its accuracy—the family and the mansion *are* in decay. He invokes female propriety to try to silence her wit because it calls his authority into serious question.

Like Mrs. Freke, Lady Honoria delights in provoking people; she particularly enjoys plaguing Mr. Delvile and her own father. She admits that defying patriarchal power has an element of danger: "[S]ometimes I am in a dreadful fright lest they should see me laugh, for they make such horrid grimaces it is hardly possible to look at them. When my father has been angry with me, I have sometimes been obliged to pretend I was crying, by way of excuse for putting my handkerchief to my face; for really he looks so excessively hideous, you would suppose he was making mouths, like the children, merely to frighten one" (497–98). Her subterfuge parodies female delicacy even as she hints that, in some cases, male anger may be nothing more than a bugbear set up to frighten women.

Lady Honoria's pitched battles with Mr. Delvile do not always skirt the issue of female rights, though; she is perfectly willing to confront him directly. When she criticizes female disempowerment, in the very last chapter of the book, Mr. Delvile contends that women should submit to men as their natural superiors. Lady Honoria, in reply, aptly points out the injustice of the marriage market: "[O]ne's fathers, and uncles, and those sort of people, always make connexions for one, and not a creature thinks of our principles, till they find them out by our conduct: and nobody can possibly do that till we are married, for they give us no power beforehand. The men know nothing of us in the world while we are single, but how we can dance a minuet, or play a lesson upon the harpsichord" (912). Mr. Delvile inquires into her notions of female education: "[W]hat else . . . need a young lady of rank desire to be known for? your ladyship surely would not have her degrade herself by studying like an artist or professor?" Not surprisingly, his own view of female learning coincides with the conservative conduct-book line: "a young lady of condition, who has a proper sense of her dignity, cannot be seen too rarely, or known too little" (912–13).

Lady Honoria gets the last laugh on this conservative patriarch, however, by throwing his concept of "dignity" back in his face:

> "O, but I hate dignity!" cried she carelessly, "for
> it's the dullest thing in the world. I always

thought it was owing to that you were so little amusing;—really, I beg your pardon, sir, I meant to say, so little talkative."

"I can easily credit that your ladyship spoke hastily," answered he, highly piqued, "for I believe, indeed, a person of family such as mine, will hardly be supposed to have come into the world for the office of amusing it."

"O, no, sir," cried she, with pretended innocence, "nobody, I am sure, ever saw you with such a thought." (913)

In view of Mr. Delvile's consistently bad behavior toward his son and Cecilia and their cowering fear of his disapproval, Lady Honoria's comic truths offer the double satisfaction of mocking a tyrant and redressing the injuries he has caused.

The last female trickster I will discuss carries her disregard of authority to dangerous lengths. Lydia Bennet's transgressions take her almost beyond redemption, yet she remains unashamed from start to finish. The narrator comments on Lydia's unshakable ease with regard to her shotgun marriage: "It was not to be supposed that time would give Lydia that embarrassment, from which she had been so wholly free at first" (317). Lydia boasts to servants about her wedding, shows off her ring, and by her own report "smiled like anything" (316). Even if we cannot respect Lydia's unconcern about the suffering she has caused, the narrator's comments draw our attention to her refusal to be burdened with an imposed sense of guilt and her complete disregard for conduct rules that urge women to put other's needs and interests first.

Although Lydia does not explicitly do battle with a male authority figure, she does thwart Mr. Collins's attempt to proselytize from Fordyce's *Sermons to Young Women*, a victory of sorts. In this scene, Lydia clearly has the author's approval; after all, Mr. Collins decides to read aloud from the sermons after protesting "that he never read novels" (68). Before Mr. Collins can get beyond three pages of Fordyce "with very monotonous solemnity," Lydia interrupts him with a piece of gossip. Mr. Collins's subsequent endorsement of conduct literature hardly testifies to its authority: "I have often observed how little young ladies are interested by books of a serious stamp, though written solely for their benefit. It amazes me, I confess;—for certainly, there can be nothing so advantageous to them as instruction" (69).

Lydia obviously disagrees. Like the other trickster characters, she enjoys transgressive behavior for its own sake. In contrast to conduct-book notions about the value of silence in women, Lydia values volubility: "I was ready to die of laughter. . . . [W]e talked and laughed so loud, that any body might have heard us ten miles off!" (222). She writes to inform Mrs. Forster about her plan to elope with Wickham as if it were an intrinsically humorous event: "You will laugh when you know where I am gone, and I cannot help laughing myself. . . . What a good joke it will be! I can hardly write for laughing" (291). By refusing to silence Lydia's laughter, Austen suggests that concern for reputation need not wholly govern a woman's life; and even though Lydia is not part of the charmed circle that surrounds Elizabeth at the novel's conclusion, she does not meet the typical fate of the seduced woman, abandonment and social ostracization. The fact that she remains "Lydia still" at the end of the novel indicates that she has managed to survive despite the odds against her.

In their pursuit of pleasure, female tricksters frequently come into conflict with the feminine ideal. They flatly refuse to be defined by their ability to please men; on the contrary, they take pleasure in openly defying patriarchal figures. Paraphrasing Woolf, feminist critics Sandra Gilbert and Susan Gubar argue that the angelic ideal must be killed to free women writers for the creative process: "women must kill the aesthetic ideal through which they themselves have been 'killed' into art. And similarly, all women writers must kill the angel's necessary opposite and double, the 'monster' in the house, whose Medusa-face also kills female creativity" (17). Female tricksters manage to transcend the angel/monster, virgin/whore dichotomy. They make it a point of honor to mock the standards that govern female behavior, and they rise above the fray by keeping their wits about them.

The four characters I have discussed by no means exhaust the list. Other characters who exhibit trickster features include Mrs. Arlbery (Burney's *Camilla*), Elinor Joddrel (*The Wanderer*),

Mrs. Beaumont (Edgeworth's *Manoeuvering* [1809]), "Araminta" (Edgeworth's *Angelina* [1801]), Lady Susan (Austen's *Lady Susan*), and Mary Crawford (*Mansfield Park* [1816]). More than any other approach, the use of female trickster characters allowed Burney, Edgeworth, and Austen to challenge directly the rules that restricted female development. While satirical commentary and female naive satirists made it possible for these authors to criticize the status quo, such devices had a major limitation: the novelists ran the risk of being identified with their fiction and censured for expressing feminist views. With trickster characters, on the other hand, they were able to stage rebellions against the restrictions on womanhood without having to fear being identified with these characters. Because tricksters are not the heroines and are often condemned within the novel by male figures, much of the reading public would not associate their views with those of the author. Those who did so would likely be people who took the tricksters seriously, as an intimate expression of their desires or fears—the female audience.

The trickster performs a vital task for the female author by ridiculing the authority of the conduct-book dictates. If women writers had played by the rules, they would never have ventured forth in print. We might even say that the female trickster stands in for the author; after all, a trickster can only be as witty as her creator.

5

Mocking the "Lords of Creation": Male Comic Characters

I like your Plan immensely of Extirpating that vile race of beings
call'd man but I (who you know am clever (VÈRRÉE) clever) have
thought of an improvement in the sistim suppose we were to Cut
of [sic][1] their *prominent members* and by that means render them
Harmless innofencive Little Creatures; We might have such
charming *vocal* Music Every house might be Qualified to get
up an opera and Piccinis Music would be still more in vogue
than it is & we might make such usefull Animals of
them in other Respects Consider Well this scheme.

—Maria Allen to stepsister Frances Burney, 1768[2]

IN THE INTRODUCTION TO A 1981 COLLECTION OF ESSAYS on
women writers' depictions of men, Janet Todd remarks somewhat wistfully upon the relative absence of men as comic targets:
"Women writers have served up men in many guises and for many
purposes. They have loved them, idealized them, bullied them,
displaced them, and humiliated them. Perhaps, though, they have
not yet learned to laugh at them enough" (*Men* 7). In a similar
vein, some theorists of women and comedy have doubted whether
women make jokes about men. Emily Toth's "humane humor
rule" sums up the widely held view that since women have suffered under centuries of misogynist satire, they tend to eschew
laughing at men.[3] According to Toth and others, women's history
has given them a more charitable sense of humor. It is more generous than male humor because its focus is more specific; rather
than condemning broadly, it mocks certain character types and
individual foibles.

We must ask, though, whether the supposition of a benevolent female comic spirit, however positive, unduly narrows the
scope of female humor. For example, does it cover up or deny the
possibility of a political component to women's humor? Benign
laughter may well be politically and socially ineffectual. In a
male-dominated society, privileges are certainly not dispersed hu-
manely or generously, and since male privileges almost always involve female deprivations, women might in fact laugh at men as a
group in order to challenge male power and further a feminist
cause. In fact, laughing at the category "man," as Maria Allen
does in the epigraph's reference to "that vile race of beings," can
be a way of solidifying ties with the oppositional and socially restricted group, woman.[4]

Folklorist Carol Mitchell suggests that assumptions about
women's "gentler" sense of humor reflect women's joke-telling
practices in public settings; she argues that women tell their most
tendentious jokes in all-female groups and that their mockery in
such circles is frequently directed against men.[5] Mitchell has discovered that joking about men allows women to comment on
their situation in a male-dominated society and to assert power by
ridiculing the source of their oppression. Although Mitchell's
studies involve women in the 1970s and 1980s, her conclusions
would seem to hold true for women in any male-dominated culture in which humor plays a social and political role. Women who
are dependent upon men in some fashion will most likely express
whatever hostility they might feel to a female audience. Because
hostile humor is more threatening to its victim than outright resentment, it will especially be reserved for a select audience, one
that will not only appreciate the aims of such humor but also respect the risk involved in its expression. We can expect secrecy,
then, to be frequently concomitant to women's telling jokes about
men.

Women's past discretion means that many of their jokes
about men are lost to us, but surviving examples of private jokes
aimed at men can help us trace the residue of such humor in published writings and can illustrate its liberating force. The section
of Maria Allen's letter to her stepsister Frances Burney that I take

as this chapter's epigraph provides a rare glimpse of two eighteenth-century women's inside jokes about men. Furthermore, it offers a new angle on Burney's sense of humor. Not only did she receive and preserve a surprisingly racy letter, but she seems to have inspired Allen's joke with some hostile humor of her own.

Although Burney's half of the correspondence is not extant, Allen alludes to her cousin's plan for "Extirpating that vile race of beings" and even suggests that Burney had come up with a "sistim" for carrying it out. In proposing routine castration, Allen continues a joke that Burney initiated. The humor of both women takes as its focus the injustice of a male-dominated culture and society. Under Allen's scheme, men could be rendered "Harmless innofencive Little Creatures" if women would just cut off their "prominent members." Her humorous proposal reverses gender roles and situates women as the dominant group, with men entertaining them as castrati and perhaps even waiting upon them as domestic servants. Burney, however, may be the more radical feminist: whereas Allen wants to invert sexual politics and put women in charge, Burney apparently would rather exterminate the brutes and live in an all-female world.

Allen's castration joke poses a challenge to twentieth-century critics who argue that early women writers like Burney, Edgeworth, and Austen could not harbor feminist views because they absorbed their culture's feminine ideal. Such a joke refutes, for example, Martha Brown's assertion that feminist readings of Burney's novels are currently "fashionable" but anachronistic (29). While acknowledging that there may be some rebellious strains in Burney's last novel, *The Wanderer,* Brown accuses feminist critics of reading backwards through Burney's canon and distorting the meaning of "the young girl who wrote *Evelina*" (38). An Austen critic, Linda Hunt, argues the same point but sees the revisionist process affecting Austen's works starting at the opposite end of her life: feminist critics transfer Austen's early feminist leanings onto her later, conservative novels. Hunt contends that although the young Jane Austen might have flirted with rebellion, the mature Austen was "convinced . . . of the importance of the social definition of femininity" (10). Hunt and Brown, along with other opponents of feminist readings of eighteenth-century women writers, seem to view feminism as a virus that might temporarily afflict an author but which—whether it comes early or late—must be considered an aberration. Those critics who most vehemently reject feminist approaches perpetuate a view of women writers as mirrors who passively reflect the manners of their time and uphold the established order.[6] If nothing else, Allen's joke allows us to see how great the difference can be between the status quo and an eighteenth-century middle-class woman.

Eighteenth-century conduct literature urged women to refrain from laughing at men as a general principle. Thomas Gisborne describes how witty women like "to lead a pert and coxcombical young man . . . to expose himself" (108). This sort of diversion, according to Gisborne, is socially disruptive and possibly addictive. Women who mock foolish men might also make respectable ones look like fools: "And if a man of grave aspect and more wakeful reflection presumes to step within the circle, they assail the unwelcome intruder with a volley of brilliant raillery and sparkling repartee, which bears down knowledge and learning before it; and convulse the delighted auditors with peals of laughter, while he labours in his heavy accoutrements after his light-armed antagonist, and receives at every turn a shower of arrows, which he can neither parry nor withstand" (109). Gisborne's worry that women will be unable to distinguish between suitable and unsuitable male targets reveals a deeper anxiety about female laughter: witty women may successfully storm the bastions of grave respectability that maintain male authority. In Gisborne's worst-case scenario, public laughter marks the man's vanquished state, giving proof to the inadequacy of his "knowledge and learning" and acknowledging female superiority. Gisborne asks his female readers to feel sorry for this unfortunate male and deny themselves the use of their exceptional skills. His message is an old one: women should not threaten men by engaging in such skirmishes because it goes against the rules. In the battle of the sexes, women must lose gracefully if they want to preserve the social order, which sanctifies male esteem.

Similarly concerned over women's potential disrespect for

men, James Fordyce preaches that a woman should cultivate her talents for listening:

> What man is not charmed with an amiable cour-
> teousness in any young woman, especially if oth-
> erwise attractive? . . . But would you be resistless
> [i.e., irresistible]? Acquire a habit of fixed atten-
> tion. It is a sort of silent flattery truly exquisite,
> and withal perfectly innocent. . . . In short, lis-
> tening to the person who speaks, with a recol-
> lected, mild, and steady aspect, *which nothing friv-
> olous can divert,* is perhaps the most valuable
> secret in the whole science of genuine politeness.
> From an agreeable young woman to an intelli-
> gent man it is incredibly soothing. (179, empha-
> sis added)

No doubt such attention can be "soothing," but one wonders about the necessity of such a studied countenance—what frivol-ity does Fordyce see lurking beneath the surface of the woman's face? An impulse to laugh *at* the male speaker? Although by pro-moting the "science of genuine politeness" and implying that men, too, would do well to listen studiously he seems to want to avoid the charge of unfairness, the structure of his argument and his choice of adjectives betray his sexism. His adjectives are those of a social code that subordinates women to men: men should be "intelligent" and use their authority with knowledge and care, whereas women are at their best, he implies, when they are "agree-able" and "young," at their most adaptable.

Nonetheless, Fordyce recognizes the equality of potential between the genders: he puts it within the female's power to bol-ster the intelligent man's ego, to soothe him, to make him feel in-teresting.[7] If, as historian Lawrence Stone posits, "patriarchy for its effective exercise depends not so much on raw power or legal authority, as on a recognition by all concerned of its legitimacy" (151), then the woman who listens quietly and reveres male au-thority plays an essential role in patriarchal culture. The conduct books' attempt to script this role for women, to secure their silent attention, suggests an awareness of the constructed nature of gen-der relations—if women were naturally docile, passive, and sub-missive, there would be no need to restrain their behavior. By attempting to script women's roles, conduct literature concedes women's potential for self-definition even as it seeks to control the avenues of expression.

We have already seen how Burney, Edgeworth, and Austen destabilize male-centered authority by making fun of absurd con-duct rules of behavior and assumptions about women's nature. They criticize and redefine gender relations in the world of fic-tion, revising the rules of the game from within. When these au-thors take males as comic targets, they subvert the game even more thoroughly. Laughing at men involves a rejection of the hi-erarchy that subordinates women and calls for a rebellion against women's so-called superiors.

In their private correspondence Allen and Burney were free to enjoy hostile humor against men that more conservative women would have repressed. Few women would have declared their cleverness, as Allen does, let alone their ambition to dominate men. Lest we fall into the error of dismissing Allen's joke as purely eccentric, though, we need to place the letter in its eighteenth-century context in order to recognize that ideas about the injus-tice of male dominance were in the air throughout the latter part of the century.

Allen's desire to invert the order of oppression was in keep-ing with a belief, widespread until the tumultuous 1790s, that men had unjustly "usurped" authority from women.[8] So common was the debate about women's enslaved condition at mid-century that Lady G. in *Sir Charles Grandison* (1753–54) could introduce a discussion of women's rights in condensed terms: "Man's usurpa-tion, and woman's natural independency, was the topic" (Vol. 6, 242). William Alexander, in his *History of Women* (1779), took "man's usurpation" as his thesis and viewed women's relative in-dependence in eighteenth-century England as an indicator of civ-ilization's progress. He presents men as sensualists who, through-out history, have conspired to keep women in ignorance to gratify their own ends: "In every age, and in every country, while the men have been partial to the persons of the fair, they have either left their minds altogether without culture, or biassed them by a culture of a spurious and improper nature; suspicious, perhaps, that a more rational one would have opened their eyes, shewn them their real condition, and prompted them to assert the rights of nature; rights, of which the men have perpetually, more or less, deprived them" (iv). Alexander's reading of men's manipulation of women—keeping them ignorant in order to keep them submissive—reflects the relatively sympathetic climate toward women's rights issues that prevailed from mid-century to the 1790s. By 1779 many shared his disgust with the hypocrisy of misogynist satire: "while we take every opportunity of telling them when present, that their persons are all beauty, and their sentiments and actions all perfection; when absent, we laugh at the credulity of their minds, and splenetically satirise and exhibit to view every fault and every folly" (iv). Alexander's comments take sexism as an avoidable but universal vice, spanning geography and history with its culturally sanctioned grips.

Allen and Burney's humorous solution to gender inequalities aligns them with the confident feminist tradition that views male supremacy as deserving of outright ridicule. When Allen slyly advocates the removal of men's prominent members, she calls into question the principle of male superiority by locating male power in the genitalia and reducing them to nonessential traits (removable appendages). Small wonder then that Burney describes her stepsister's letters as "uncommon, lively, comical, entertaining, frank, and undisguised" (*Early Diary* 1.106). No doubt, Allen's brand of humor provided Burney with a welcome release from the burdens of dutiful daughterhood. Often silenced by male authority figures, Burney was able in Allen's company to laugh at men.

In her journal Burney records one incident in which her stepsister's behavior leads her to laugh at a man she both disrespected and feared. She describes this man—Mr. Featherstone—as "a weak-Hearted, dirty, pettish, absurd Creature . . . equally ugly & cross" (*Early Journals* 158–59). In a complex scene, male smugness (Featherstone), female subversion (Allen), and moral ambivalence (Burney) combine to portray some of the social dis-

117

locations caused by sexism. Allen shocks Burney by boldly ap-
proaching Mr. Featherstone to ask if she can borrow his clothes in
order to play a male role in some amateur theatricals. Burney herself would have hesitated to make a request of Featherstone and
certainly not such an intimate one. Gradually, however, Burney's
timidity dissolves into mirth as Allen and another female friend
invade Featherstone's chambers with multiple requests for clothing and accessories. According to Burney, Featherstone does not
suspect that Allen and her friend are mocking him, but instead
feels flattered at being let in on a secret: "Mr. Featherstone enjoyed it prodigiously, sniggering & joking, & resting upon his
Crutches to Laugh: for my own part, the torrent of their ridiculous requests, made me every minute march out of the Room to
laugh more freely" (160). The episode concludes with Burney's
flight: "I now ran away with all speed, not able any longer to keep
with them, both from laughter, & really from shame" (161).
However much she may have been ashamed, Burney clearly
found this scene diverting.[9]

The incident with Featherstone illustrates how the open
laughter of women of different moral temperaments may conceal
a similar hostility. The source of both Allen's and Burney's laughter is the same, as is the quality of their laughter. By Burney's own
report, she might have remained in the room and shared in the
general laughter. The only, and significant, difference is their behavior. Burney eventually hides herself because she is disturbed
by her friends' and her own duplicity, knowing that the girls'
laughter differs from Featherstone's in motive.

According to Mitchell, "women, taught that they should
not be openly aggressive and hostile, express hostility in a somewhat more disguised form than males do" ("Some Differences"
173). For Allen and her friend, one disguise involved pretending
to laugh *with* Featherstone while enjoying a laugh *against* him; for
Burney it meant leaving the room to laugh. Another form of
masking was their excessive interest in male clothing: Who would
want to be a male when the immediate representative figure of
the sex was one such as Featherstone? Allen's and Burney's laughter had an individual and a generic target that doubled them up
until Burney felt morally obliged to leave. In fiction, however,

Burney found ways to make sure that her laughter would satisfy
her sense of honor by not reaching the ears of males instigating it.

What Wollstonecraft accomplishes by bringing patriarchal texts
into her work to mock them, Burney, Edgeworth, and Austen
achieve by attributing sexist assumptions to comic male characters. These authors reduce male supremacy to a laughing matter,
the mainstay of fops and fools. Edgeworth's Lady Cecilia jokingly
pronounces a maxim on the respect women should accord to male
authority: "It is always permitted . . . to woman to use her intellects so far as to comprehend what man says; her knowledge, of
whatever sort, never comes amiss when it serves only to illustrate
what is said by one of the lords of creation" (*Helen* 95). As she
makes clear, sexist maxims always place men at the center of the
universe and situate women in peripheral positions. Lady Cecilia's maxim had a special relevance for these women writers:
they indeed used their intellects to comprehend what the "lords
of creation" were saying; what they learned caused them in turn
to laugh at the myth of male superiority.[10]

Comic male characters in works by eighteenth-century female writers provided opportunities for women living in a sexist society to laugh at men. Since the characters are also faulty human beings, they could make male readers laugh as well, but the quality of
laughter would probably be different. Like male writers of comedy
such as Fielding or Smollett, women novelists ridicule egotistical
characters in their fiction; but unlike their masculine counterparts,
they reserve the brunt of their scorn for men who have a low opinion of women, and they show no indulgence toward this fault.
Joyce Tompkins comments on the "strong satiric vein" in eighteenth-century novels by women: "In a generation whose humour
mostly took the form of whimsical sentiment or of horse-play, the
women show a keen sense of the ludicrous, but none of the charity
of humour. They have taken notes of all the stupidities, all the selfishness and clumsy motions of conceit with which for centuries
their sex had been affronted. They observe with a scornful eye and
record with a dry intolerance of phrase, and where their fastidious-
ness is offended they punish without mercy" (131–32). Although
Tompkins does not explore comic male targets in any detail, she

accurately pinpoints the feminist source of such comedy: "Their laughter covers a sore, and they can scarcely regard with equanimity any of those qualities which undermine the dignity of woman, or of a man in his relations with woman" (134).

Numerous comic male characters appear in the works of Burney, Edgeworth, and Austen. Most of these comic males batten on a belief in male supremacy and female inferiority. They generally make sexist remarks and offer some form of insult or impertinence to women. Many, especially those who try to court the heroines, conceive of women as men's rightful property. In situations involving comic male characters, the authors depict social injustices and deconstruct the maxims that bolster an unequal system. By mocking specimens of the "lords of creation," these women novelists attack the basis of patriarchal society and encourage in their readers a similar insouciance toward male supremacy.

Sexist males make pronouncements upon women's capacities, restrict women's ability to choose, and demand that women pay homage to male supremacy. In novels by women, male comic characters may very well exert a substantial amount of pressure upon female development; nonetheless, by subjecting male power to laughter, women novelists register their rejection of male authority. Burney, Edgeworth, and Austen engage the central issues of the Enlightenment debate on gender relations in their choice of social topics and comic male characters. In three widely discussed areas— the marriage market, the educational system, and the structure of authority—women writers found countless absurdities and contradictions. When these writers make fun of male suitors, "educated" men, and fathers, they take a stand against the established order.

The most frequent site of satiric exposure in feminist comedy is the marriage market. As women's only path to social advancement, the marriage market (like society in general) was skewed in men's favor. To men belonged all power of choice; to women at most the negative power of refusal. Burney, Edgeworth, and Austen so frequently call attention to the inhuman dimension of the marriage market by bringing together exceptional heroines and foolish suitors that the comic proposal scene is practically a fixture in their fiction. What makes these scenes important from a feminist point of view is not only the heroine's opportunity to exercise her power of refusal, but also the sexist nonsense that the heroine laughs at when she rejects the foolish suitor.

The prevalence of comic suitors in the works of women novelists has received little critical attention, but even a short list reveals a pattern of shared feminist views. In each case the comicality of the male suitor has a serious edge. In *Evelina*, Sir Clement's comic antics place the heroine in compromising, even dangerous, positions, and his callousness toward Madame Duval belies his florid lovemaking style. Mr. Smith, a minor contender for Evelina's hand who professes to be "never so happy as in obliging the ladies," nonetheless boasts of his bachelor's contempt for marriage: "I have not yet the cares of the world upon me,—I am not *married*,—ha, ha, ha,—you'll excuse me Ladies,—but I can't help laughing" (179, 188). In *Cecilia*, Sir Robert Floyer argues that there is no point in making an effort to talk to women; he feels that since men have all the advantages to offer, women should make the effort to attract them. In Edgeworth's *Patronage*, Buckhurst Falconer, initially a suitor for Caroline Percy, ends up marrying an older woman for her money even though he refers to her as an "old, ugly, cross, avaricious devil" (423). Finally, in *Emma* (1816), Mr. Elton makes gallant speeches of courtship that were "very apt to incline [Emma] to laugh" and that result in her leaving the room to "indulge the inclination" (82). All tenderness disappears, however, as soon as he discovers that his own plan of marrying an heiress will not succeed. These male suitors come across as comical precisely because their egotism is self-evident; they wear their hypocrisy on their sleeves.

When we laugh at comic male suitors, we must keep in mind the political implications of such laughter. If women were supposed to make men feel good about themselves, they certainly were not permitted to make sport of courtship rituals. Hannah More, who stresses the gravity of courtship in *Coelebs in Search of a Wife* (1808), alludes to the unacceptability of laughter as a response to a proposal by describing an outrageous household:

> In one, where the young ladies had large fortunes,
> they insinuated themselves into the admiration,

and invited the familiarity of young men, by attentions the most flattering, and civilities the most
alluring. When they had made sure of their air, and
the admirers were encouraged to make proposals,
the ladies burst out into a loud laugh, wondered
what the man could mean; they never dreamt of
any thing more than common politeness; then pet-
rified them with distant looks, and turned about to
practise the same arts on others. (77)

Only the exceptional economic independence of the women
could account for the self-confidence behind such radically unconventional behavior; in reality, women would have seldom
been able to extract proposals from men at will or afford to reject
them. Besides making it clear that the marriage market is a very
serious business, More expresses an anxiety that she perhaps
shared with Fordyce: that women's character, when freed of social
restraint, would prove as volatile as men's.

Burney, Edgeworth, and Austen were less inclined to constrain female power, particularly with regard to the marriage market. By mocking comic suitors, these authors denounce a ludicrous
system that inflates male egos. Whether he is a minor annoyance
to be brushed off like a fly or a persistent source of trouble for the
heroine, the comic suitor represents sexist nonsense ranging from
the valorization of everything male to the denigration of all
things female. Burney, Edgeworth, and Austen strip away romantic pretensions from the courtship practices of egotistical men and
discredit the sexism of the marriage market. In the process, they
teach their readers that women are not to be treated as objects of
exchange. Once the reader sees how foolish sexist men look next
to sensible women, she or he might begin to rethink the entire
notion of gender-based social privileges.

Austen may have drawn the curtain in her novels upon serious proposals of marriage, but in *Pride and Prejudice* she does not
hesitate to disclose a humorous one. Mr. Collins's proposal to Elizabeth Bennet dramatizes the absurdity of woman's place in the
marriage market. Austen gives free play in this scene to the clash

between sexist foolishness and common sense. Mr. Collins's notions about female delicacy mirror those expressed in the conduct literature of writers such as Fordyce. By contrast, Elizabeth, while politely suppressing her laughter, tries to talk some sense into him. Mr. Collins's rigidly applied cultural standards give him no chance for success with Elizabeth; that the reader wishes him none is to Austen's, and feminism's, credit.

His self-confidence in the eventual success of his proposal taints every remark he makes; the more inflated his rhetoric, the more his self-interest comes out with comic effect. Austen lets us know that for Mr. Collins a marriage proposal is a business matter, a formality with its own guiding conventions: "having no feelings of diffidence to make it distressing to himself even at the moment, he set about it in a very orderly manner, with all the observances which he supposed a regular part of the business" (104). From the start, Mr. Collins reveals an ignorance of individual female will in his mistaken interpretation of Elizabeth's unwillingness to be alone with him: "your modesty, so far from doing you any disservice, rather adds to your other perfections" (105). When he claims to risk being "run away with" by his feelings, Elizabeth can barely stifle her laughter at his cant. After listing his reasons for proposing marriage to her, which include Lady Catherine de Bourgh's explicit command that he marry soon, he adds, "And now nothing remains for me but to assure you in the most animated language of the violence of my affections" (106). Austen's juxtaposition of hackneyed romantic phrases and pompous, insincere behavior as standard aspects of courtship makes this scene politically relevant as well as ludicrous.

Mr. Collins's egotism prevents him from comprehending either women in general or Elizabeth's individuality. The possibility of a distinction between gender and role could never occur to him, given his commitment to social forms, and the conventional proposal script that he blindly follows does not take female resistance into account. When Mr. Collins invokes what he believes to be women's custom of making false refusals, his appropriation of romantic rhetoric reveals the cynicism behind courtship conventions. He feels assured of her subordination:

I am not now to learn . . . that it is usual with
young ladies to reject the addresses of the man
whom they favour; and that sometimes the refusal is repeated a second or even a third time. I
am therefore by no means discouraged by what
you have just said, and shall hope to lead you to
the altar ere long. (107)

I am far from accusing you of cruelty at present, because I know it to be the established custom of your sex to reject a man on the first appli-
cation, and perhaps you have even now said as
much to encourage my suit as would be consis-
tent with the true delicacy of the female character. (108)

The dialogue between this confident suitor and the sensible heroine seems like something out of *Alice in Wonderland,* but with a
feminist thrust. Elizabeth grounds her refusal in rational argument; Mr. Collins steadfastly rejects her negative by referring to
an absurd system in which women have scarcely any choice and
are not allowed to express desire when it *is* present.

Mr. Collins's confidence reflects unfavorably upon the society that subordinates women to men. When interpreting Elizabeth's refusal, he remains unshaken in his worldview: "it is by no
means certain that another offer of marriage may ever be made
you. . . . As I must therefore conclude you are not serious in your
rejection of me, I shall chuse to attribute it to your wish of in-
creasing my love by suspense, according to the usual practice of elegant females" (108). Though Mr. Collins's delivery of this message is comical, the syllogism motivating his persistence has the
sinister reasoning of commercial exploitation: a woman must
marry; her opportunities for marriage are dependent on her financial situation; Elizabeth has little money; therefore, Elizabeth must
accept any offer she gets. Faced with this logic, she has good reason to be contemptuous of the marriage market. In a desperate
plea to be heard, she begs him to treat her "not . . . as an elegant
female intending to plague you, but as a rational creature speaking
the truth from her heart." But Mr. Collins only replies with yet an-

other assertion of confidence and "an air of awkward gallantry" (109). In the situation at hand he confuses commerce with chivalry and property with love, envisioning himself as a conquering hero and Elizabeth as the distressed damsel whom he must rescue. By placing the bumbling Mr. Collins in this courtship scene, Austen punctures the sexism inherent in the plot of rescue and salvation, reveals its exploitative values, and tries to release the female character from at least one set of conventional chains.

Her recognition of the power of convention, however, allows for only a partial victory. Even in the midst of the comic proposal, Austen lets us know that the odds are stacked in Mr. Collins's favor. Elizabeth's own mother takes his side and agrees with him on the advantages of his proposal. For, despite his buffoonery, Mr. Collins exerts a certain influence because of his gender. As the consequence of an entailment preventing the Bennet females from owning property, their home will eventually belong to him; and as an example of male commercial power, his interpretation of women's position in the marriage market proves to be correct in Charlotte Lucas's case. Elizabeth represents an exception to the conventional script, but only because she is outspoken. Her rejection of the marriage-market mentality no doubt reflected the wishes of many eighteenth-century women denied her freedom of choice. Had her father united with Mrs. Bennet in favor of the match, *Pride and Prejudice* might have been a tragedy, like *Clarissa*, instead of a brilliant comedy.

Belinda depicts another comic male suitor who questions women's capacity for choice. In a footnote to a later edition of the novel, Edgeworth registers her view of Sir Philip Baddley's role and his expletives: "The manners, if not the morals, of gentlemen, have improved since the first publication of this work. Swearing has gone out of fashion. But Sir Philip Baddley's oaths are retained, as marks in a portrait of the times held up to the public, touched by ridicule, the best reprobation" (79). Along with his oaths, his view of women is "touched by ridicule" as well and receives adequate reprobation in the course of the novel.

When Sir Philip first contemplates proposing to Belinda, his confidence, oaths, and sexism blend in a ludicrous speech of self-persuasion:

I could make her sing to another tune, if I pleased, . . . but, damme, it would cost me too much—a wife's too expensive a thing, now-a-days. Why, a man could have twenty curricles, and a fine stud, and a pack of hounds, and as many mistresses as he chooses into the bargain, for what it would cost him to take a wife. Oh, damme, Belinda Port- man's a fine girl, but not worth so much as that comes to; and yet, confound me, if I should not like to see how blue Clary would look, if I were to propose for her in good earnest. (133)

Considering a wife as yet another piece of property, Sir Philip per- suades himself to propose to Belinda in order to get a jump on Clarence Hervey. Immediately after having thought of proposing, his mind is made up: "At last, what he called love prevailed over prudence, and he was resolved, cost him what it would, to have Belinda Portman." To resolve, for Sir Philip, is the same thing as to gain his point: "He had not the least doubt of being accepted, if he made a proposal of marriage; consequently, the moment that he came to this determination, he could not help assuming *d'avance* the tone of a favoured lover" (133). His overstated arrogance springs from a conviction that all women aim at monetarily advan- tageous matches and that Belinda is in no position to reject his advances.

Like Mr. Collins, Sir Philip wastes no time in making his proposal in proper form; he "determined the next day upon the grand attack" (135). A central comic feature of this proposal scene is his playing with a "stick," a masturbatory activity that he repeats throughout his visit: "He twirled and twisted a short stick that he held in his hand, and put it into and out of his boot twenty times" (135). His "little stick," like his masculine author- ity, is something that he flourishes to small effect. In spite of his flattery—calling Belinda a "charming girl" with "charming lips" and claiming to like "pride in a handsome woman, if it was only for variety's sake"—Sir Philip makes no great impression upon his intended prey. When Belinda flatly refuses his offer of marriage, he cannot comprehend her: "Confusion seize me . . . if this isn't the most extraordinary thing I ever heard!" (136).

Their conversation resembles Mr. Collins's proposal to Elizabeth in that both exchanges portray a man unable to accept the truth of the woman's statements:

> "Oh, curse it!" said he, changing his tone, "you're only quizzing me to see how I should look— damn me, you did it too well, you little coquet!"
>
> Belinda again assured him that she was entirely in earnest, and that she was incapable of the sort of coquetry which he ascribed to her.
>
> "Oh, damme, ma'am, then I've no more to say—a coquet is a thing I understand as well as another, and if we had been only talking in the air, it would have been another thing; but when I come at once to a proposal in form, and a woman seriously tells me she has objections that cannot be obviated, damme, what must I, or what must the world, conclude, but that she's very unaccountable, or that she's engaged—which last I presume to be the case." (137)

His logic, like that of Mr. Collins, leads him to conclude that no personal objections to his proposal make sense; he must account for her refusal by either considering her irrational or positing another suitor. Once Belinda calmly assures him that she is unengaged, neither explanation remains available to him. He attempts to take refuge in his stick, but finds no comfort there: "after twisting his little black stick into all manner of shapes, [he] finished by breaking it, and then having no other resource, suddenly wished Miss Portman a good morning, and decamped with a look of silly ill-humour" (137). The broken stick represents his lack of potency as a suitor, his failed attempt to bully Belinda into submission, and the inability of conventional thinking to account for rational, unconventional female behavior.[11] In Sir Philip's case, as in that of Mr. Collins, the comic suitor's failure represents a triumph in the novel—the triumph of sense over folly and a victory over the myth of male superiority. Like Elizabeth, Belinda demonstrates a degree of self-assertiveness and speaks the minds of many when she repeatedly states her own preference.

A particularly foolish male suitor, *Camilla*'s Mr. Dubster, is described by Burney as "a figure distinguished only as a mark for ridicule" (69). Unlike Mr. Collins and Sir Philip, Mr. Dubster plays the marriage market to his monetary advantage: as a result of two previous marriages, he acquired enough money to get out of business and to assume, albeit awkwardly, the role of a gentleman. He reveals his sense of masculine entitlement when he holds forth on female beauty for Camilla's edification: "That young lady, ma'am, . . . cuts you all up, sure enough. She's as fine a piece of red and white as ever I see. I could think of such a young lady as that myself, if I did not remember that I thought no more of my wife that was pretty, than of my wife that was ugly, after the first month or so. Beauty goes for a mere nothing in matrimony, when once one's used to it" (91). Mr. Dubster's vulgar description of a woman as a fine "piece of red and white" and his freedom in suggesting a comparison between her and Camilla demonstrate his confidence in male supremacy; he feels entitled to evaluate women as objects.[12]

Mr. Dubster's leading comic feature, parsimony, accentuates his ingratitude to his two dead wives, the source of the money that raised him into the leisured class. His description of how his wives wasted money stands as a satire on property relations within marriage: "They was always a thinking they had a right to what they had a mind, because of what they brought me; so that I had enough to do to scrape a little matter together, in case of outliving them" (91). His miserliness is so excessive that he even begrudges one wife her medical expenses in dying: "She cost me a mort of money to the potecary before she went off. And she was a tedious while a dying, poor soul" (279). His term of endearment is at best reflexive; Mr. Dubster's motives for marrying are unabashedly mercenary and inhumane. His experience in the marriage market has only given him confidence in the propriety of his demeanor.

When Mr. Dubster makes his formal visit to Sir Hugh to ask

for Camilla's hand and learns that she is not an heiress, he changes his mind. He declares, "Matrimony's a good thing enough, when it's to help a man forward: but a person must be a fool indeed, to put himself out of his way for nothing" (603). Completely oblivious to Camilla's dislike for him, Mr. Dubster is convinced that she tried to lure him into marriage. Without knowing whether she would have accepted his proposal or not, he congratulates himself on escaping from her clutches: "He then formally wished the baronet a good day, and hastened from the house, puffed up with vain glory, at his own sagacious precautions, which had thus happily saved him from being tricked into unprofitable wedlock" (603). Although he is more extreme than either Mr. Collins or Sir Philip, all three view women as chattel. Mr. Dubster's assumption that Camilla is his for the taking underscores the absurdity of the marriage market system. His projection of fraud onto Camilla reveals the lack of character women appear to have for many men in the market. She is what he makes of her. While an ill-bred man can still exercise his right of choice, women are not regarded as having the minimal equipment with which to choose. Because Mr. Dubster is so extreme, he is the most comic of all the suitors; Burney's portraits of him are delightful miniatures in self-made character assassination.

Mr. Collins, Sir Philip, and Mr. Dubster each serves as a comic contrast to the true suitor; even though Darcy, Clarence Hervey, and Edgar Mandlebert have a good deal to learn about relationships with women, they never approach the sexism of the comic characters. In *Helen*, the heroine compares the exceptional Granville Beauclerc to her comic suitor Horace Churchill on the basis of how they treat women: "he always speaks of women in general with respect—as if he had more confidence in them, and more dependence upon them for his happiness. Now Mr. Churchill, with all the adoration he professes, seems to look upon them as idols that he can set up or pull down, bend the knee to or break to pieces, at pleasure—I could not like a man for a friend who had a bad, or even a contemptuous, opinion of women" (149). Her classification of men into two categories—those who respect women and those who do not—indicates the difference between the successful suitor and his comic counterpart in novels by women. In comic works, men who have bad opinions of women come across not as villains, but as fools.

Among the masculine privileges that eighteenth-century feminists attacked, no area received as much attention as education. The issue of women's education became even more pressing as educational opportunities were extended to males of the lower classes. By the end of the eighteenth century, most educational theorists agreed that women should learn, but there was a good deal of disagreement about what subjects were suitable for women, and there were many skeptics about women's potential talents.

Burney, Edgeworth, and Austen refuse to pay tribute to men's capacity for learning; in fact, they ridicule male pretension and express resentment against an educational system that allowed ignorant men to claim superiority over women through their association with male-dominated institutions of higher learning. They show that common sense may be superior to booklearning and that it transcends gender as an indicator of people's worth; in their depictions of humorous encounters between heroines and male egotists, common sense belongs exclusively to the woman.

The attitude of Miss Margland, a governess in Burney's *Camilla*, toward the schooling of her fair charge reflects the late-eighteenth-century opinion that too much learning constitutes a liability for women: "Miss Lynmere . . . though both beautiful and well brought up, could never cope with so great a disadvantage as the knowledge of Latin" (46). As Miss Margland indicates and Camilla's younger sister Eugenia's case bears out, the rewards of a classical education for most women would include social ostracism.[13] In this same novel, however, Burney makes fun of the male scholar Dr. Orkborne, "whose life had been spent in any study rather than that of human nature" (38) and whose obsession with books and study seals him off from the human community. In Dr. Orkborne's capacity as tutor, he commands the respect of all around him, but in other areas he comes across as a foolish specimen of humanity.

Dr. Orkborne's lack of common sense makes him the focus of several comic scenes in the novel that call into question his ability to put any of his knowledge into practical use. When, during a walk in the country, everyone panics over a charging bull, Dr. Orkborne remains oblivious to the screams, roars, and shrieks: "intent upon his annotations, [he] calmly wrote on, sensible there was some disturbance, but determining to evade inquiring whence it arose, till he had secured what he meant to transmit to posterity from the treachery of his memory" (132).

Dr. Orkborne carries his work with him wherever he goes and, as a result, often forgets where he's going. A servant provides a humorous report of Dr. Orkborne's behavior on one occasion when he has been sent to pick up Camilla and Eugenia:

> [A]s soon as we come to the Grove, I goes up to the coach door, to ask the Doctor if he would get out, or only send in to let the young ladies know he was come for them; but he was got so deep into some of his larning, that, I dare say, I bawled it three good times in his ears, before he so much as lifted up his head; and then it was only to say, I put him out! and to it he went again, just as if I'd said never a word; till, at last, I was so plaguy mad, I gives the coach such a jog, to bring him to himself like, that it jerked the pencil and paper out of his hand. So then he went straight into one of his takings, pretending I had made him forget all his thoughts, and such like out of the way talk, after his old way. (200)

Dr. Orkborne's singlemindedness would be almost Quixotic were it not for his bad temper. His propensity for venting his scholarly frustrations on whoever gets in his way makes him appear more egotistic than idealistic. Through Dr. Orkborne, Burney portrays the anxieties and exertions of the exclusively book-learned man as laughable idiosyncrasies and, in doing so, indirectly challenges the benefit he has received from so much "larning."

John Thorpe, in *Northanger Abbey*, is an excellent example of a comic male egotist upon whom an education has been wasted. Not only is his conversation limited to himself and his interests; he continually brags and exaggerates in order to prove his importance. Although Thorpe preens himself on his worldliness, his pretensions make his speeches comic and allow Austen to indict the masculine culture that produces such figures. Austen makes fun of his stated areas of expertise—drinking and equipage—and hints that if such is the stuff of male superiority they're welcome to it.

To defend male drinking, for example, Thorpe irrationally attacks women's perception of liquor's effects. He downplays the amount he and his fellows actually drink and then emphasizes that liquor has a positive value that men, in their fraternal knowledge, appreciate and that women underestimate. According to Thorpe, Catherine is naive in thinking that one bottle is enough to incapacitate a man: "You women are always thinking of men's being in liquor. Why you do not suppose a man is overset by a bottle? I am sure of *this*—that if every body was to drink their bottle a-day, there would not be half the disorders in the world there are now" (63). His emphasis on the difference between what "you women" think and what he, as a man, knows indicates his assumption of male superiority.

Thorpe's pride in his capacity for drink not only gives the lie to his claim of the healthiness of a "bottle a-day," it also provides an avenue for Austen to poke fun at the male privilege of a university education. When Catherine mentions having heard that a great deal of wine is consumed by Oxonians, Thorpe recounts his own experiences at that bastion of learning[14]: "Oxford! There is no drinking at Oxford now, I assure you. Nobody drinks there. You would hardly meet with a man who goes beyond his four pints at the utmost. Now, for instance, it was reckoned a remarkable thing at the last party in my rooms, that upon an average we cleared about five pints a head. It was looked upon as something out of the common way. . . . [T]his will just give you a notion of the general rate of drinking there" (64). So much for male continence and the merits of a university education! Rather than having improved Thorpe's mind, Oxford has merely provided a site for his reckless dissipation.

Austen goes one step further to laugh at the triviality of Thorpe's concerns in a tongue-in-cheek summary of his conversation with Catherine:

Thorpe's ideas then all reverted to the merits of his own equipage, and she was called on to admire the spirit and freedom with which his horse moved along, and the ease which his paces, as well as the excellence of the springs, gave the motion of the carriage. She followed him in all his admiration as well as she could. To go before, or beyond him was impossible. His knowledge and her ignorance of the subject, his rapidity of expression, and her diffidence of herself put that out of her power; she could strike out nothing new in commendation, but she readily echoed whatever he chose to assert, and it was finally settled between them without any difficulty, that his equipage was altogether the most complete of its kind in England, his carriage the neatest, his horse the best goer, and himself the best coachman. (64–65)

Austen's use of the terms "knowledge" and "ignorance"—to describe Thorpe's and Catherine's relative understanding of equipage—is ironic, as the excessive superlatives of the last clause make clear. Thorpe may be knowledgeable about carriages, but his bragging makes the value of that knowledge dubious. Like an agreeable female, Catherine goes along with Thorpe's assertions, but the reader, who knows better, is openly invited to laugh at him.

Indeed, Catherine's ignorance about Thorpe's interests testifies to her common sense: "she had not been brought up to understand the propensities of a rattle, nor to know to how many idle assertions and impudent falsehoods the excess of vanity will lead" (65). Catherine learns from her encounter with Thorpe that, contrary to what her brother James says about women liking "rattles," no woman of sense can tolerate their foolishness. In a humorous understatement, the narrator reports Catherine's conclusion about Thorpe's character: "It was a bold surmise . . . she had been assured by James, that his manners would recommend him to all her sex; but in spite of this, the extreme weariness of his company . . . induced her, in some small degree, to resist such

high authority, and to distrust his powers of giving universal pleasure" (66–67). Underlying James's view of female taste is an assumption that women enjoy being treated like fools. Austen
shows how even a novice in the world like Catherine can take a
stand against "high authority" and make an educated guess that is
accurate as well as independent. Thus, the comic treatment of
Thorpe goes beyond simply attacking one man's foibles; Austen
pulls down the system of male privilege with him.

In *Helen*, Edgeworth depicts another version of a male who
offers a poor return for his educational advantages when the foppish Horace Churchill has a bad day: "everyone knows how men,
like children, are in certain circumstances, affected miserably by
a rainy day" (141). Unable to find any useful occupation, Horace
tries to show off in front of anyone who will observe him, but because he continually blunders, his efforts only make him look
foolish. At last, he resorts to the library where he nonetheless
cannot escape the prying eyes of the narrator, who sports over his
puerility: "He retreated to the book-room, but there the intellectual Horace, with all the sages, poets, and novelists of every age
within his reach, reached them not; but, with his hands in his
pockets, like any squire or schoolboy under the load of ignorance
or penalties of idleness, stood before the chimney-piece, eyeing
the pendule, and verily believing that this morning the hands
went backward" (142). For all of his pretensions, Horace has no
resources when left to himself. Edgeworth underscores his childishness and indicates the gulf that may exist between the self-
indulgent ego and the self-establishing individual. In her comic
treatment of this "male coquette," she turns the tables on smug
males such as Lord Chesterfield who referred to women as "children of a larger growth." Moreover, she implies that when males
such as Horace are given free reign, there will be an end to progress. Just as Horace discovers himself a child alone in a large house,
a nation of Horaces will watch itself go backwards in time until
the existence of even the potential for culture—a room full of
books—will be a memory.

A particularly subversive comic male character is the incompe-
tent authority figure. By mocking authority figures in their novels,

as Wollstonecraft did in her *Vindication*, Burney and Austen re-affirm their own authority over and against male domination.[15] They illustrate that cultural sanctions are not enough to make a person authoritative. Under the system which Mary Hays called "a bundle of contradictions and absurdities," women are forced to submit to arbitrary male power. But like the child in Andersen's fairy tale who shouts that the emperor has no clothes, these female writers expose the inadequacy of figures who are given power simply because they are male.

In the repressive atmosphere of late-eighteenth-century England, assaults on the established order were regarded with even more anxiety than usual by conservatives. Claudia Johnson argues that conservative authors use extreme caution in their handling of authority figures: "[H]aving pointedly committed themselves to an anti-Jacobin position, conservative novelists have little choice but to idealize authority per se—the authority of laws, of conventions, of customs, and of course of standard figures embodying them: fathers, husbands, clergymen. To do any less would be to surrender their first position and grant that the reformers they tried to discredit as maniacal and treasonous had legitimate grievances after all" (*Jane Austen* 8). As Johnson points out, Austen's treatment of clergymen like Mr. Collins, Mr. Grant, and Mr. Elton would be enough to evict her from the conservative camp, and her treatment of fathers is even more critical. When we keep in mind that "conservative novelists preach submission without repining, and fault fathers for being too indulgent" (Johnson, *Jane Austen* 9–10), Austen's comic depictions of Mr. Woodhouse and Sir Walter Eliot come across as downright radical.

Eighteenth-century thinker Edmund Burke drew a common analogy between family and state when he advised the social critic to "approach to the faults of the state as to the wounds of a father, with pious awe and trembling solicitude" and urged the critic not to "hack that aged parent in pieces" (417). The force of such an argument depends upon an emotional acceptance of the father as an unassailable social authority and an undeniable object of affection. For those who endorsed this vision of paternity, and there were many, an author who ridiculed parental authority offered a direct challenge to society at large. Were it not for her subtle, subversive talent, Austen would have been branded a radical at the time. Her fathers are by no means exemplars of social responsibility. Mr. Woodhouse's hypochondria and Sir Walter's vanity make them not only comic figures, but also instances of social criticism.

In *Emma*, Mr. Woodhouse represents the contradictions within conservative thinking: he dislikes change so thoroughly that even the traditional source of social stability, "[m]atrimony, as the origin of change, was always disagreeable" to him (7). Mr. Woodhouse's attitude toward marriage also exemplifies the conservative double standard, especially as it affects parents and others who are in a position to determine the lives of women: he reveres social forms as long as they indulge his comfort, but dismisses them when they interfere with it. For example, he accords a privileged status to brides, which allows him to play out his fantasies of courtly behavior, yet he does not want his dependents to marry and break up his own domestic court. When Emma interrogates her father on holding contradictory views, he calls upon etiquette to defend his duplicity:

> "I never encouraged any body to marry, but I would always wish to pay every proper attention to a lady—and a bride, especially, is never to be neglected. More is avowedly due to *her*. A bride, you know, my dear, is always the first in company, let others be who they may."
>
> "Well, papa, if this is not encouragement to marry, I do not know what is. And I should never have expected you to be lending your sanction to such vanity-baits for poor young ladies."
>
> "My dear, you do not understand me. This is a matter of common politeness and good-breeding, and has nothing to do with any encouragement to people to marry."
>
> Emma had done. Her father was growing nervous, and could not understand *her*. (280)

This discussion shows Mr. Woodhouse's parochial "gentle selfishness" (8) at work. His courtly notions about how to treat ladies and brides mask his disregard for women and his distaste for marriage. Emma lets her father off the hook, but the narrator informs us that the subject has touched a nerve in Mr. Woodhouse. His nervousness represents an inability to unite his general principles with his particular selfishness. Austen playfully underscores the two "hers" in the passage, suggesting that Mr. Woodhouse's ideas about what is due to a bride have very little connection in his mind to the real woman in front of him.

By lodging high-flown notions of women in the feeble mind of Mr. Woodhouse, Austen pokes fun at excessive—and ultimately sexist—courtliness. Emma describes her father's view of women as one of sentimental chivalry: "He loves . . . any thing that pays woman a compliment. He has the tenderest spirit of gallantry towards us all!" (77). Emma's indulgence of her father prevents her from recognizing the foolishness of his behavior and values. The vulgar Mrs. Elton, however, casts a different light upon Mr. Woodhouse's treatment of women: "Here comes this dear old beau of mine, I protest!—Only think of his gallantry in coming away before the other men!—what a dear creature he is;—I assure you I like him excessively. I admire all that quaint, old-fashioned politeness. . . . But this good old Mr. Woodhouse, I wish you had heard his gallant speeches to me at dinner. Oh! I assure you I began to think my caro sposo would be absolutely jealous. I fancy I am rather a favourite" (302). Not only does Mr. Woodhouse's behavior justify this familiar commentary from Mrs. Elton, but his attitude toward women puts him on her level. His stylized gallantry matches her bravado, as is evident from the way she relishes his attentions. Her tags for her husband—"caro sposo" and "lord and master"—publicize an affection and subservience that are as phony as Mr. Woodhouse's "gallant speeches." Mr. Woodhouse bears authority in name only; the petty tyranny he exercises can barely mask his intellectual impotence. By casting a father as a comic character and mocking his view of women, Austen deflates the myth of paternal solicitude.

In *Persuasion* (1818), Austen scoffs at male power in a more radical fashion. Austen caricatures the world history of masculine authority in the opening paragraphs of her last work. Unlike Austen's own preferred reading—novels, which deal with life in all its variety and complexity—Sir Walter's favorite book, the Baronetage, celebrates male lineage and, more specifically as he sees it, himself. Austen ironically describes his relish for this book as a travesty of literary pleasure:

> [T]here he found occupation for an idle hour, and consolation in a distressed one; there his faculties were roused into admiration and respect, by contemplating the limited remnant of the earliest patents; there any unwelcome sensations, arising from domestic affairs, changed naturally into pity and contempt, as he turned over the almost endless creations of the last century—and there, if every other leaf were powerless, he could read his own history with an interest which never failed. (1)

Although the "domestic affairs" which he chooses to retreat from are left unspecified, his use of the book as an escape indicates that Sir Walter's interactions at home make him aware of his own powerlessness. He turns specifically to the book because it legitimates his supreme narcissism: through the medium of the patriarchal text, the "unwelcome sensations" of daily life become objects of "pity and contempt," instead of grounds for personal and social development.

Austen lampoons Sir Walter's conceit: "Few women could think more of their personal appearance than he did; nor could the valet of any new made lord be more delighted with the place he held in society" (4). With these comparisons, Austen attacks both gender and class pretensions. The description of Sir Walter's vanity challenges the notion that vanity appertains only to women; that his pride of place resembles the coxcombry of a servant hints at the folly of hierarchical preening. Like Emma with her father, Lady Elliot coddled Sir Walter and attempted to make up for his shortcomings: "She had humoured, or softened, or concealed his failings, and promoted his real respectability for seventeen years" (4). Unlike *Emma*, however, *Persuasion* contains no fond daughter to shield Sir Walter; with his wife dead, his failings receive no indulgence in the novel.

Austen states outright that Sir Walter is a bad father: "Three girls . . . was an awful legacy for a mother to bequeath; an awful charge rather, to confide to the authority and guidance of a conceited, silly father" (4–5). To explain his having remained a widower, Austen blends Sir Walter's own account with a more objective one and chuckles at his hypocrisy: "Be it known then, that Sir Walter, like a good father, (having met with one or two private disappointments in very unreasonable applications) prided himself on remaining single for his dear daughter's sake" (5). However much Sir Walter might be fond of Elizabeth—the daughter "for whose sake" he remains single—he cannot be called a "good father," except perhaps by himself. In fact, Austen hinges the plot of the novel upon Sir Walter's weaknesses. The story begins at the point when Sir Walter is no longer able to mask his growing debts, the public sign of his moral bankruptcy.

His younger daughter Anne's desire for a radical solution to the Elliot family's troubles reveals the seriousness behind Austen's comic treatment of Sir Walter's egotism: "She wanted more vigorous measures, a more complete reformation, a quicker release from debt, a much higher tone of indifference for every thing but justice and equity" (12). When the boisterous Crofts take over the Elliot home, Kellynch Hall, a new order begins to take shape. Admiral Croft duly recognizes the vanity of Sir Walter's numerous mirrors and sends them away: "Such a number of looking-glasses! oh Lord! there was no getting away from oneself" (128). Anne finds the Crofts to be a delightful embodiment of reform. By marrying into their family, she rejects the "instant oppression" of her father's presence and embraces a model of marriage in which a wife and husband "go shares" in everything (226, 168).

Although male authority figures in Burney's novels can be as tiresomely serious as Mr. Villars and Mr. Tyrold, when she chooses to cast a comic light on authority the results are generally quite lively, even radical. Recent feminist criticism has begun to take note of this aspect of Burney's comedy. For instance, Margaret Doody has called *Evelina* "an antimasculinist satire" (65). And Kay Rogers has admirably discussed how Burney's treatment of the guardians in *Cecilia* serves "to highlight comically the pretensions of patriarchal theory and the inadequacies of individual patriarchs" (95–96).

In her novel of the 1790s, *Camilla*, Burney's comic handling of Sir Hugh indicates her uneasiness with established authority. His patronage, on which many rely, is capricious. He decides to make Camilla his heiress simply because she pleases him, but then he disinherits her and endows Eugenia to ease his guilt at having caused Eugenia's deformity. His benevolence is inextricably bound up with egotism. An amiable man Sir Hugh may be, but his negligence brings about serious consequences in the novel.

Burney calls attention to Sir Hugh's incompetence in a carnivalesque scene at the beginning of the novel. Acting as the "fairy mistress of the ceremonies" during her birthday celebration, Camilla enacts a symbolic inversion of gender roles:

> Sir Hugh . . . entered into all their plays, he forgot all his pains, he laughed because they laughed, and suffered his darling little girl to govern and direct him at her pleasure. She made him whiskers of cork, powdered his brown bob, and covered a thread paper with black ribbon to hang to it for a queue. She metamorphosed him into a female, accoutring him with her fine new cap, while she enveloped her own small head in his wig; and then, tying the maid's apron round his waist, put a rattle into his hand, and Eugenia's doll upon his lap, which she told him was a baby that he must nurse and amuse. (18)

This scene of role reversals in which Camilla transforms Sir Hugh into a "grotesque figure" (18) makes use of a classic comic trope that Ian Donaldson identifies as "the world upside down": "such comedy characteristically represents society collapsing under the strain of scandalous and widespread folly and ineptitude, centred in particular in those traditionally thought to be society's very pillars" (8). Donaldson points out that the comedy of inversion subversively suggests that the social order is not based upon merit. Kristina Straub has correctly identified Camilla's role in this scene as that of a "little mistress of misrule" (212); however, Straub overlooks the particularly dangerous atmosphere in which Burney envisioned this scene of comic inversion.

In 1796, when Burney published *Camilla*, the violence of the French Revolution had barely spent its fury, and England suffered bitter battles between Jacobins and Anti-Jacobins. When Hannah More came to write *Coelebs in Search of a Wife* at the beginning of the nineteenth century, she connected children's unruliness with revolutionary philosophy: "I know not . . . whether the increased insubordination of children is owing to the new school of philosophy and politics, but it seems to me to make part of the system. . . . There certainly prevails a spirit of independence, a revolutionary spirit of independence, a separation from the parent state. IT IS THE CHILDREN'S WORLD" (398). By beginning *Camilla* in a children's world with the heroine in charge of the man who is supposed to be her guardian, Burney dramatizes the difference between female childhood optimism toward the world and the realities of the social gauntlet they will be forced to run.[16] When Camilla dons Sir Hugh's wig, forces him to nurse a baby, puts a maid's apron on him, and commands him to do her bidding, she entertains the possibility of further female insubordination. She exercises the sort of power that Maria Allen imagined wielding over the race of castrated males.

In spite of the different tempers of Sir Hugh, Mr. Woodhouse, and Sir Walter Elliot, they share a gender-based cultural prestige which Burney and Austen show to be unmerited. In their depiction of comic authority figures, Burney and Austen accomplish what Todd refers to as "demythifying," an act of deflating "the heroic myths men have created for themselves" (*Men* 2). But whereas Todd sees this kind of activity only occurring in texts by twentieth-century writers during "peak moments of feminism" (1), I contend that a similar kind of debunking takes place in the works of eighteenth-century women when they represent sexist ideology in the form of comic male characters.[17]

In their depictions of comic men, Burney, Edgeworth, and Austen expose the egotism behind arguments for male supremacy by portraying men who make such claims as fools and buffoons. They parody the system that grants even foolish males a higher social status than women and demonstrate that not all men deserve the privileges society bestows upon them.[18] By laughing at sexist men, Burney, Edgeworth, and Austen criticize male domination and hold out the possibility of social reform.

"There is as severe a punishment for men of gallantry (as they call themselves) as sword or pistol," declares Lady Euston in Elizabeth Inchbald's *I'll Tell You What*, "laugh at them—that is a ball which cannot miss; and yet kills only their vanity." According to one twentieth-century psychoanalyst, female laughter can have drastic results: "There is hardly anything more mortifying for a young man than to be laughed at. Laughter may make him impotent" (Grotjahn 61–62). Although not all women writers share Maria Allen's wish to bring about such dire physical effects, Burney, Edgeworth, and Austen certainly aim to curtail men's political potency, and comedy supplied them with a formidable weapon.

6

The Limits of Sisterhood:
Satirizing Women

It was said by Christiana, Queen of Sweden, that she sought the
company of men, merely because they were not women.
A severe and pointed sarcasm!

I blush for the folly, the frivolity in which we have consumed so
many of our best days; too long have we been slaves to vanity
and giddy flutterers of the hour: it is fit we should now rise
superior to this empty trifling. . . . If we would but unite
in intention, great would be our power, and extensive
our influence; the character of one sex has ever
been found to affect that of the other.

—Mary Hays (*Letters and Essays* 92, 157)

I HAVE ARGUED THAT WHEN BURNEY, EDGEWORTH, and Austen
mock sexist male characters in their novels, they turn the tables on misogynist satirists and challenge the notion of male superiority. In other words, they disrupt the hierarchy that places
men above women. But lest we assume that these authors saw
"women" as an undifferentiated or united group, we must consider the women who come under attack in their writings. It is
one thing for the authors to laugh at their supposed superiors (i.e.,
men), but it is another thing for them to laugh at women's faults
and foibles, because this laughter entails a different set of risks.

In this chapter, I will discuss the double-edged sword that
Burney, Edgeworth, and Austen wield when they satirize women's
shortcomings. I contend that by creating satirical portraits of
women they were able to criticize those who went along with the
debilitating standards imposed on them by conduct writers and
other proponents of female subordination, yet in the process they

143

risked being identified as misogynist satirists. Before looking at particular examples of satirized female characters, we should consider how the issue of feminist solidarity, or sisterhood, was both congruent and in conflict with critiques of women's complicity in bolstering male authority that appear in eighteenth-century feminist discourse.

In the epigraph to this chapter, Mary Hays wrestles with questions of female identification and difference.[1] Citing the alleged statement of Christiana, Queen of Sweden, Hays calls attention to its "pointed sarcasm"; that is, she recognizes there might be some reason for Christiana to distance herself from the company of women. The citation appears in Hays's *Letters and Essays, Moral, and Miscellaneous* (1793), a work that came out the year after Wollstonecraft's *Vindication*, and an allusion to feminist solidarity directly precedes Hays's mention of Christiana's detachment from other women. "I cannot help," Hays writes, "on every occasion, joining my feeble efforts to those of the admirable assertor of female rights [Wollstonecraft], in endeavouring to stimulate, and rouse my sex from the state of mental degradation, and bondage, in which they have so long been held" (92). Like her role model Wollstonecraft, Hays sees the need to issue a wake-up call to the women of England in order to "rouse" them into activity that will benefit women as a group. She acknowledges the importance of collective awareness of oppression as a key starting point for a feminist movement. However, as we can see in the second epigraph, identifying with other women causes Hays some pain: she "blushes" for what she views as women's collective "folly," "frivolity," and slavery to vanity. Her use of the first-person plural marks the extent of her identification, while her use of the first person singular complicates her call for a united front. She locates herself both inside and outside of her own gender, as one of "us" and as one who can see how (other) women have gone astray—and feel embarrassed by their errors. At the same time that she points the way to a reformation of gender relations through combined female action, she characterizes women as the dupes and perpetuators of these imbalanced relations.

Yet Hays overtly denies any satirical intent in her discussion of women's faults: "I mean not to satirize your foibles, I wish not

to restrain your vivacity; it is not ill humour; it is not affected singularity: no! it is benevolence,—it is virtue, that stimulate me to
take up my pen" (157). She takes great pains to ensure her readers (the fictional recipient of the letters and her wider audience)
that she means well when she offers corrective advice: "May I flatter myself that, for once, you will attend to the words of advice
which come from your equal, your friend?" (156).

I call attention to the efforts Hays made to cast herself as a
benevolent mentor of those whom she called her equals in order
to illustrate the fine line a woman writer had to walk if she wished
to satirize female behavior without indicting the entire sex, as
misogynist satirists did. For the misogynist writer, particular foolish female actions were simply manifestations of an already flawed
female nature: woman as a defective creature whose faults revealed
her inferiority to men.[2] Hays wanted to make it clear that she
thought well of women as a group and that she did not attack her
sex indiscriminately. Similarly, she wanted her comments to have
a direct bearing on women's lives, to encourage women to live up
to their potential rather than subordinating themselves to men
through frivolous and irrational behavior.

In order to negotiate her own authority with a female audience, Hays must be both a friend (equal) and an instructor (superior) to her readers. Similarly, women authors who created satirical sketches of female behavior had to face issues of identification
and difference: if they presented themselves as completely implicated in the actions of their satirized female characters, they
risked being dismissed as foolish and silly; if they distanced themselves too completely from these characters, they risked being
deemed misogynistic. Those who satirized female shortcomings
with the aim of reforming female foibles and making women more
rational and worthy individuals could provide fodder for their
own enemies by contributing to the list of comic female types.[3]

But either way, whether a female writer identified with or
separated herself from other women, her subordinate role in the
culture as a woman meant that she was always implicated in the
behavior, values, and situations of women as a group. If Hays
blushed at her fellow women's follies, she did so in part because
she saw their behavior as reflecting badly upon her. In her strug-

gle to prove that women could be just as reasonable and sensible as men, the eighteenth-century feminist was constantly alert to the fact that her efforts at reform could be undermined by other women's behavior. Audre Lorde comments on her own sense of competition with other black women in terms that shed light on Hays's ambivalence and embarrassment:

> We are Black women, defined as never-good-enough. I must overcome that by becoming better than you. If I expect enough from myself, then maybe I can become different from what they say we are, different from you. If I become different enough, then maybe I won't be a "nigger bitch" anymore. If I make you different enough from me, then I won't need you so much. I will become strong, the best, excel in everything, become the very best because I don't dare to be anything else. It is my only chance to become good enough to become human. (170)

Here Lorde explains how her early drive for self-improvement was fueled by a radical differentiation of herself from other black women. Like Lorde, Hays and other early feminist writers aspired to "become human" by showing that they could succeed in embodying the definition of humanity that their culture accepted. For Lorde, acceptance by the dominant culture meant distancing herself from other black women, since neither blackness nor femaleness has been highly prized in the United States; for Hays, such acceptance entailed distancing herself from debased models of femininity and embracing an ostensibly genderless platform of rationality.

If being "good enough" means to be better than a woman, then other women represent threats to a striving female's self-image because they serve as living reminders of how "woman" falls short of "human." However, as Lorde came to recognize, women need to work together to change the paradigms that shape definitions of humanity, and separating oneself from other women only helps to perpetuate patriarchy. Critic Helena Michie has coined the useful (and witty) term "sororophobia" to describe the tensions between women that interfere with the building of feminist coalitions: "[Sororophobia] attempts to describe the negotiation of sameness and difference, identity and separation, between women of the same generation, and is meant to encompass both the desire for and the recoil from identification with other women" (9). In the works of eighteenth-century women writers, we can see the simultaneous longing and revulsion that can characterize women's relations with other women, a longing for some kind of female community coupled with a revulsion toward those whose behavior gives women a bad name. In the feminist writing of the period, we can also see an awareness of the dangers of women's isolation from one another.

One of the key points of Enlightenment feminism, as expressed by writers from Astell to Hays, is that women were prevented from achieving their full humanity by sexist stereotypes. These feminists pointed out that many of the things women were satirized for (an absorption in dress, makeup, scandal, manipulation, and light reading) were direct effects of their limited opportunities for improvement. Wollstonecraft contends that "if women are not permitted to enjoy legitimate rights, they will render both men and themselves vicious, to obtain illicit privileges" (6). Likewise, Hays justifies women's use of "back-door" power by arguing that they have no better alternatives:

> And if indeed, women do avail themselves of the only weapons they are permitted to wield, can they be blamed? Undoubtedly not; since they are compelled to it by the injustice and impolicy of men. Petty treacheries—mean subterfuge— whining and flattery—feigned submission—and all the dirty little attendants, which compose the endless train of low cunning; if not commendable, cannot with justice be very severely censured when practised by women. Since alas!— THE WEAK HAVE NO OTHER ARMS AGAINST THE STRONG! Since alas!—NECESSITY ACKNOWLEDGES NO LAW, BUT HER OWN! (*Appeal* 91)

Just because women appeared outwardly to accept their subordinate status did not mean that they gave up the desire to wield power and "weapons." In fact, Hays indicates that "cunning" is a sanctioned weapon for women in a society that prohibits overt acts of self-assertion. She argues that women's state of inequality hurts everyone: if women were not forced into the position of the "weak," they would not need to practice dirty politics.

Hays's account of the weapons women use to gain some power in an imbalanced world could serve as a rationale for the appearance of numerous female comic characters in Burney, Edgeworth, and Austen. Like Hays, these novelists indict the source of women's bad behavior along with the particular female characters; they carefully contextualize negative portraits of women and imply that if society were structured differently, such individuals might have better things to do. Burney, Edgeworth, and Austen would have recognized that what was generalized as *human* nature in satires on male characters would be viewed as *female* nature in satires involving women characters.

A good example of how this disparity operates can be seen in two eighteenth-century *memento mori* engravings: one entitled "An Abridgement of Mr. Pope's Essay on Man," the other "An Essay on Woman" (1769).[4] Each print depicts a figure (male in the first case, female in the second) that is half skeleton and half flesh, clothed in the fashion of the day; each includes a number of quotations selected to make the viewer reflect upon the brevity of existence. However, the print with the male figure stresses humanity over gender. For instance, it cites Shakespeare's "What a piece of work is Man . . ." and Pope's "The proper study of mankind is man." Such declarations are typically read as being applicable to all humans, and in the context of the engraving imply that the wonder one feels about human power or glory should be tempered by an awareness of death as our common final end. By contrast, the captions in the "Essay on Woman" engraving contain pronouncements about women as a group, such as the following anonymous statements: "Women are like Tricks by sleight of Hand / Which to admire we should not understand" and "The proper study of womankind is their own sex." In keeping with this gendered perspective, satires on women do not aim to chasten the generic viewer or to reform any particular faults; rather, they promulgate the notion that women are in and of themselves flawed humans.

All-encompassing condemnatory statements about women's nature do not appear in the works of Burney, Edgeworth, and Austen. Instead of focusing on women as the weaker sex, they focus on the social conditions that lead to weaknesses and faults in many women. Women who accept conventional views about female potential are frequently the targets of their satire. In their heroines, they carry on the tradition of Enlightenment feminism by presenting women who transcend negative stereotypes about females and behave as rational creatures. Each author has her own approach to satirizing women, and they all present a good number of silly, foolish, and deluded female characters who contrast sharply with their more sensible heroines. For the purposes of discussion, I have selected an assortment of female characters whose faults allow the authors to criticize the social conditions that gave rise to such creatures.

Women's participation in the marriage market offers numerous occasions for satire and a host of comic characters. For example, Burney satirizes the naivete of young girls such as Miss Dennel (*Camilla*) and Selina Joddrel (*The Wanderer*) who mistakenly believe that they will be able to do what they want once they get married. Edgeworth and Austen draw attention to the lack of appropriate role models for such young girls by portraying manipulative mothers and mother figures who wheel and deal in the marriage market without regard for the feelings of their daughters. As examples of this type, Edgeworth gives us Mrs. Stanhope (*Belinda*), and Austen offers up Mrs. Bennet (*Pride and Prejudice*). In connection with the marriage-market mentality, we can find many competitive females in the works of these authors: Lady Margaret (Burney's *Cecilia*), Lady Angelica (Edgeworth's *Patronage*), Lady Katrine Hawksby (Edgeworth's *Helen*), and Fanny Dashwood and Lucy Steele (Austen's *Sense and Sensibility* [1811]) compete with the heroines for male attention and, in general, try to make other women look bad.

In the satirical portraits of Miss Arbe (*The Wanderer*) and Isabella Thorpe (*Northanger Abbey*) we can see figured the false sister, the woman who claims to be on the side of female solidarity but who is actually motivated by self-interest. Such characters help to spotlight the vulnerability of the heroine who lacks assistance and who seeks in vain some kind of fellowship with other women. Burney and Austen give us several female characters who seem to be just plain nasty—for example, Mrs. Ireton (*The Wanderer*) and Mrs. Norris (*Mansfield Park*) both deliberately cause pain to the heroines of their novels. However, even the behavior of these women is contextualized as belonging to a system that typically restricts female power. Given a modicum of independence and authority, they behave as badly as any authoritarian male and abuse anyone whose status is lower than theirs.

Although these authors use a wide range of female comic characters, it is important for us to see the family resemblances that pertain among their satirical caricatures of women. Rather than engaging in antifeminism or misogyny in their works, Burney, Edgeworth, and Austen aim to promote solidarity among women by dramatizing the failures of female isolationism and duplicity. Whereas the marriage market casts women as competitors for husbands, these novelists make it clear that women should pay attention to one another's interests; their heroines are more likely to long for sisterhood than to shun it. Unlike the trickster characters I discussed in Chapter 4, who criticize the status quo and who use laughter as a weapon, the comic female characters I will discuss here are more directly butts of the novels' satire. But the criticism that falls upon them falls even more heavily on the unjust system that produced them.

In an early journal entry, Burney registers her surprise at the shortness of a wedding ceremony she attended, using terms that reveal her skepticism about the merits of marriage *per se:* "how short a time does it take to put an eternal end to a Woman's liberty! I don't think they were ¼ of an Hour in the Church altogether—lord bless me! it can not be time enough, I should think, for a poor creature to see where she was" (*Early Journals* 17). By joking about the "poor creature's" inability to get her bearings, Burney implies that if a girl had her eyes open, she might think twice about putting an end to her "liberty." In her fiction, she created two notable female characters who mistakenly believe that marriage will give them greater freedom than they could possibly enjoy within their own family unit. *Camilla*'s Miss Dennel and *The Wanderer*'s Selina Joddrel comically represent the self-deception that might lead a woman to think of marriage as a pathway to autonomy.

From her perspective as a fourteen-year-old, Miss Dennel takes a dim view of women's maturation, declaring in her first appearance in the novel that seventeen is already almost too late for a woman to get married and that she plans to marry by the time she is eighteen (190). The narrator provides significant details about her background in order to account for the limitations of her point of view: "Miss Dennel was a pretty, blooming, tall girl, but as childish in intellect as in experience; though self-persuaded she was a woman in both, since she was called from school to sit at the head of her father's table" (259). While Miss Dennel is faulted here for her childish intellect, the narrator links intellect to experience and indicates that "childishness" is not the basic state of the female mind. Even though we are told that Miss Dennel is "self-persuaded" that she has reached womanhood, we can clearly see that her father is to blame for withdrawing her from school— the place where she might have developed greater faculties— and for prematurely placing her in a woman's role at the head of his table.

With her lack of experience and education, it is not surprising that Miss Dennel forms mistaken notions about where her life is heading. The following conversation discloses her fantasy of married life as an escape from present restraints; she discusses how she would like to be free to enjoy home theatricals in the style of Mrs. Arlbery, who dedicates a room in her attic to this activity:

> "I'm determined when I've a house of my own,
> I'll have just such a room as this at the top of it,
> on purpose to act a play every night."
> "And when, my dear," said Mrs. Arlbery,
> "do you expect to have a house of your own."
> "O, as soon as I am married, you know."
> "Is your marrying, then already decided?"
> "Dear no, not that I know of, aunt. I'm sure

I never trouble myself about it; only I suppose it
will happen some day or other."

"And when it does, you are very sure your
husband will approve your acting plays every
night?"

"O, as to that, I shan't ask him. Whenever
I'm married I'll be my own mistress, that I'm resolved upon. But papa's so monstrous cross, he
says he won't let me act plays now." (263)

Miss Dennel's self-delusion is clear from the moment she refers to
having a "house of her own," as Mrs. Arlbery's pointed question
indicates. The passage highlights her blindness by juxtaposing expressions of Miss Dennel's will—"I'm determined," "I'll be my
own mistress," "I'm resolved"—with expressions of her passive acceptance of whatever comes her way—"I never trouble myself
about it," "I suppose it will happen." A reader who was familiar
with the marriage laws in England would have seen that her haste
to escape from an authoritarian parent could catapult her into an
equally restrictive marriage.

As it turns out, Miss Dennel's choice of a partner is decided
not by her own desires but by an agreement between her father
and his preferred suitor, Mr. Lissin. She confides to Camilla her
surprise at this choice: "Mr Lissin never once came into my head,
because of his being so old. I dare say he's seven and twenty! only
think!—But I believe he and papa had settled it all along, only
papa never told it me, till just before hand. I don't like him much;
do you?" (782). When Camilla urges her to "endeavour to like him
better," the now Mrs. Lissin reveals her continuing self-delusion
and her absorption in trivialities:

I don't much care whether I do or not, for I shall
never mind him. I always determined never to
mind a husband. One minds one's papa because
one can't help it: But only think of my being
married before you! though you're seventeen
years old—almost eighteen, I dare say—and I'm
only just fifteen. I could not help thinking of it all

> the time I was dressing for a bride. You can't
> think how pretty my dress was. Papa made Mrs.
> Mittin buy it, because, he said, she could get
> every thing so cheap: but I made her get it the
> dearest she could, for all that. Papa's monstrous
> stingy. (782)

Mrs. Lissin's triumphs—getting married before Camilla, wearing a pretty dress, subverting her father's stinginess—are no compensation for the enormity of the step she has taken. Like the bride whose fifteen-minute ceremony made Burney's head spin, the fifteen-year-old Mrs. Lissin makes no attempt to evaluate what she is doing.

Mrs. Lissin's conference with Camilla is interrupted by her new bridegroom, whose "violent ringing" at the gate precedes his entrance "without any ceremony" into the private chamber in which the two ladies are speaking (782–83). The satirical aim of Burney's portrait of Miss Dennel/Mrs. Lissin becomes all too clear after he scolds her for absconding from the house without his permission and for letting dinner get cold on the table while he waited for her return:

> She looked frightened, and he took her hand,
> which she had not courage to draw back, though
> in a voice that spoke a sob near at hand, "I'm
> sure," she cried, "this is not being treated like a
> married woman! and I'm sure if I'd known I
> might not do as I like, and come out when I'd a
> mind, I would not have married at all! (783)

Unlike a female trickster such as Lydia Bennet, Mrs. Lissin must suffer for her delusions. The aggression of her husband and her frightened looks tell us that she will pay a high price for being ignorant about women's position in society.

Mrs. Arlbery supplies the ironic moral of Mrs. Lissin's story:

> Poor simple girl! . . . Mr. Lissin, who is a country
> squire of Northwick, will soon teach her another

lesson, than that of ordering her carriage just at dinner time! The poor child took it into her head that, because, upon marrying, she might say, "my house," "my coach," and "my servants," instead of "my papa's;" and ring her bell for [whom] she pleased, and give her own orders, that she was to arrive at complete liberty and independence, and that her husband had merely to give her his name, and lodge in the same dwelling: and she will regard him soon, as a tyrant and a brute, for not letting her play all day long the part of a wild school girl, just come home for the holidays. (783)

These comments interpret the unfortunate Mrs. Lissin's plight as, on the one hand, the result of arrested development—the "wild school girl" who has not progressed to the level of adult responsibility that is required in marriage. On the other hand, and more seriously, Mrs. Lissin is the product of a defective system: her biggest mistake is thinking that she will ever be able to call anything her own, least of all herself. She goes from living as a dependent among her father's possessions to living in dependence under her husband. Both states make it difficult for her to see her own situation with any clarity. Her desire for "liberty and independence" is as unfocused as any of her other goals and prevents her from taking a stand on how the rest of her life would be spent. By agreeing to marry Mr. Lissin because she believes that one husband is as good as another, Miss Dennel seals her own fate. And, as Mrs. Arlbery's commentary indicates, her complaints about the married state and thus her use of feminist rhetoric (calling husbands "tyrants" and "brutes" is very much in the Wollstonecraftian tradition) are compromised by her self-indulgent, competitive, and ultimately sexist reasons for entering into marriage.[5]

Although Miss Dennel is a minor character in *Camilla*, her story served as a cautionary tale for women of the period. So significant did Edgeworth find this tale that she includes a reference to Miss Dennel in *Patronage*, during a discussion of marriage that takes place between sisters Caroline and Rosamond Percy. Caroline tells Rosamond that love is the only thing that would induce her to get married and leave home:

> "For what else *could* I marry," continued Caro-
> line, "I who am left by the kindest of parents
> freely to my own choice—could I marry,—for a
> house in Leicestershire? or for a barouche and
> four? . . . or on the *Missy* notion of being married,
> and having a house of my own, and ordering my
> own dinner, and, like Miss Dennel in Camilla,
> having every day minced veal and mashed pota-
> toes?" (201)

Caroline's speech emphasizes her freedom to choose, which gives her more options than Miss Dennel had, but it also exposes the economic and social factors that influence many women to marry. Clearly, Edgeworth took the message of Miss Dennel's history to be representative of a wider social issue, and by having one of her characters cite one of Burney's as a negative example, she pays tribute to the force of her predecessor's satire.

Burney evidently enjoyed the satirical potential of Miss Den-nel so much that she gave her another incarnation as Selina Joddrel in *The Wanderer*. Like Miss Dennel, Selina makes her ap-pearance at age fourteen; at this point she is already engaged and described as a "conceited little thing" by her sister, Elinor, who quips that "it is a rule . . . to deny nothing to a bride elect; proba-bly, poor wretch, because every one knows what a fair way she is in to be soon denied every thing!" (44). Elinor's rule simultane-ously illuminates the prestige that is generally accorded the bride-to-be and casts aspersions on married life. Giving free reign to the young woman because she will be "denied every thing" as a wife is like leading a lamb to slaughter, and as we saw in the case of Miss Dennel, a cloud of illusion can prevent a girl from clearly seeing her fate.

Selina shares Miss Dennel's view that getting married will lead to greater freedom: "she related, with earnest injunctions to secresy, all the little incidents of her little life, finishing her narration by intimating, in a rapturous whisper, that she should very soon have a house of her own, in which her aunt Maple would have no sort of authority. 'And then,' added she, nodding, 'perhaps I may ask you to come and see me!'" (51). The adjective "little" calls attention not only to Selina's limited experience and development, but also to her self-centeredness and inability to see beyond the trivialities of her life. Speaking to Juliet, the heroine of the novel, Selina alludes to the possibility of Juliet's finding a future asylum at "her" house in an offhanded and unfocused way that reveals her lack of concern for Juliet—who has been buffeted by circumstances beyond her own control and who desperately needs community and fellowship. Even though she likes to have Juliet around as a confidante for her little "secrets," Selina ignores her completely in public unless someone else pays attention to Juliet first.

Because of her snobbery, Selina is more deeply castigated for her delusions than is Miss Dennel. Whereas Miss Dennel receives a direct punishment for her ignorance about married life in her union with Mr. Lissin, Selina is called to task in the course of *The Wanderer* for her lack of character. Although her marriage to Mr. Ireton is not depicted in the novel, we can guess that it will be less than satisfactory: he sexually harasses Juliet and develops a crush on Elinor for the perverse reason that he would like to have a woman attempt suicide out of love for him. In a novel in which personal responsibility is so highly prized and acts of kindness so few and far between, Selina comes across as morally bankrupt, and her last mention in the novel enumerates her sins. After being told that "No one to whom Juliet had ever owed any good office, was by her forgotten, or by Harleigh neglected," we learn of those who will be "excluded from the happy Hall, as persons of minds uncongenial to confidence; that basis of peace and cordiality in social intercourse." Here we find listed "Selina, who, in presence of a higher or richer acquaintance, ventured not to bestow even a smile upon the person whom, in her closet, she treated, trusted, and caressed as her bosom friend" (835).

Burney's satirical treatment of Miss Dennel and Selina Joddrel underscores the facts that women must behave like morally responsible beings and that the culture that applauds them for marrying early is overlooking the cultivation of their characters. In *Camilla*, the heroine must learn through experience and reflection to behave in a responsible manner. Likewise, the unknown, friendless Juliet in *The Wanderer* is able to survive in a hostile environment by relying on her moral principles and standards. Women like Miss Dennel and Selina abdicate their personal responsibility and in doing so become fit targets of satire. As Burney makes abundantly clear, their flaws do not spring from their gender, but rather from a combination of their circumstances and what they choose to do with themselves.

Edgeworth and Austen satirize the marriage market from another angle and show that if the Miss Dennels and Selina Joddrels of the world put too much of an emphasis on getting married and neglect their own development, then adult role models may be contributing greatly to their slanted perspectives. In the novels of Edgeworth and Austen, mothers and mother figures who work to find husbands for their daughters and who regard marriage as the culmination of a woman's life provide extremely poor models for female maturation. Such women often think more about social status and about how they will be affected by their daughters' choices than they do about their daughters' well-being. They excel in the weapons of the weak that Hays disparages. They tend to scheme and manipulate behind the scenes, encouraging their daughters to follow suit and promoting a vision of courtship and marriage as exercises in deception.

Edgeworth satirizes Mrs. Stanhope of *Belinda* for engaging in vulgar matchmaking tactics, and she directly represents the effect of this woman's behavior on other women by showing the pain Mrs. Stanhope causes the heroine. The opening paragraph of the novel indicates the bent of Mrs. Stanhope's schemes:

> Mrs. Stanhope, a well-bred woman, accomplished in that branch of knowledge which is called the art of rising in the world, had, with but a small fortune, contrived to live in the highest company. She prided herself upon having established half a dozen nieces most happily, that is to say, upon

having married them to men of fortunes far superior to their own. One niece still remained unmarried—Belinda Portman, of whom she was
determined to get rid with all convenient expedi-
tion. Belinda was handsome, graceful, sprightly,
and highly accomplished; her aunt had endeavoured to teach her that a young lady's chief business is to please in society, that all her charms
and accomplishments should be invariably subservient to one grand object—the establishing
herself in the world. (1)

Mrs. Stanhope focuses on external aspects of character and encourages the young woman who wishes to marry to mold herself
to her surroundings. The narrator defines Mrs. Stanhope's view of
a "happy" marriage in purely financial terms; the "art of rising in
the world" is Mrs. Stanhope's specialization, and getting rid of
nieces is her preoccupation.

Mrs. Stanhope's reputation for selling her product—that is,
her nieces—puts Belinda's reputation in jeopardy, since those
who know about the prowess of the aunt harbor suspicions about
the niece. The novel's hero, Clarence Hervey, gives voice one
evening to his mistrust of Belinda: "There's danger in flirting . . .
with an arrant flirt of Mrs. Stanhope's training. There's a kind of
electricity about that girl. I have a sort of cobweb feeling, an
imaginary net coming all over me" (16). Other young men express similar reservations, praising Mrs. Stanhope for her cleverness in catching husbands for her female relatives, but laughing at
the kind of "novice" who could be "taken in at this time of day by
a niece of Mrs. Stanhope's" (16). As the men recount how Mrs.
Stanhope married off niece after niece through trickery and deception, they also point out the flaws of the resulting unions. Not
surprisingly, the marriages she arranged neither have solidity nor
provide the partners with satisfaction.

The discussion of Mrs. Stanhope's "talents" takes place at a
pre-masquerade gathering, and Belinda, in costume and mistaken
by Clarence for Lady Delacour, hears every word the men say and
even comments at one point on her cousins' marriages: "What

miseries spring from these ill-suited marriages! The victims are sacrificed before they have sense enough to avoid their fate" (17). As Belinda recognizes, Mrs. Stanhope's methods subvert her own ends, and by tricking the prospective bridegrooms, she condemns the brides to unhappiness. Among the reports that Belinda hears, one involves Mrs. Stanhope's handling of her particular case.

> "As for this Belinda Portman, 'twas a good hit to send her to Lady Delacour's; but, I take it she hangs upon hand; for last winter, when I was at Bath, she was hawked about every where, and the aunt was puffing her with might and main. You heard of nothing, wherever you went, but of Belinda Portman, and Belinda Portman's accomplishments: Belinda Portman, and her accomplishments, I'll swear, were as well advertised as Packwood's razor strops."
>
> "Mrs. Stanhope overdid the business, I think," resumed the gentleman who began the conversation: "girls brought to the hammer this way don't go off well. It's true, Christie himself is no match for dame Stanhope. Many of my acquaintance were tempted to go and look at the premises, but not one, you may be sure, had a thought of becoming a tenant for life." (17–18)

Here we see the "market" aspect of the marriage game deployed in a series of metaphors that satirize the inhumanity of selling off young women as if they were shaving goods or pieces of property. In spite of Belinda's numerous strengths and her freedom from guile or cunning, she is made available for public abuse because of her aunt's marketing tactics.

Mrs. Stanhope fails in her attempts to "train" Belinda in the art of trapping a husband, even though she sends her disapproving letters and threatens continuously to withdraw support if Belinda does not fall into line. Her letters are filled with self-incriminating remarks that amplify the satire on female duplicity. For example, she writes at one point, "What you can mean by principles and delicacy I own I don't pretend to understand, when I see you . . . forget the respect that is due to the opinions and advice of the aunt to whom you owe every thing" (71–72). Obviously, Mrs. Stanhope knows little about "principles and delicacy" and is not above stooping to emotional blackmail. In her view, a dependent's obligations to a patron should dictate all aspects of behavior: "Now I look upon it that a young girl who has been brought up, and brought forward in the world as you have been by connexions, is bound to be guided implicitly by them in all her conduct. What should you think of a man who, after he had been brought into parliament by a friend, would go and vote against that friend's opinions?" (72). The "correct" answer to Mrs. Stanhope's question is clearly not what she thinks it should be: such a person would be acting as a free agent, not as a paid political lackey. By associating domestic and political patronage in Mrs. Stanhope's philosophy, Edgeworth underscores the moral seriousness of a young girl's choices and her need for autonomy rather than coercion. In a gesture that epitomizes her manipulative ploys, Mrs. Stanhope signs herself, "Yours *affectionately* (if you follow my advice)" (73).

The more Mrs. Stanhope tries to change Belinda's behavior, the more clearly she exposes the flaws of the marriage market. Her advice to her niece to accept Sir Philip Baddley's proposal shows how thoroughly she shares the sexist values that make him unable to believe and accept Belinda's rejection: "Sir Philip hints in his letter, that my influence might be wanting with you in his favour; but this surely cannot be. As I have told him, he has merely mistaken becoming female reserve for a want of sensibility on your part, which would be equally unnatural and absurd." She then proceeds to enumerate his many good qualities, which consist entirely of his finances, titles, and estates, concluding, "So I see no possible objection to Sir Philip"; she further dismisses any reservations Belinda might have about his lack of "genius" as "childish" and "romantic" (182). In Mrs. Stanhope's view, "there is no managing" a man of genius, so it is better for a woman to marry a fool like Sir Philip.

Mrs. Stanhope is sent up at the conclusion of the novel by Lady Delacour, who jokes about how one tidy ending for the story would be "a characteristic letter of congratulation from Mrs. Stanhope to her *dearest* niece, Belinda, acknowledging that she was wrong to quarrel with her for refusing Sir Philip Baddley, and giving her infinite credit for that admirable *management* of Clarence Hervey, which she hopes will continue through life" (433). The irony, of course, is that Mrs. Stanhope's plan of sending Belinda to Lady Delacour's has indeed resulted in a "good catch" for her seventh and last niece. Fortunately, however, Belinda will not need to "manage" or manipulate Clarence Hervey; theirs promises to be a companionate marriage, one in which their "happily ever after" is "happy in a rational manner," as Lady Delacour's mother-in-law puts it (433).

It is a short step from Edgeworth's Mrs. Stanhope to the familiar Mrs. Bennet in Austen's *Pride and Prejudice*. As most readers of English literature know, the "business of [Mrs. Bennet's] life was to get her daughters married," and by the end of the novel her record of success is almost as good as Mrs. Stanhope's: three out of five daughters have found husbands, and two of those men are well-off. Like Mrs. Stanhope, however, Mrs. Bennet almost defeats her own purposes by indulging in vulgar publicity. Just as Belinda's reputation suffers from her aunt's excessive advertising of her accomplishments, Jane and Elizabeth find themselves damaged by their mother's loose tongue. For example, Elizabeth overhears Mrs. Bennet talking "freely" and "openly" at a gathering to Lady Lucas about the expectation that Jane will marry Mr. Bingley: "It was an animating subject, and Mrs. Bennet seemed incapable of fatigue while enumerating the advantages of the match." In Mrs. Bennet's view, one of the greatest advantages is that Jane's marriage would increase her other daughters' chances of finding mates. Although Elizabeth tries to "check the rapidity of her mother's words, or persuade her to describe her felicity in a less audible whisper" (99), Mrs. Bennet will not be dissuaded from boasting and projecting. As a result of her volubility, Darcy associates Mrs. Bennet's superficiality with Jane and is unable to see Jane's sincere regard for Bingley.

Mrs. Bennet's speech leads Darcy to steer Bingley away from Jane and causes much pain and uncertainty to her daughters, whose well-being she ought to have in mind. Ironically, whereas

Darcy is all ears to Mrs. Bennet's boasts, her immediately intended audience could hardly care less: "At length however, Mrs. Bennet had no more to say; and Lady Lucas, who had been long yawning at the repetition of delights which she saw no likelihood of sharing, was left to the comforts of cold ham and chicken" (100). That Lady Lucas prefers such "comforts" to Mrs. Bennet's discourse is no surprise, considering the extent to which Mrs. Bennet is only concerned about herself. Both ladies reveal a good deal of self-centeredness when it comes to marrying off their daughters, and Mrs. Bennet's failure to be heard by another woman indicates the kind of boundaries that marriage-market business places between women. Later, when Lady Lucas gloats over her daughter Charlotte's marriage to Mr. Collins, Mrs. Bennet hears nothing in this news but her own daughter's missed opportunity.

Mrs. Bennet's efforts to make Elizabeth marry Mr. Collins have been discussed in Chapter 5, and, as I pointed out, Elizabeth would be in dire straits if Mr. Bennet had joined his mandate to his wife's. The disappointment Mrs. Bennet feels in her lack of success finds expression in a comic speech filled with empty threats and self-pitying remarks. Following on the heels of her accusation that Elizabeth cares for no one but herself "provided she can have her own way," Mrs. Bennet's tirade reflects her own lack of maternal concern:

> I tell you what, Miss Lizzy, if you take it into your head to go on refusing every offer of marriage in this way, you will never get a husband at all—and I am sure I do not know who is to maintain you when your father is dead.—I shall not be able to keep you—and so I warn you.—I have done with you from this very day.—I told you in the library, you know, that I should never speak to you again, and you will find me as good as my word. I have no pleasure in talking to undutiful children.— Not that I have much pleasure indeed in talking to any body. People who suffer as I do from nervous complaints can have no great inclination for talking. Nobody can tell what I suffer!—But

it is always so. Those who do not complain are
never pitied. (113)

Like Mrs. Stanhope, Mrs. Bennet incriminates herself with practically every statement. A standard feature of her discourse is the
sentence that seems to make sense on the surface, but that comes
apart upon examination. Her warning to Elizabeth, for instance,
is not advice but tautology (i.e., if Elizabeth refuses every offer of
marriage, she cannot possibly get married, unless—and this would
be virtually inconceivable at the time—she makes the proposal
herself). Similarly, Mrs. Bennet's threat of not speaking to Elizabeth again had been made earlier, yet this speech makes clear that
she will *not* stop speaking to her. In fact, we are told by the narrator that Mrs. Bennet continues on in this manner for some time.
When she groups Elizabeth among "undutiful children," then, we
are led to consider the reciprocal quality of duty and the rational
fact that Elizabeth is not obliged to blindly follow the will of a de-
cidedly undutiful parent.

But the novel does not fault Mrs. Bennet in isolation. With
the Bennet marriage, Austen dramatizes the deleterious effects of
a union formed on unsuitable grounds. Mr. Bennet marries because he is "captivated by youth and beauty," and when he discovers too late that his new partner has a "weak understanding
and illiberal mind," he chooses to find amusement in her "ignorance and folly" rather than attempting to help raise her mind to
his own level (236). After Mr. Bennet disregards Elizabeth's request that Lydia be prevented from going to Brighton (the trip
that results in her elopement), Elizabeth contemplates the "im-
propriety of her father's behaviour as a husband": "She had always
seen it with pain; but respecting his abilities, and grateful for his
affectionate treatment of herself, she endeavoured to forget what
she could not overlook, and to banish from her thoughts that
continual breach of conjugal obligation and decorum which, in
exposing his wife to the contempt of her own children, was so
highly reprehensible" (236). In the mode of misogynist satirists,
Mr. Bennet ridicules with no intention of reforming; his behavior
tends to encourage Mrs. Bennet's follies instead of making her re-

flect upon them. So even though Mrs. Bennet is more consistently comic in the novel, Mr. Bennet's role in the marriage is faulted as "reprehensible" because of the "evils arising from so ill-judged a direction of talents; talents which, rightly used, might at least have preserved the respectability of his daughters, even if incapable of enlarging the mind of his wife" (237). Although Mrs. Bennet might not have responded to reason, the novel contends that Mr. Bennet should, for the sake of his daughters, have played a more active role in family life.

In spite of the infelicities of her own marriage, Mrs. Bennet sees a wedding as the proper goal of each of her daughters. When she gets her wishes, however, she has to face the fact that marriage takes her daughters out of her life. In the case of Lydia, she expresses regret: "I often think . . . that there is nothing so bad as parting with one's friends. One seems so forlorn without them." In characteristic fashion, she focuses only on herself here, which leads Elizabeth to counter, "This is the consequence you see, Madam, of marrying a daughter. . . . It must make you better satisfied that your other four are single" (330). Of course, Mrs. Bennet cannot think beyond her well-worn paradigms; she replies that had Lydia married someone in their neighborhood, then the transition would not have been difficult. Ironically, Jane, who does marry a man from nearby, decides to move away after a year: "So near a vicinity to her mother and Meryton relations was not desirable even to *his* easy temper, or *her* affectionate heart" (385).

The shortsightedness of Mrs. Bennet's goals and the reciprocity of relations between Mr. Bennet and his wife give rise to an ironic reflection by the narrator in the concluding chapter: "I wish I could say, for the sake of her family, that the accomplishment of her earnest desire in the establishment of so many of her children, produced so happy an effect as to make her a sensible, amiable, well-informed woman for the rest of her life; though perhaps it was lucky for her husband, who might not have relished domestic felicity in so unusual a form, that she still was occasionally nervous and invariably silly" (385). Besides benefiting from Mrs. Bennet's comic speeches, the novel promotes the companionate model of marriage by contrasting the Bennets with the more sensible Gardiners. Mr. and Mrs. Gardiner provide advice for Elizabeth and help facilitate Lydia's marriage to Wickham, playing the role of responsible parents much better than the Bennets ever could. The Gardiners receive special commendation in the final paragraph of the novel as "the means of uniting" Darcy and Elizabeth (388).

Even though Burney, Edgeworth, and Austen criticize the marriage market from different angles in their depiction of misguided young women (Burney) and misguiding mothers (Edgeworth and Austen), they unite in their penchant for satirizing women who compete with one another for men. Their creation of a number of scheming, competitive women indicates the foolishness of a system that offers limited options for female life and then pits woman against woman for available positions as wives. The competitive woman reinforces notions of male superiority by striving exclusively for the attention of men and disregarding even the possibility of friendship with other women.

Even a married woman might still feel threatened by other women, as Burney makes clear in her darkly satirical portrait of a competitive female in *Cecilia*. Lady Margaret, wife of the book's arch-dissimulator Mr. Monckton, correctly identifies her husband's inappropriate attachment to Cecilia, but rather than castigating him for his attentions toward another woman, she treats her perceived rival badly: "Lady Margaret received [Cecilia] with a coldness that bordered upon incivility; irascible by nature and jealous by situation, the appearance of beauty alarmed, and of cheerfulness disgusted her" (6). Cecilia, who sees only the good side of Mr. Monckton, "pitied in secret the unfortunate lot of her friend" (6); however, the events of the novel disclose that Lady Margaret is more pitiable than her husband.

In fact, Lady Margaret ultimately dies as the direct result of her husband's cruelty. When she goes to his sickbed after he has been wounded in the duel with Delvile, he uses her "almost inhumanly," raging at her for her "age and infirmities" and blaming her for his sufferings: "Lady Margaret, whom neither jealousy nor malignity had cured of loving him, was dismayed and affrighted; and in hurrying out of the room upon his attempting, in his frenzy, to strike her, she dropt down dead in an apoplectic fit" (833). The irony here is that Lady Margaret has placed her trust in the wrong person; her realization of the enormity of her husband's malice leads to her death. Upon hearing of Lady Margaret's fate, Cecilia sums up her life: "Poor Lady Margaret! her life has been as bitter as her temper! married from a view of interest, ill used as a bar to happiness, and destroyed from the fruitless ravings of despair!" (833). As Cecilia sees it, the root of Lady Margaret's troubles was a marriage based on interest rather than mutual regard. What she overlooks is that she, too, was deceived by Mr. Monckton and that Lady Margaret's fate could have been her own. Had Mr. Monckton succeeded in keeping Cecilia in isolation from the world and in marrying her after the death of his wife, he would have gained control of her fortune and person, and his cruel nature would have eventually come out against her. Although Lady Margaret makes only brief appearances in the book, we can see that, in light of Mr. Monckton's abuse and treachery, the two women would have been better off as allies than as enemies.

In Edgeworth's *Patronage*, Lady Angelica Headingham actively competes with Caroline Percy for the attention of male suitors. To account for Lady Angelica's coquettishness and theatricality, the narrator tells us that "[d]uring the early part of her life she had been much and injudiciously restrained." "The moment the pressure was taken off," we are told, "the spirit boiled with surprising rapidity" (178). This explanation accords with Edgeworth's views on a liberal education as the key to shaping character and gives a rationale independent of gender determinism for Lady Angelica's behavior. When she first encounters Caroline, Lady Angelica is in the process of reigning supreme at a gathering and at first feels confident in her ability to hold her own against another female: "There was beauty enough to alarm, but simplicity sufficient to remove all fears of rivalship.—Caroline entered, without any prepared grace or practised smile, but merely as if she was coming into a room" (180). The terms that Lady Angelica uses to comfort herself in her mental evaluation of Caroline are precisely the terms that condemn Lady Angelica herself in the book's moral vocabulary. To enter a room as though one were entering a room is a demonstration of honesty that puts coquetry to shame.

In Lady Angelica's numerous maneuvers to win out over Caroline, she is continually faulted by the narrator for her lack of sincerity. In a sense, the narrator puts the women in competition on a moral level in order to satirize the triviality of the competition that Lady Angelica practices. The two women are frequently contrasted, as in the following passage: "Now and then her Ladyship condescended to join the young people, when they went out to walk, but never, unless they were attended by gentlemen.—The beauties of nature have come into fashion of late, and Lady Angelica Headingham could talk of bold outlines, and sublime mountains, the charming effects of light and shade, fine *accidents*, and rich foliage—spring verdure and autumnal tints,—whilst Caroline could enjoy all these things without expecting to be admired for admiring them" (181–82). Here Lady Angelica's need for a specifically male audience differs sharply from Caroline's self-sufficiency. Caroline genuinely appreciates nature; Lady Angelica affects the style of a Romantic writer and discusses nature in order to draw attention to herself: "She became too hot or too cold, or she was tired to death the moment she ceased to be the principal object of attention" (182).

To hone her conversational skills, Lady Angelica spends her nights pouring over "dictionaries and extracts, abridgments and *beauties* of various authors" so that she can appear to be familiar with "a vast extent of literature, and to be deeply skilled in matters of science, of which she knew nothing, and for which she had no taste" (182). Just as she uses tricks to play the social game, she engages in endless ploys to impress and tease her suitors. That Lady Angelica is meant to stand as a criticism of women's general behavior within the marriage market can be seen in the narrator's approval of Caroline's straightforwardness: "It may seem small praise, that she avoided all coquetry and deception by word or look; yet those who know the world and the fair sex best will be inclined to have the highest opinion of a young lady, who entirely deserved this praise" (193). This formulation may appear to smack of misogyny in its apparently negative generalization about the "fair sex"; however, in the portraits of Caroline, of the women in her family, and of the women who applaud her, we can see that, in the view of the book, coquettes err by choice and not by nature.

Another competitive female, Lady Katrine Hawksby in Edgeworth's *Helen,* is described as having "come to that no particular age, when a remarkable metaphysical phenomenon occurs; on one particular subject hope increases as all probability of success decreases" (179). That subject, of course, is matrimonial prospects, and Lady Katrine sees herself as competing with Helen for suitors. She also resents Helen's close relationship with Lady Cecilia: "Lady Katrine had always, even when she was quite a child, been jealous of Lady Cecilia's affection for Helen; and now her indignation and disappointment were great at finding her established at Clarendon Park—to live with the Clarendons, to *go out* with Lady Cecilia" (178). Because she regards Helen as a rival, she "longed for an opportunity to discomfit Helen, which supreme pleasure her ladyship promised herself upon the first convenient occasion,—convenient meaning when Lady Davenant was out of the room; for Lady Katrine, though urged by prompting jealousy, dared not attack her when under cover of that protection" (180). A bully and a coward, Lady Katrine practices her incivilities only when she can avoid any repercussions from her powerful hostess. From her envious perspective, she can only see Helen's gains as her losses; what she does not recognize is that Lady Cecilia would not necessarily care more for her if she loved Helen less. Lady Davenant exposes Lady Katrine's superficiality when she cuts her down to size for openly resenting Helen's place in Lady Cecilia's affections: "In justice to my daughter [Lady Cecilia], I must say her love has not been won by flattery, as none knows better than the Lady Katrine Hawksby" (181).

But family solidarity is no guarantee against the spirit of competition society generates among women. Another source of resentment for Lady Katrine is her own sister's marriage: "since Lady Castlefort's marriage, the younger, the beautiful being now the successful lady of the ascendant, the elder writhed in all the combined miseries of jealousy and dependence, and an everyday lessening chance of bettering her condition" (179). In a manner most unsisterly, Lady Castlefort contributes to Lady Katrine's discomfort and wants to remove her from the premises. Despite Lady Katrine's bad temperament, the narrator shows some sympathy for the plight of the unmarried dependent: "Lady Castlefort had no decent excuse for her ardent impatience to get rid of her sister. She had magnificent houses in town and country, ample room everywhere—but in her heart" (179). The comparative situations of the two sisters illustrate the extreme poles at which women are placed within the marriage-market economy. Lady Castlefort's success on the market does not constitute good news for her sister even though she has the means—and space—to make Lady Katrine comfortable. Instead, the two women continue to be pitted against one another, and Lady Castlefort's desire for admiration and attention urges her to subvert Lady Katrine's slim chances of catching a man by diverting attention to herself.

If so much competition exists so close to home for Lady Katrine, it is no wonder that she puts such energy into tormenting Helen with "ill-natured raillery" and "perpetual sneers, innuendos, and bitter sarcasms" (205). Her malice leads her to deceive Helen by telling her that the novel's hero, Beauclerc, is engaged, a lie that prevents Helen and Beauclerc from communicating their mutual regard (and extends the book for several hundred more pages). Because of her own unhappiness in spinsterhood, Lady Katrine feels threatened by all women who have a man of their own or who might be capable of obtaining one. According to Lady Castlefort, she obsessively envies other women's good fortune: "Katrine naturally hates everybody that is going to be married. If you were to see the state she is in always reading the announcements of marriages in High Life!" (347–48). Like an addict, Lady Katrine takes pleasure from the very thing that causes her most harm. Her hatred for other women allows her to shift responsibility for her unhappiness onto their shoulders; in the process, she overlooks both her own culpability and the injustices of the system that offers so few alternatives for adult female life.

Women's limited opportunities give rise to the plots of almost all of Austen's novels, and like Burney and Edgeworth, Austen satirizes the competitiveness that interferes with female solidarity. In *Sense and Sensibility*, she foregrounds woman's inhumanity to woman in the early part of the book in the infamous negotiation scene that takes place between John and Fanny Dashwood about how much money to give Mrs. Dashwood and the Dashwood sisters. A firm believer in the nuclear family, Fanny wants to keep as much as possible for her "dear little boy." She tells John that his half sisters are "no relationship at all" and summons up a commonly held belief to support her view that they therefore have no corresponding claim on his resources: "It was very well known that no affection was ever supposed to exist between the children of any man by different marriages" (8). Fanny's restrictive definition of family allows her to ignore the specifics of other people's conditions and to be callous to the wants of the other Dashwood women. If the famous dialogue in which she whittles away at the proposed sum is comic, the message about relations between married women and dependent ones is not.

Less successful in her efforts to compete is *Sense and Sensibility*'s Lucy Steele. Lucy's manipulative qualities are in evidence from her first appearance in the novel as she ingratiates herself with Lady Middleton by showing "excessive affection and endurance" toward the Middleton offspring. The narrator comments wryly on Lucy's ability to win Lady Middleton over in this arena: "Fortunately for those who pay their court through such foibles, a fond mother, though in pursuit of praise for her children, the most rapacious of human beings, is likewise the most credulous; her demands are exorbitant; but she will swallow anything" (120). When we learn of the treatment the Steele sisters receive at the hands of the Middleton offspring, then, we laugh at the price they pay for winning Lady Middleton's approval and at the mother who observes with indulgence the "impertinent incroachments and mischievous tricks" her children force upon the Steeles: "She saw their sashes untied, their work-bags searched, and their knives and scissars [sic] stolen away, and felt no doubt of its being a reciprocal enjoyment" (120–21). By accepting such treatment without protest and even praising the children for their behavior, Lucy and her sister are able to convince Lady Middleton that they are the "sweetest girls in the world" (119). That such manipulations might be necessary for dependent females is implied by Elinor's reflection on Lady Middleton's labeling of the Steeles: "Elinor well knew that the sweetest girls in the world were to be met with in every part of England, under every possible variation of form, face, temper, and understanding" (119). Her skepticism about the real virtues of the Steeles takes in all "girls" who are required to be "sweet" in order to maintain a foothold in society.

In the report of Elinor's disparagement of Lucy, Austen upholds the Enlightenment feminist value on education as necessary for female development and on the need for women to build their characters on a foundation of sound principles:

> Lucy was naturally clever; her remarks were often just and amusing . . . but her powers had received no aid from education, she was ignorant and illiterate, and her deficiency of all mental improvement, her want of information in the most common particulars, could not be concealed from Miss Dashwood, in spite of her constant endeavour to appear to advantage. Elinor saw, and pitied her for, the neglect of abilities which education might have rendered so respectable; but she saw, with less tenderness of feeling, the thorough want of delicacy, of rectitude, and integrity of mind, which her attentions, her assiduities, her flatteries at the Park betrayed. (127)

Elinor contextualizes Lucy's limitations and shows some sympathy for her lack of opportunities; nonetheless, she condemns Lucy for making such poor use of her faculties.

Lucy thinks she is playing her cards well when she pretends to confide in Elinor about the man in whom they both have an interest. By misrepresenting Edward's point of view and saying that he looks upon Elinor as a sister, Lucy hopes to prey on her rival's insecurities and to force her off the field. But Lucy errs in believing that Elinor is like her. Rather than feeling overpowered by a superior talent, Elinor trusts in her own strength of character and in Edward's affection for her, correctly identifying his attachment to Lucy as a youthful infatuation. Rather than focusing on Lucy as rival, Elinor considers Edward's fate in a remarkable act of self-transcendence: "she wept for him, more than for herself" (140). She even tries to ascertain whether Lucy feels any genuine regard for Edward in order to fortify herself against his loss.

In the scenes that take place after Lucy has told Elinor of her secret engagement, the satire against hypocrisy is heightened by the reader's knowledge that Elinor understands Lucy's game. Well-versed herself in social lying for the sake of establishing comfort, Elinor is able to operate on two levels in her dealings with Lucy: on one, she maintains the polite surface veneer; on the other, she evaluates Lucy's dishonesty and deplores her vulgar methods. The following exchange illustrates Lucy's maneuvering and Elinor's ability to keep her in check:

> At length Lucy exclaimed with a deep sigh,
> "I believe it would be the wisest way to put an end to the business at once by dissolving the engagement. We seem so beset with difficulties on every side, that though it would make us miserable for a time, we should be happier perhaps in the end. But you will not give me your advice, Miss Dashwood?"
> "No;" answered Elinor, with a smile, which concealed very agitated feelings, "on such a subject I certainly will not. You know very well that my opinion would have no weight with you, unless it were on the side of your wishes."
> "Indeed you wrong me," replied Lucy with great solemnity; "I know nobody of whose judgment I think so highly as I do of yours; and I do really believe, that if you was to say to me, 'I advise you by all means to put an end to your engagement with Edward Ferrars, it will be more for the happiness of both of you,' I should resolve upon doing it immediately."
> Elinor blushed for the insincerity of Edward's future wife, and replied, "this compliment would effectually frighten me from giving any opinion on the subject had I formed one. It raises my influence much too high; the power of dividing two people so tenderly attached is too much for an indifferent person."
> "'Tis because you are an indifferent person,"

said Lucy, with some pique, and laying a particular stress on those words, "that your judgment
might justly have such weight with me. If you
could be supposed to be biassed in any respect by
your own feelings, your opinion would not be
worth having." (149–50)

This dialogue contains multiple ironies: Lucy knows that Elinor
can see through her feint about calling off the engagement; Elinor
knows that Lucy knows this, but does not want to show her own
hand by indicating just how affected she is by Lucy's engagement
to Edward; further, Elinor suspects Lucy's feelings for Edward to be
false, while Lucy rightly suspects that Elinor may have sincere
feelings for him; and both women believe that Edward's heart belongs to Elinor. Each weighs her words carefully, making full use
of ambiguous phrasings to insinuate her true assessment of her adversary. If Elinor were a stereotypically competitive female, this
verbal sparring match would have been ugly; however, Elinor's
empathy for Lucy comes out in the midst of the fray when she
blushes for Lucy's insincerity, demonstrating her ability to step
outside her own pain and to feel for someone else.

In other similar conversations between Elinor and Lucy, we
can see that, though Lucy has enough wit to engage in pointed
repartee with Elinor, she lacks her adversary's sincerity and strength
of mind. When Lucy switches camps and marries Edward's
brother, Robert, she demonstrates her market-driven view that
men are basically interchangeable; she even manages to get her
mother-in-law to see things this way, too, insofar as Mrs. Ferrars
ends up slighting Edward, the elder son and heir, in favor of his
younger brother.

Significantly, when competition occurs in the novels of Burney, Edgeworth, and Austen between the heroine and another
female character, the heroine does not initiate it. The only exception to this rule occurs when the heroine herself is being satirized, such as Austen's Lady Susan or Edgeworth's Mrs. Beaumont
(*Manoeuvring*). These novelists' heroines typically subscribe to
an unwritten code of conduct that prescribes good will toward
other women and a belief in the possibility of female friendship.

Although the competitive woman appears frequently in the novels, her efforts to malign the heroine or to steal suitors actually highlight the virtues of that heroine by force of contrast. Whereas competitive female characters make use of duplicitous and manipulative tactics—the weapons of the weak—the heroines, when most true to character, behave straightforwardly, sensibly, and rationally.

Because of their honesty and integrity, heroines in the novels of Burney, Edgeworth, and Austen are susceptible to the treachery of those who approach them in the guise of friendship. For example, Elizabeth Bennet trusts Wickfield on the basis of his amiable demeanor and has trouble accepting the fact that he is a self-centered schemer. Similarly, Cecilia is taken in by Mr. Monckton's assertions of friendship and has no idea of the elaborate plots he launches behind her back until after her husband fights a duel with him. And Belinda is almost ready to accept Mr. Vincent's proposal before his history of gambling becomes known. Such deceptions between men and women form the basis of many plots in eighteenth- and nineteenth-century fiction, ending in seduction and abandonment for tragic heroines and for countless secondary characters. Deceptions between women, however, can also result in serious consequences for the comic heroine who seeks fellowship and aid in female friendship. Two such heroines, Austen's Catherine Morland (*Northanger Abbey*) and Burney's Juliet (*The Wanderer*), are mistreated by women in whom they put their trust, and their experience demonstrates the need for greater female solidarity.

As part of its satire on novelistic conventions, *Northanger Abbey* is critical of people who rely on bad fiction for cues about how to live their lives. Isabella Thorpe, for example, treats the people around her as characters she can force to conform to her plot; in the end, she has lost all credibility and stands exposed as a crass fortune hunter. When Catherine meets Isabella, she is overwhelmed by the older girl's knowledge of "dress, balls, flirtations, and quizzes" (33), and she does not realize that Isabella has ulterior motives in cultivating her friendship. Isabella has her eye on Catherine's brother and sees an intimacy with the sister as a step in the right direction; she mouths the words of friendship, but her real motivations are seldom altruistic. Nowhere is this more clear than when she claims to be an avid proponent of female solidarity: "There is nothing I would not do for those who are really my friends. I have no notion of loving people by halves, it is not my nature. My attachments are always excessively strong. I told Capt. Hunt at one of our assemblies this winter, that if he was to tease me all night, I would not dance with him, unless he would allow Miss Andrews to be as beautiful as an angel. The men think us incapable of real friendship you know, and I am determined to shew them the difference" (40). Here she is making what on the surface looks like a feminist argument: men accuse women of being false to one another, and she aims to show them better. However, her statements about loving with strength are fictionalizations of her own persona. She obviously thinks that the appearance of loyalty to other women will make a good impression, and she also is not adverse to Captain Hunt's teasing her all night if necessary. Ironically, her advocacy of female friendship is merely a way for her to distinguish herself from other women—and, by extension, to support the accusation that women are incapable of real friendship. Miss Andrews is the vehicle for Isabella's self-aggrandizement, both at the dance and later as a ploy for Catherine's friendship.

Unable to conceive of people saying one thing and meaning another, Catherine is constantly being thrown into confusion by Isabella's statements. For instance, when Isabella claims that she wants to get away from two young men who she says are staring at her, Catherine cannot understand why she decides to walk in a direction that might put her into contact with them:

> Catherine readily agreed [to walk in the direction Isabella recommended]. "Only," she added, "perhaps we may overtake the two young men."
>
> "Oh! never mind that. If we make haste, we shall pass by them presently, and I am dying to shew you my hat."
>
> "But if we only wait a few minutes, there will be no danger of our seeing them at all."

> "I shall not pay them any such compliment,
> I assure you. I have no notion of treating men
> with such respect. *That* is the way to spoil them."
>   Catherine had nothing to oppose against
> such reasoning; and therefore, to shew the inde-
> pendence of Miss Thorpe, and her resolution of
> humbling the sex, they set off immediately as fast
> as they could walk, in pursuit of the two young
> men. (43)

Again, Isabella uses pseudo-feminist rhetoric—asserting her "independence" and disregard for male approval—to cover up her
own desire to chase after the men. Her actions tell the true story,
though, and the narrator lets us in on what Catherine, bemused
by her own sensible nature, cannot understand about Isabella's
"reasoning."

    Throughout the novel, Isabella's professions of intimacy and
her self-presentation are highly suspect, but only when Isabella
shows her hand by throwing over James for Captain Tilney does
Catherine see the falseness of her supposed friend. When the
Captain Tilney engagement evaporates and Isabella writes to try
to get Catherine to put in a good word for her to James, Catherine
is able to properly read the emptiness of Isabella's words: "Such a
strain of shallow artifice could not impose even upon Catherine.
Its inconsistencies, contradictions, and falsehood, struck her from
the very first. She was ashamed of Isabella, and ashamed of having ever loved her. Her professions of attachment were now as dis-
gusting as her excuses were empty, and her demands impudent"
(218). The reader knows that Isabella has not changed; it is
Catherine who has grown and matured. Fortunately for Catherine, she finds a more genuine friend in Eleanor Tilney than she
had in Isabella. Like the excesses of gothic terror that Catherine
suffers during her early stay at the Abbey, Isabella's false friendship disappears when held to the light of reason and common
sense. Similarly, the stereotype of women as being incapable of
friendship is dismissed by the actual representation of a solid and
caring friendship between Eleanor and Catherine.
    Equally manipulative and more harmful than Isabella, *The*

Wanderer's Miss Arbe pretends to serve as patron to Juliet (known throughout most of the novel as "Ellis") in order to avail herself of Juliet's skills and to receive free lessons on the harp. In spite of her "assurance of protection" for Juliet (209), Miss Arbe shamelessly takes advantage of her. For example, she insists that Juliet rent an expensive instrument rather than a cheaper one and then shows up at Juliet's lodgings with a large stack of music on the day after the harp arrives, saying that she wants to try the instrument: "What Miss Arbe called trying the instrument, was selecting the most difficult passages, from the most difficult music which she attempted to play, and making [Juliet] teach her the fingering, the time, and the expression, in a lesson which lasted the whole morning" (209). What Burney reveals in the sections which discuss Miss Arbe's style of patronage is that this woman gets more than she gives, yet she expects gratitude without showing any in return.

Her good deeds are cancelled out by her inconsiderate execution of them. For instance, although she does apply herself to recruiting students for Juliet and attempts to set up a benefit on her behalf, she refuses to take Juliet's straitened circumstances into account:

> The gratitude of [Juliet] was, however, by no means unruffled, when Miss Arbe insisted upon regulating the whole of her proceedings; and that with an expence which, however moderate for any other situation, was for hers alarming, if not ruinous. But Miss Arbe declared that she would not have her recommendation disgraced by any meanness: she engaged, therefore, at a high price, the best apartment in the house; she chose various articles of attire, lest [Juliet] should choose them, she said, too parsimoniously. . . . In vain [Juliet] represented the insufficiency of her little store for such expences. Miss Arbe impatiently begged that they might not waste their time upon such narrow considerations; and, seizing the harp, devoted the rest of the visit to a long, though unacknowledged lesson. (211)

Juliet had hoped that Miss Arbe's influence would save her from having to take a position as a humble companion; instead, what she learns here is that dependence of any sort can be dangerous. Ironically, the more Juliet "benefits" from Miss Arbe's assistance, the more she gets into debt. Miss Arbe's dismissal of Juliet's financial concerns as "narrow considerations" shows how little she is motivated by a desire to assist the needy heroine.

Even though Miss Arbe causes problems for Juliet, she is still one of the few people who even pretend to be kind to her and thus can easily manipulate Juliet into giving freely of her time. The other woman who plays patron to her, Miss Bydel, is frequently rude to Juliet and, like Miss Arbe, makes constant demands upon her time, seeking gossip about the families of Juliet's students. By their intrusiveness, Miss Arbe and Miss Bydel threaten the livelihood of the person they supposedly aim to patronize: "And but that these ladies had personal engagements for their evenings, [Juliet] could not have found time to keep herself in such practice as her new profession required; and her credit, if not her scholars, might have been lost, through the selfishness of the very patronesses by whom they had been obtained" (224). Miss Arbe and Miss Bydel both lack the capacity to understand Juliet's delicate position and to act with true generosity. For all her pretenses to gentility and her professions of friendship, Miss Arbe is really no better to Juliet than the more vulgar and uncivil Miss Bydel is. In fact, Miss Arbe comes off looking worse than Miss Bydel because she masks her incivilities and self-interest more thoroughly.

The Wanderer illustrates how difficult it is for a woman to survive alone in a world that defines women according to their connections. True friendships in the novel—as seen in the partnership that exists between Juliet and Gabriella or in the empathy that Lady Aurora evinces for Juliet's situation—provide only short breathing spaces for the heroine, who is constantly assailed by hostile contacts. Asylum with either Gabriella or Lady Aurora would rescue Juliet from the trials of being an anonymous outsider; however, the book's sweeping social criticism indicates that such a refuge is hard to maintain in a society that stacks the deck against women in the first place.

One woman who contributes consistently to Juliet's sufferings is Mrs. Ireton, who specializes in what Jane Collier dubbed "the art of ingeniously tormenting."[6] Mrs. Ireton surrounds herself with subordinates so that she can humiliate and abuse them. This female tyrant reflects another side of the authoritarianism inherent in patriarchy: in order to compensate for the power denied women in the wider culture, a woman might feel no qualms in exploiting the power she is allowed within the domestic realm. In satirizing Mrs. Ireton's bad behavior, the novel discloses the interconnectedness of systems of oppression, whether based upon gender, class, or race.

In the first two-thirds of the novel, Juliet tries to avoid taking a position as Mrs. Ireton's humble companion, knowing that service under such a vicious woman would be torture. After a series of failed attempts to achieve self-sufficiency, however, she reluctantly places herself at Mrs. Ireton's disposal. During her brief period with Mrs. Ireton, Juliet struggles to preserve her own dignity in the face of perpetual insults, innuendos, and threats. She is shocked by the "general tyranny" that Mrs. Ireton exercises and by the "authoritative tone" with which this woman addresses her (456).[7]

Mrs. Ireton's speeches reveal class- and gender-consciousness as the basis for much of her tyrannical behavior. For instance, when the housemaid becomes frustrated with trying to clean up after Mrs. Ireton's ward and her lapdog, saying that "she had wiped up the grease and the slops till her arms ached; for the little boy made more dirt and nastiness than the cur himself," Mrs. Ireton calls upon decorum and claims to be physically threatened by working-class nomenclature:

> "The boy?—The cur?—What's all this?" cried Mrs. Ireton; "who and what, is the woman talking of? The boy? Has the boy no name?—The cur? Have you no respect for your lady's lap dog?—Grease too?—Nastiness!—you turn me sick! I am ready to faint! What horrible images you present to me! Has nobody any salts? any lavendar-water? How unfortunate it is to have

such nerves, such sensations, when one lives
with such mere speaking machines!" (458)

Mrs. Ireton's pretense of excessive delicacy is ludicrous, as is her
demand that her servant respect her mistress's lapdog. In her
view, employees are nothing but robots, paid to do her bidding
and expected to obey mindlessly.

On a more ominous note, Mrs. Ireton's tyranny extends to
an involvement in the slave trade (which would have still been
legal during the 1790s, when the events in the book take place).
She keeps a black youth, identified as the "favourite, because the
most submissive servant" (456). In chastising this servant for
laughing during her speech to the housemaid, Mrs. Ireton's sarcasm has a particularly biting edge:

> So this amuses you, does it, Sir? You think it very
> comical? You are so kind as to be entertained, are
> you? How happy I am to give you so much plea-
> sure! How proud I ought to be to afford you such
> diversion! I shall make it my business to shew my
> sense of my good fortune; and, to give you a
> proof, Sir, of my desire to contribute to your gai-
> ety, to-morrow morning I will have you shipped
> back to the West Indies. And there, that your joy
> may be complete, I shall issue orders that you
> may be striped till you jump, and that you may
> jump—you little black imp!—between every
> stripe! (458)

With threats like this, it is no wonder that the black servant is so
submissive to Mrs. Ireton. She mimics the style of a domestic
angel by ostensibly emphasizing her happiness at giving pleasure
to this young man and her willingness to accommodate him to
her utmost ability, but Mrs. Ireton's real message is that she literally owns his life and can send him "back" into a more brutal slavery at a moment's notice.

With more freedom than the black servant, Juliet can stren-
uously resist being claimed as Mrs. Ireton's property, responding

to her impertinent questions with silence and repeatedly asserting her desire to be considered as a person independent of the title "humble companion." Nonetheless, she endures endless trials at her employer's hands, and her experience satirizes the abuse of power by those who hire impoverished young women to do their every bidding:

> If a new novel excited interest, or a political pamphlet awakened curiosity, [Juliet] was called upon to read whole hours, nay, whole days, without intermission; even a near extinction of voice did not authorize so great a liberty as that of requesting a few minutes for rest. Mrs. Ireton, who regarded all the world as robust, compared with herself, deemed it an impertinent rivalry of a delicacy which she held to be unexampled, ever to pronounce the word fatigue, ever to heave a sigh of lassitude, or ever even to allude to that part of the human frame which is called nerves, unless with some pointed reference to herself. (469)

Mrs. Ireton designates Juliet's fatigue an "impertinent rivalry" because she finds it necessary to emphasize the difference in status between herself and her companion. Versed in genteel accomplishments such as reading, playing music, singing, and embroidering, the humble companion shares elements of her mistress's class privilege and could thus be perceived as a rival for other aspects of that privilege. Even though Juliet's exhaustion is genuine—she is being overworked—it resembles too closely Mrs. Ireton's feigned "delicacy" and threatens to disrupt the employer's monopoly on power. If Mrs. Ireton were to allow Juliet the "liberty" of a few minutes rest, she would be making a concession to Juliet's subjective experience of oppression, something that Mrs. Ireton deliberately avoids doing.

The satire on Mrs. Ireton succeeds so well because Juliet manages to avoid degradation and is able to subvert her tyrannical employer's authority. When Mrs. Ireton carries her mockery too far, Juliet typically leaves her presence. On one occasion, Mrs.

Ireton calls out after her, "Permit me, Madam, . . . if it is not taking too great a liberty with a person of your vast consequence,—permit me to enquire who told you to go?" Juliet's retort, though quietly pronounced, is a scathing critique of authoritarianism: "A person, Madam, who has not the honour to be known to you,—myself" (501). By claiming herself as the final arbiter of her actions and by asserting her free will in the face of Mrs. Ireton's demands, Juliet strikes a blow for all women who must pay the high price of dependence. Mrs. Ireton falls within my discussion of comic strategies precisely because Juliet so completely unmasks her through verbal exchanges and autonomous acts. In Mrs. Ireton's extended speeches and memorable dialogues with Juliet, we can see the skeleton of tyranny laid bare.

Lest we doubt the comic appeal of a character like Mrs. Ireton, we would do well to consider the comments of Jane Austen's relations and friends on a similar character in *Mansfield Park*. Of the six readers who made reference to Mrs. Norris in the "Opinions of *Mansfield Park*," assembled and recorded by Austen, five expressed their appreciation of this character who torments the heroine of the novel. For instance, Anna Lefroy, Austen's niece, was "delighted with Mrs. Norris"; Mrs. James Austen "Enjoyed Mrs. Norris particularly" (432); and Mr. J. Plumtre wrote, "Mrs. Norris amused me particularly" (*Minor Works* 434). It is possible that the enjoyment of Mrs. Norris bore some correspondence to one's feelings about the novel's heroine, since Miss Lloyd and Austen's mother expressed contrasting views on the two characters' relative merits:

> Miss Lloyd . . . —Delighted with Fanny.—Hated Mrs. Norris.—
> My Mother—not liked it so well as P. & P.—Thought Fanny insipid.—Enjoyed Mrs. Norris.— (432)

Some polarization of opinion on Fanny and Mrs. Norris could be due to the fact that Mrs. Norris is a more colorful figure than Fanny. Whatever the case, it is clear that in spite of her numerous incivilities, many of Austen's contemporaries took pleasure in the satire against Mrs. Norris.

Like Mrs. Ireton, Mrs. Norris wants to maintain a sense of hierarchy in her dealings with the dependent heroine. Her desire to make distinctions of rank between Fanny and the Bertram sisters is explicitly connected with the masculinist order of the Bertram household, in which Mrs. Norris feels authorized to participate. Sir Thomas urges her to understand in her dealings with his daughters and niece that "they cannot be equals." He calls upon Mrs. Norris to help him "choose exactly the right line of conduct" toward Fanny so that she will not become too intimate with her stepsisters and consequently forget her own subordinate status, and Mrs. Norris agrees to be "quite at his service" (11). In fact, she carries his mandates to (logical) extremes that even he will later reject when he comes to see the flaws in his authoritarian model of family relations. Sir Thomas reflects upon the bond that existed between him and Mrs. Norris: "she seemed a part of himself, that must be borne forever" (465–66). By this time, Mrs. Norris is in exile from Mansfield Park, along with the disgraced Maria Bertram, and Fanny has taken an affectionate hold on Sir Thomas's heart. During the reign of Mrs. Norris, however, Fanny lives in fear of both her uncle and this formidable aunt.

A consummate dissimulator, Mrs. Norris dislikes her niece from early on because Fanny is unable to suppress her true feelings. On Fanny's first trip to Mansfield Park, Mrs. Norris oppresses her by "talking to her the whole way from Northampton of her wonderful good fortune, and the extraordinary degree of gratitude and good behaviour which it ought to produce." The effect of this coaching is to increase Fanny's sense of misery for feeling homesick when it is "a wicked thing for her not to be happy" (13). Consequently, when Fanny winds up in tears shortly after her arrival at the Bertrams, Mrs. Norris begins to identify her as ungrateful for not recognizing how lucky she is.

Mrs. Norris's own behavior is at odds with what she expects from Fanny. Having only a small income herself, Mrs. Norris schemes to get the most out of any situation that comes her way. For example, when the Bertram family visits the Rushworths,

Mrs. Norris comes away laden with gifts of food and plants. She deflects attention away from her own successes by accosting Fanny: "Well, Fanny, this has been a fine day for you, upon my word! ... I am sure you ought to be very much obliged to your aunt Bertram and me, for contriving to let you go" (105). In fact, Mrs. Norris was opposed to Fanny's accompanying them, but she took great care to garner a place for herself on the trip. Maria Bertram calls attention to Mrs. Norris's hypocrisy in trying to make Fanny feel grateful: "I think *you* have done pretty well yourself, ma'am. Your lap seems full of good things, and here is a basket of something between us, which has been knocking my elbow unmercifully" (105). As Maria recognizes, Mrs. Norris has benefited conspicuously from the excursion and the "spunging" that went along with it (106).

Unable to see the parallels between her own financially strapped position and Fanny's dependent one, Mrs. Norris looks only to her own interests, courting the favor of those whose status she perceives to be above hers and abusing Fanny because she can. She adores the Bertram daughters and treats any privilege Fanny receives as an encroachment on their entitlements. Whereas Maria and Julia can spend their time in leisurely pursuits (and Lady Bertram seldom leaves the couch), Mrs. Norris expects Fanny to keep herself gainfully occupied. In one instance, Mrs. Norris makes Fanny cut roses in the sun and then walk back and forth to deliver them in two trips to her house; when Fanny retreats onto the sofa with a headache later that day, Mrs. Norris scolds her for idleness: "That is a very foolish trick, Fanny, to be idling away all the evening upon a sofa. Why cannot you come, and sit here, and employ yourself as *we* do? ... You should learn to think of other people" (71). Of course, it is Mrs. Norris who needs to learn to think of others, and Fanny is effectively vindicated in this scene when Edmund nurses and comforts her.

In spite of Fanny's lowly status, Mrs. Norris comes to see her as an enemy. Like other female characters who set themselves in opposition to other women, Mrs. Norris sees Fanny's gains as her own (and the Bertram daughters') losses. She is offended when Sir Thomas holds a ball in Fanny's honor, but she is mortified when Fanny receives a proposal of marriage from Henry Crawford. For her misplaced allegiances and her abusive nature, Mrs. Norris pays the penalty of being forced to spend the rest of her narrative life in exile with Maria in "another country—remote and private, where, shut up together with little society, on one side no affection, on the other, no judgment, it may be reasonably supposed that their tempers became their mutual punishment" (465). Dante could not have come up with one more suitable.

In their depictions of tyrannical females, Burney and Austen illustrate that authoritarian politics are untenable, whether they are practiced by men or women. Furthermore, they condemn women who oppress other women as complicit in a system that enforces female subordination. Just as Mrs. Ireton finds fault with Juliet because of her lack of a clear affiliation with a powerful name (and hence a male protector), Mrs. Norris devalues Fanny because of the low status of her family ties. Both women are satirized for their selfishness, their thoughtless values, and the discomfort they cause those who most need their aid.

The characters I have examined are not the only women that Burney, Edgeworth, and Austen satirize in their fiction, but the circumstances in which they appear provide a good picture of the range of social issues the authors engage in their handling of such characters. Other areas of satire would include the following: for Edgeworth, women who involve themselves in partisan politics without fully weighing the issues (Mrs. Falconer [*Patronage*], Lady Bearcroft and Lady Masham [*Helen*]); for Burney, silly women who talk nonsense (the Miss Branghtons [*Evelina*], Miss Larolles and Miss Leeson [*Cecilia*], Juliet's harp students [*The Wanderer*]); for Austen, women who gossip mindlessly (Mrs. Allen [*Northanger Abbey*], Miss Steele [*Sense and Sensibility*], Mrs. Elton [*Emma*]). In their depictions of women as the butts of satire, they go to great lengths to show that, while these women might represent categories of female behavior, they by no means reflect woman's nature or intrinsic flaws. Even as they dramatize the pain that heroines feel at being associated by gender with such women, they debunk the notion of a common stain upon the sex. Their works promote the feminist principle that women are capable of reason and sound judgment, but that such faculties must be culti-

185

vated by a society that values women as individuals rather than denouncing them as innately frivolous or exalting them as inherently angelic.

As a teenager, Burney wrote in her journal that she was "provoked . . . for the honour of the sex" by what she perceived to be misogyny in Homer's representation of Helen in the *Iliad*: "Thus has Homer proved his opinion of our poor sex—that the Love of Beauty is our most prevailing passion." Disturbed by this revelation, she proceeds to question the veracity of portraits of women in literature by men: "It really grieves me to think that there certainly must be reason for the insignificant opinion the greatest men have of Women—At least I *fear* there must.—But I don't in fact *believe* it—thank God!" (*Early Journals* 37). The movement of Burney's recorded thoughts traces her negotiation of distance from and closeness to women in terms of statements about women as a group. She begins by defending the stereotypes, appealing to their widespread usage by "the greatest men" and thinking that women must have given rise to the negative views. Next, she registers her fear that women might deserve to be lumped together and condemned. But she concludes on a strong note of skepticism, adding an expletive of praise to God either for her disbelief or for the fact that women are not to be dismissed so quickly. What Burney discovers in her reading of Homer is her own identification with women and her ultimate involvement in any generalizations about female nature. She takes her stand firmly on the side of women, discrediting the authority of men and confirming her own sense of women's significance.

In Burney's journal entry we can see the poignancy of one girl's experience of sexual politics in literature; in her novels, we can see the politics of gender rewritten on her own terms. She rejects sexist stereotypes of women as intrinsically vain, frivolous, and weak-minded. Like Edgeworth and Austen, she concerns herself with setting the record straight about whom or what to blame for many female shortcomings. Their satires against women have much in common with Wollstonecraft's assertion that "From the tyranny of man, I firmly believe, the greater number of female follies proceed; and the cunning, which I allow makes at present a part of their character, I likewise have repeatedly endeavoured to prove, is produced by oppression" (193). By satirizing foolish and manipulative women, Burney, Edgeworth, and Austen criticize the perversions of character that take place within a male-dominated culture; by presenting rational, sensible heroines as counterexamples, they promote a positive vision of female potential and give women readers something to be proud of.

7

Goblin Laughter:
Violent Comedy and the
Condition of Women

Mrs. Hall, of Sherbonne, was brought to bed yesterday of a dead
child, some weeks before she expected, owing to a fright. I
suppose she happened unawares to look at her husband.

—Jane Austen (*Letters* 24)

VIOLENT COMEDY TESTS THE LIMITS of comic response. Taken out of context, violent comedy can easily elicit the reaction "That's not funny." In fact, violent comedy is often faulted for transgressing against appropriate standards of humor. To call attention to its disturbing qualities, André Breton coined the phrase "black humor" (*humour noir*) to describe this brand of comedy. The hallmark of black humor, according to Mathew Winston, is a disparity between content and form: "The contents provide the blackness, and the style mitigates that blackness with humor" (33). For my purposes, the phrase "violent comedy" provides a more adequate description of a comic mode in which brutal and painful events are described in a setting or tone that invites laughter. Even when violence is not an element, as in the Austen quotation above, such humor itself does violence to the reader by asking her or him to laugh at something that would ordinarily cause pain. Violent comedy has been primarily associated with male writers.[1] Yet, as I will show, women writers produced violent comedy as a response and a challenge to oppressive conditions.

Unlike other comic strategies we have examined, which derive their force from rationality, violent comedy treads a fine line between humor and horror. Social criticism merges with unbridled rage. By taking pleasure in violence, the woman writer flaunts her own violation of tradition; she refuses to bury female pain, but she also refuses to succumb to despair. In order to evaluate violent comedy and to recognize its implicit message, we must keep in mind the social conditions that give rise to it. Before exploring violent comedy in Burney, Edgeworth, and Austen, I will first examine the violence in eighteenth-century women's lives and then look at examples of violent comedy in feminist writers Jane Collier and Mary Wollstonecraft to establish a connection between this mode of comedy and broad critiques of women's oppression. Without some consideration of the darker side of eighteenth-century women's lives, the violent comedy that crops up in the works of Burney, Edgeworth, Austen, and other women writers is likely to seem exaggerated or out of place.

When we imagine the lives of eighteenth-century middle-class women, we may think of family parties, drawing rooms, card-playing, and embroidery as standard features of the domestic environment. In their construction of an ideal femininity, many conduct-book writers of the time intended the possessor of feminine virtues to dwell in an equally ideal domestic setting. But the realities of women's lives could fall far short of paradise. One eighteenth-century woman, for example, records how her recently widowed friend refused an offer of marriage because of the potential for violence within the family: "Her answer to his proposal was not a bad one if she has resolution to stick to it. She said that at home her Mother pinched her, when she married her husband horsewhipped her. She was now her own mistress and very much at her ease" (qtd. in Brophy 174).

Lord Chesterfield's insulting description of women as "children of a larger growth" (66) accurately adumbrates women's legal status in the eighteenth century. From the cradle to the grave, most women were utterly dependent on family ties. If a woman married, her legal identity was subsumed by her husband's. If she remained single, she was subject to the will of her parents and, upon their deaths, to that of her eldest brother. Only in rare cases did women have the financial wherewithal to lead independent lives; as Austen quipped, "Single Women have a dreadful propensity for being poor—which is one very strong argument in favour of Matrimony" (*Letters* 483). Middle-class women cut off from connections by multiple deaths in the family found themselves in dire, and sometimes dangerous, straits. The eighteenth century offered few career choices for single women of the middle class; most available options involved daily dependence—as governesses or humble companions. But even these positions would not have been available to single women unable to procure the necessary references and referrals.

"Female Difficulties," as Burney termed them in *The Wanderer*'s subtitle, went far beyond the indignities of enforced dependence. Conduct literature urged women to be modest, submissive, and gentle, but it neglected to either discuss or prepare them for many of life's real dangers. Women who achieved the ultimate goal of conduct-book training (marriage) still had a perilous path to tread. Austen's humorous reference to the unfortunate Mrs. Hall, "brought to bed . . . of a dead child," attests to the high rate of infant mortality in the eighteenth century and the resulting acceptance of infant death as a fact of life.[2]

Rape and domestic violence were, no doubt, as common in the eighteenth century as our own. Rousseau might argue, "Rapes are hardly ever spoken of anymore, since they are so little necessary and men no longer believe in them," but his view that "for the attacker to be victorious, the one who is attacked must permit or arrange it" suggests that he has merely defined rape out of existence (360, 359). In fact, women's dependence on masculine protection created countless opportunities for abuse. John Gregory warns his daughters, "Thousands of women of the best hearts and finest parts have been ruined by men who approached them under the specious name of friendship" (75).

Although Gregory sees marriage as the most desirable position for a woman, his underlying pessimism asserts itself when he advises his daughters not to marry merely for the sake of being married: "Heaven forbid you should ever relinquish the ease and independence of a single life, to become the slaves of a fool or a tyrant's caprice" (109–10). In a similar tone, conduct-book author Lady Sarah Pennington worries about her daughters' odds of achieving marital bliss: "Happy is her lot, who in a husband, finds [an] invaluable friend!—Yet, so great is the hazard, so disproportioned the chances, that I could almost wish the dangerous die was never to be thrown for any of you!" (56). Nonetheless, society set such a high premium upon marriage that numerous women ended up in disastrous unions with men who could inflict both mental and physical punishment on them on a daily basis. Until 1891, husbands maintained the right to imprison their wives in their own homes.[3]

Some women learned to transcend brutal circumstances by laughing in the face of suffering and converting pain into violent comedy. Consider, for example, the following excerpt from an eighteenth-century woman's letter concerning Christmas festivities that got out of hand: "The evenings have some of them been concluded among the gentlemen with swearing, fighting, spoiling furniture, breaking windows, snoring, and such like masterly performances. Among the wives some have added a wrinkle to their foreheads, which I condemn, for if by chance a drinking husband should die, a disconsolate widow would certainly look better with a smooth brow than a furrowed one" (qtd. in Brophy 173). This woman exhibits an admirable talent for rising above the unpleasantness in her life. Her list of the men's "masterly performances" includes behavior that would have caused much distress and labor for the women in the house: someone would have to clean up afterward and bear the loss of favorite trinkets or furnishings. Her deadpan delivery of the final sentence perfectly illustrates the tension between form and content in violent comedy. In a single clause, the writer kills off the offending husband and then proceeds to affirm her solidarity with the long-suffering wife by humorously reducing the significance of the man's worth to that of wrinkle-producer. Like the woman whose now-deceased husband had horsewhipped her, this woman sees the widowed state as a potential haven from domestic misery, but until then she claims another haven in her humor.

As we have seen throughout this study, laughter can represent a significant triumph over adversity. Gloria Kaufman views humor as a way to preserve mental health under duress: "When the social situation becomes so oppressive that madness is a potential survival response, humor is also a possibility" ("Feminist Humor" 86). Likewise, Freud argues that humor provides psychological relief for people in dire circumstances: "humour is a means of obtaining pleasure in spite of the distressing effects that interfere with it" (228). "Gallows humor," Freud's term for the most extreme form of survival humor, exhibits a fierce rejection of suffering: "there is something like magnanimity . . . in the man's tenacious hold upon his customary self and his disregard of what might overthrow that self and drive it to despair" (229). People in unbearable conditions—imprisoned, enslaved, tortured—use gallows humor to exert control over their environment. Violent comedy by eighteenth-century women writers serves as a powerful vehicle for feminist protest. Like gallows humor, it asserts witty control over life's paradoxes and absurdities.[4]

To grasp more fully how violent comedy can dramatize the subjection of women, we will turn to an example halfway between polemic and fiction. Jane Collier's *Essay on the Art of Ingeniously Tormenting*, a satire on power relations, urges its readers to "ALWAYS DO UNTO EVERY ONE, WHAT YOU WOULD LEAST WISH TO HAVE DONE UNTO YOURSELF" (161). This book enjoyed some popularity in the eighteenth century, going into a second edition and being reprinted in the 1790s and as late as 1808. A sustained piece of violent comedy, it provides a model for exploring the uses of such comedy by the woman writer.

The essay suggests methods for disposing of unwanted children, making servants' lives miserable, mortifying humble companions, and causing spouses to suffer. Collier makes an important distinction by addressing her essay mainly to women; her sport is intended for those who do not have it in their power to employ brute force themselves. She points out that husbands, for example, have no need to torment: "[T]he sport of tormenting is not the husband's chief game. If he grows indifferent to his wife, or comes to hate her, he wishes her dead or absent; and therefore, if in low life, often takes such violent measures, as to break her bones, or to break her heart: and if in high life, he keeps his mistresses abroad, and troubles not his head, one way or other, about his wife" (65–66). In part because men can and often do resort to actual violence, Collier provides guidelines for those hampered by law and custom from indulging in such explicit behavior. The art of tormenting belongs to those who can only aim to torture, not to kill.[5]

In effect, Collier's violent comedy is an indictment of a society based on unjust gender and class hierarchies. If she gives female readers a vicarious thrill, she does so by acknowledging the omnipresence of sexism and by salvaging from society what little power there is available to women. But even then the reader's pleasure contrasts sharply with her sense of outraged justice. Collier's exploitation of female ambition must be read in the context of male domination—as a satire on masculine and class privilege.

Collier depicts the pain that an expert tormenter can inflict in terms that become comic through exaggeration. In one particularly graphic passage, she encourages mothers to use their children as agents of tormenting the humble companion and to evade moral responsibility by taking refuge in social hierarchy. Here, content and form are drastically at odds: violent acts and outrageous brutality get brushed aside by the urbane voice of the didactic narrator, whose tone mimics that of the advice literature.

> If your son, Mr. Jacky, should have cut Miss Lucy across the face with his new knife; or your daughter Miss Isabella, should have pinched her arms black and blue, or scratched her face and neck, with her pretty nails, so as to have fetched the blood; and poor Lucy, to prevent any farther mischief to her person, should come and make her complaint to you; do you, in the first place, rate her soundly for provoking the poor children, who, you may affirm, are the best natured little things in the world, if they are not teazed and vexed. But if, by the blood streaming from her face and arms, it appears plainly, that the girl has

194

been very much hurt, you may (to show your great impartiality) say, that you will send for the children in, and reprimand them. . . .

As soon as the children come into the room, begin to rate them most severely.—But for what?—Why for disobeying your commands, and condescending to play, and be familiar with any thing but their equals! You may conclude also, by threatening them with the greatest punishment, if ever they are again guilty of so high an offence, as that of speaking to a wretch so much beneath them in birth, fortune, and station, as Miss Lucy. (47–49)

Blood and bruises outwardly mark poor Lucy's plight, but the malicious taunts of her mistress form her invisible crown of thorns. By satirizing one who could invoke class hierarchy in the face of such extreme suffering, Collier faults the unlimited indulgence of upper classes guided by an ideology of dominance and submission. Such a chronicle of cruelty relies for its humor on a better standard of behavior than the mistress maintains. But the described behavior must at least seem plausible for its humor to be appreciated. The humor response to this passage involves three aspects: shock at the blood and the injustice, recognition of the realistic depiction of power relations, and pleasure at the iconoclastic portrait of the mother and child. Whereas shock gets the reader's attention, realism promotes a reformist agenda made unsanctimonious by humor.

Collier worried that her satirical message would go unheeded. Lest her readers take too much pleasure in laughing at the torments she describes and neglect to reform their behavior, she includes a parable that aims to separate the tormented from the tormenters. In the fable, anthropomorphized animals discover a poem "in which was strongly described the misery that is endured from the entrance of teeth and claws into living flesh." The poem paints "[i]n the strongest colours . . . the pain which the poor sufferer sustains, his agonizing faintness from loss of blood, with the exquisite torment he undergoes, until his heartfelt anguish is relieved by death." Since the poem is signed only with the letter "L," a dispute arises among the lion, the leopard, the lynx, and the lamb about whose ancestor could have written it. Initially, the lamb is thrown out of the competition by general consent "as knowing nothing of the subjects treated of in the poem." After much bickering, however, the horse interposes and declares that no predator could evince such sympathy for the "tortured wretches." He thus deduces that the writer of the poem must have been the ancestor of the lamb, "As it is from suffering, and not from inflicting torments, that the true idea of them is gained" (n.pag.).

Collier's fable responds directly to critics who detect malice in the propensity of women writers to injure female characters in their violent comedy. Sympathy, as she illustrates, distinguishes the oppressor from the victim; moreover, a sympathetic response separates the discerning from the superficial reader. By inciting uncomfortable laughter, violent comedy enlists the reader in the process of reform. At the point where laughter ends, change can begin.

In previous chapters, we have examined female laughter at the follies of male domination; this laughter, though subtle at times, is confident. Wollstonecraft's comic treatment of Rousseau, Fordyce, and Gregory in *A Vindication* reveals feminist humor at its best, defiantly laughing in the face of pompous sexism. Comedy aimed at stereotypes of women, restrictive rules of conduct, and the male monopoly on education generates hope for social progress. In spite of the pressure for reform, however, in actuality many men felt no compelling need to treat women better, and so women writers had to find ways to express their frustration with male control over social change. Wollstonecraft and other women writers resorted to violence as a comic outlet.

Wollstonecraft introduces violent comedy in the concluding paragraphs of *A Vindication* when she refers to the possibility that male domination might be justified:

> Let woman share the rights and she will emulate
> the virtues of man; for she must grow more per-
> fect when emancipated, or justify the authority
> that chains such a weak being to her duty.—If

the latter, it will be expedient to open a fresh
trade with Russia for whips; a present which a father should always make to his son-in-law on his
wedding day, that a husband may keep his whole
family in order by the same means; and without
any violation of justice reign, wielding this scep-
tre, sole master of his house, because he is the
only being in it who has reason. (194)

Wollstonecraft's confidence in the justice of her cause allows her
to mock men for their tyranny; at the same time, she recognizes
that the subject of her mockery is no laughing matter. Uneasiness
about whether men will participate in the revolution in gender
relations gives rise to her violent humor. As anthropologist Peggy
Reeves Sanday has shown in her comparative study of primitive
cultures, "male dominance in myth and everyday life is associated
with fear, conflict, and strife" (35). By alluding to the brutality of
male dominance, Wollstonecraft makes one final appeal to her
potentially hostile audience.

In the context of *A Vindication*, we readily recognize the political implications of a sardonic joke about husbandly tyranny.
When violent comedy occurs in novels, however, the political
message may be misunderstood. Margaret Doody argues that critics have found Austen's comedy more satisfying than Burney's because of mixed feelings about Burney's violent comedy: "Austen
may or may not have 'superior' comic vision—it depends partly
on one's feelings about violence in comedy" (2). Although Doody
herself claims to only be a fan of violent comedy about "half the
time," she makes a strong case for the necessity of violence in
comedy that dramatizes women's lot in a male-dominated society.

Other critics do not see it this way. Katharine Rogers, in a
1990 book on Burney, repeatedly faults the author for resorting to
"inappropriately violent farce" (*Frances Burney* 30). Rogers's comments on Madame Duval's beating illuminate the complexity of
possible reactions to violent comedy: "Beating an elderly woman
and leaving her tied up in a ditch is not funny, nor is it appropriate punishment for her rude self-assertiveness, nor does it throw
light on the subjection of women. If Burney's point was that it was

acceptable to bully women in her society, she had already made it far more convincingly through the long-suffering Mrs. Mirvan, who spends her life accommodating to her brutish husband" (30). Rogers argues that since she already understands the subjection of women, she does not need the graphic reminders of violent comedy. However, her implication—that Mrs. Mirvan's persecution at the hands of Captain Mirvan would have been as clear to Burney's contemporaries as was Madame Duval's—does not take into account the numerous advice manuals that counseled women to accommodate their husbands at all costs. Some readers may have needed the example of Madame Duval in order to understand the example of Mrs. Mirvan.

Rogers views Burney's violent comedy as an aesthetic failing, as does Elizabeth Bergen Brophy, who calls the female footrace in *Evelina* "completely gratuitous," complaining that "it in no way furthers the development of the novel or significantly differentiates Orville and Evelina from the other characters" (262). Neither Brophy nor Rogers finds the female footrace at all humorous. Interestingly enough, in at least one of Burney's contemporary readers, "the race between the old women excited a roar of laughter" (*Early Diary* 241). Burney took it as high praise that her father laughed himself to tears while rereading *Evelina*, and she singled out his response to the old women's race for particular notice. One can only speculate on Burney's feelings about the footrace episode, but she must have taken some pleasure in getting a powerful male to read a satire on the brutal condition of women and to respond by laughing, notwithstanding the fact that he probably did not appreciate its subtlety.

We may distinguish two related types of violent comedy: the comedy of transgression and the comedy of exposure. The comedy of transgression exploits the author's self-consciousness about rules and boundaries by shamelessly violating conventions. In its overt aggression, this comedy takes too many liberties to appear often in published works, but it can occur with regularity in private writings, such as Austen's juvenilia. The comedy of exposure serves the less extreme purpose of revelation. Women writers may use it to dramatize society's brutal treatment of women by simultaneously ridiculing and sympathizing with outrageous female characters. Burney and Edgeworth produce scenes of comic exposure to challenge the system that makes women acceptable targets for comedy; female grotesques stand in for their creator's rebellious individuality. More than any other mode, violent comedy foregrounds the perilous position of the woman writer as one who transgresses against feminine decorum and exposes herself in the public sphere. Defiant, aggressive, and completely unladylike, violent comedy forces itself upon the reader's attention.

Confronted with the comedy of transgression in Austen's juvenilia, biographer John Halperin marvels at her early "perception and understanding of heartlessness." He puzzles over the darker side of *Lady Susan:* "Perhaps the most striking thing about the tale is the young Jane Austen's insight into the lower depths of the human character. Where, one cannot help wondering, did such a perspective come from?" (39, 47). Although Halperin connects what he refers to as Austen's "cynicism" to her position as a woman in a sexist society and admits that the juvenilia bear some relation to Austen's later work, he has little sympathy for the complexity of a woman's lot. By associating her acerbic wit with "a certain old-maidish waspishness" (54), he implies that it is something a good man could have eliminated from her character and forgets that it appeared long before Austen could have been termed an old maid.

Unruly women populate the comic landscape of Austen's juvenilia (collected in *Minor Works*). Self-assertive *and* self-conscious, these characters aggressively impose their will over and against a society which insists that they have none. Alice of "Jack and Alice" is one such transgressive heroine, a woman with "many rare & charming qualities, but Sobriety is not one of them" (23). Drinking reddens her cheeks and arouses her pugnacity; she almost punches a lady who declares that a woman can have too much color.[6] Alice's brusque defense of her sex comically suggests a need for women to overcome the restraints that make females colorless. "The Beautiful Cassandra," dedicated to Austen's sister, recounts a day in the life of a young girl who steals a bonnet, eats six ices and refuses to pay for them, knocks down a pastry cook, refuses to pay for a lengthy coach ride, and declares at the conclusion of her adventures, "This is a day well spent" (47). In Cassandra, we see a beloved sister asserting her female will in a comedy of social transgression, which Austen applauds for its critical self-liberation.

Topping the list of transgressive heroines, the murderous Anna Parker appears in a segment dedicated to Austen's niece Fanny as "my personal instructions" and "my Opinions & Admonitions on the conduct of Young Women" (170). The author describes Anna as "a Young Lady, whose feelings being too Strong for her Judgement led her into the commission of Errors which her Heart disapproved." Anna's letter punctures the lofty tones of this introduction. Sentimental phrasing clashes comically with the gravity of the heroine's offenses:

> Many have been the cares & vicissitudes of my past life . . . & the only consolation I feel for their bitterness is that on a close examination of my conduct, I am convinced that I have strictly deserved them. I murdered my father at a very early period of my Life, I have since murdered my Mother, and I am now going to murder my Sister. I have changed my religion so often that at present I have not an idea of any left. I have been a perjured witness in every public tryal for these past twelve Years; and I have forged my own will. In short there is scarcely a crime that I have not committed—But I am now going to reform. (174–75)

In spite of her contrite tone, Anna does not abandon her murderous course; the letter concludes with a reiteration of her declaration "I am now going to murder my Sister."

Whereas transgressive heroines in Austen's juvenilia provide cathartic releases from feminine restraints, comic sketches allowed her to transgress against the demands of modesty and voice some nasty truths about the condition of women. In "Sir William Montague," the eponymous hero would rather give up his beloved fiancé than sacrifice the first day of hunting for his wedding. He proceeds to murder a rival suitor, marry the woman who allegedly loved the rival, and privately marry the sister of the man he murdered. At the end of the fragment, Sir William is "violently in love" with yet another woman to whom he hopes to gain "free access" (42). Sir William's rampant abuse of women and unmitigated self-indulgence leave no doubt as to the young Austen's view of male power.

"Henry and Eliza," one of Austen's early "novels," contains examples of violent comedy that would be incomprehensible without reference to the negligent treatment of women in the eighteenth century and to conventional models of female development. Eliza's history of female degradation burlesques the family romance plot: the beginning of the tale finds Eliza an orphan in the custody of foster parents; the conclusion unravels her identity as the real daughter of that same couple.

In the comic recognition scene that takes place at the end of the "novel," Eliza's mother explains how she managed to lose her own daughter. After reminding her husband of a trip he took to America, at which time he "left [her] breeding," she recounts a series of flagrant misdeeds:

> Four months after you were gone, I was delivered of this Girl, but dreading your just resentment at her not proving the Boy you wished, I took her to a Haycock & laid her down. A few weeks afterwards, you returned, & fortunately for me, made no enquiries on the subject. Satisfied within myself of the welfare of my Child, I soon forgot I had one, insomuch that when, we shortly after found her in the very Haycock, I had placed her, I had no more idea of her being my own, than you had, & nothing I will venture to say would have recalled the circumstance to my remembrance, but my thus accidentally hearing her voice, which now strikes me as being the very counterpart of my own Child's. (38–39)

Austen clearly has fun taking potshots at the implausibility of conventional recognition scenes and domestic relations. However, the central message of this passage has more to do with social condemnation than with literary criticism. When Eliza's mother admits to having feared her husband's "just resentment" at the baby's gender, she discloses her complicity in an ideology that discounts female worth. A woman herself, the mother is nonetheless ready to leave her girl child exposed rather than take responsibility for bearing what society defines as an unworthy human being. Sexist ideology—as represented both by her assumption about the husband's displeasure and her own assimilation of it as "just"—demands that the girl be punished for her gender, that she be abandoned to the elements.

The mother's subsequent amnesia about her daughter can be viewed as an exaggerated version of the father's inability to remember details about his own wife. Immersed in an ideology that negates women's worth, Eliza's mother first rejects the daughter and then forgets her existence. Parodic elements of maternal solicitude—her confidence that the abandoned child is safe and her claim of being able to recognize her own child's voice—highlight the contradictions inherent in a woman's position as wife and mother within a culture that devalues women in part by sentimentalizing them. Austen shows in "Love and Freindship [sic]" that the devaluation of women affects how even young women see themselves and their sex. Laura and Sophia are united with and then abandoned by their grandfather, who gives them money and bids them remember that he has "done the Duty of A Grandfather" (92). The heroines later learn by accident that their mothers have both starved to death. Their immersion in masculinist values is so complete that they fail to link possible male neglect, such as their grandfather exhibited toward them, to their mothers' starvation. Instead, they casually accept the news.

Sophia suffers a comically feminine fate—she dies from one swoon too many. Her deathbed advice to Laura is deservedly famous: "Run mad as often as you chuse; but do not faint—" (102). In their embodiment of "femininity," Laura and Sophia reveal the masochism demanded by society of women in general. Their comic displays of sentiment typify the reflexive behavior of the unself-conscious female, a creature for whom Austen never shows much sympathy.

Throughout the juvenilia, Austen demonstrates an acute awareness of women's claustrophobic circumstances and a willingness to laughingly transgress against the strictures of ideal femininity. Austen felt free to indulge in violent comedy when she was writing for her immediate circle of friends and family; her juvenile comedy plays around with events that most people take dead seriously.

Significantly, none of Austen's early comic efforts was published during her lifetime, and her mature fiction seldom relies upon violent comedy. One striking exception occurs in *Persuasion*, in her seemingly callous reference to Mrs. Musgrove's "large fat sighings" over the untimely death of a son whom the narrator deems worthless. Unlike the unapologetic iconoclasm of the juvenilia, here Austen appends an explanation to her apparently cruel humor: "Personal size and mental sorrow have certainly no necessary proportions. A large bulky figure has as good a right to be in deep affliction, as the most graceful set of limbs in the world. But, fair or not fair, there are unbecoming conjunctions, which reason will patronize in vain,—which taste cannot tolerate,—which ridicule will seize" (68). Austen's comic handling of Mrs. Musgrove's grief has made many readers uncomfortable and has been seen as malicious and not in the least bit funny.[7] Indeed, Mrs. Musgrove seems like one of those characters that Virginia Woolf describes as having been "born merely to give Jane Austen the supreme delight of slicing their heads off" ("Jane Austen" 140).

But Claudia Johnson suggests a possible reading for the passage which partially de-fangs it: "The narrator . . . brings up the grotesqueness of Mrs. Musgrove's grief only to ponder the irrationality of our response to it" (150). Johnson sees Austen as taking on the authority of cultural aesthetic standards in order to expose their irrationality. According to such standards, large bodies, such as Mrs. Musgrove's, must express grief differently than small bodies do. The disjunction between Mrs. Musgrove's size and her expression of grief parallels the sexist assumption of a disjunction in stature and strength in women. Rationally, we should know that the sincerity of Mrs. Musgrove's grief has nothing to do with her size and that a small woman like Anne Elliot can be as strong in some ways as a man like Wentworth.

Johnson believes that Austen deliberately seeks to undermine cultural perspectives, implicitly in the case of Mrs. Musgrove, more explicitly in Anne Elliot's. But to take Johnson's insight in a different direction, we might also say that the perspective that deems a large woman's grieving sighs worthy of ridicule belongs to the broader system that endorses frailty in women as attractive to look at and that eroticizes female suffering. Mrs. Musgrove's intrusiveness is undeniably physical—in the scene above, she sits between Wentworth and Anne—and the narrator's commentary draws attention to her physicality. Besides pointing out the injustices of her culture's aesthetics, Austen underscores the physical foundation of some of these standards, in particular, the enfranchised physical vulnerability of women.

In this rare example of violent comedy in her adult novels, Austen strikes a different chord than in her juvenilia. There, the comedy laughingly violates social restrictions upon female behavior; here, she suggests the extent to which these restrictions determine society's perception of "the female"—an epistemological category. To challenge social constructions of the female, Austen employs a brand of comedy that Edgeworth and Burney develop at greater length—the comedy of female exposure.

Mary Russo has described the danger of exposure as "a specifically feminine danger." A woman who makes "a spectacle of herself" invites ridicule and gossip; she brings shame upon herself. The trouble is, Russo makes clear, that it can happen to any woman in an unguarded moment and, more disturbingly, that it often happens to those whose bodies refuse to conform to social norms:

> For a woman, making a spectacle out of herself had more to do with a kind of inadvertency and loss of boundaries: the possessors of large, aging, and dimpled thighs displayed at the public beach, of overly rouged cheeks, of a voice shrill in laughter, or of a sliding bra strap—a loose, dingy bra

strap especially—were at once caught out by fate and blameworthy. It was my impression that these women had done something wrong, had stepped, as it were, into the limelight out of turn—too young or too old, too early or too late—and yet anyone, any *woman*, could make a spectacle out of herself if she was not careful. (213)

Boundaries between acceptable feminine pageantry and disorderly female display vary from culture to culture and shift over time, but the danger of becoming a spectacle poses a constant threat in societies that objectify women. The culture that expects women to practice what Rousseau called "the art of getting looked at" (373) offers no guarantees that they will get looked at for the right reasons.

Sexist societies objectify women in order to control them more thoroughly. When the female body is laden with sexual significance for men and subject to violation by prying eyes, women must voluntarily restrict themselves to their socially sanctioned spheres or suffer the consequences. Standards of beauty almost always reflect the viewpoint of the male gaze, a gaze that reduces women to the sum total of their body parts.[8]

In eighteenth-century fiction, women's bodies tend to mirror their inner character. Thus, heroines are generically attractive, and only comic characters—or "female grotesques," as Russo calls them—have distinctive physical traits. But it is important to recognize that not all female grotesques carry the same kind of cultural baggage and that gender may alter the inflections of an author's comedy.[9] In antifeminist fiction, the female grotesque usually functions to censor and punish women who threaten male power.[10] Fiction with feminist sympathies, on the other hand, offers up female grotesques as challenges to male-centered definitions of femininity.

Feminist writers position the grotesque female in a context that dramatizes the violence of a male-dominated society. Since, as Dorinda Outram points out, eighteenth-century novelists imply a connection between "the history of the heroines' bodies and the nature of the public order itself" (140), the status of female grotesques in women's fiction should tell us something about the author's negotiation between submission to male authority and outright rebellion. In their scenes of comic exposure, Edgeworth and Burney display an understanding of the problems of objectifying women. They invite readers to laugh, but they also refuse to blame the victims and instead ask us to blame the system that allows women to be made into spectacles.

Edgeworth was herself victimized in physical and violent ways by the reigning standards of feminine beauty. At boarding school, she endured "all the usual tortures of backboards, iron collars, and dumb-bells, with the unusual one of being swung by the neck to draw out the muscles and increase the growth, a signal failure in her case" (qtd. in Butler 72). Self-described as "little, and ugly" (qtd. in Butler 73), Edgeworth was acutely aware of conventional standards of beauty and of her shortcomings (at the age of twenty-one, she stood four feet seven inches tall). Moreover, her father's succession of wives provided her with firsthand experience of the disposable nature of female life in the eighteenth-century world. Her father's first two wives died young (one at thirty, the next at twenty-nine) and his last of four marriages involved a woman a year younger than Maria herself. Edgeworth's position as the eldest daughter in a family of twenty ensured her the labor of a wife and mother even though she bore the stigma of being an old maid.

Authorship not only freed Edgeworth from the confining circumstances of female existence, it offered her a means of self-presentation independent of physical appearance. Sadly, Edgeworth thought of herself as a being whose form and content were at odds. When, for example, her father suggested taking her on a trip abroad to seek a husband, Edgeworth expressed confidence in her intellect, but doubted that any man could overlook her body for her mind: "The idea . . . of being shewn, & stared at & criticised as the author of Prac Ed &c would be highly disagreeable to me—I know my own defects of person too well to wish to be placed in 'horrid relief'—The chance of my meeting, abroad, with any person who should have so much judgment & so little taste as to overlook these defects & in spite of them to become sincerely attached to me is I think scarcely worth calculating—

There is 34 to one against me" (qtd. in Butler 187). To make a spectacle of herself, Edgeworth thought, she had only to make an appearance and her celebrity as an author would draw unwelcome attention to her physicality. The standards of conventional beauty, then as now, probably made the majority of women feel inadequate and made women with unusual features, such as Edgeworth's petite stature, feel particularly vulnerable to exposure.

Edgeworth incorporated female grotesques into her fiction as rampant feminists. Mrs. Freke in *Belinda* is the most fully developed of these comic butts, and her name betrays Edgeworth's ambivalence toward contemporary radical feminism. I have already discussed Mrs. Freke's role as a trickster figure, but placing her between two other feminist grotesques will help us see her importance in the violent comedy of exposure. In Edgeworth's versions of this comedy, the feminist character either draws attention to herself or leads other women into situations in which people watch and ridicule them. Edgeworth clearly understood the dangers inherent in radical feminism, and her feminist grotesques reveal a degree of conservatism in the author. But they also function to tear away "the thin veil with which politeness covers domestic misery" (*Belinda* 4).

In *Angelina; or, L'amie Inconnue*, the heroine is led astray by a caricatured Wollstonecraftian, "Araminta." When Anne Warwick reads Araminta's autobiographical novel, she changes her name to Angelina (a romanticized version of her own name) and runs away from home to seek the author who has stirred up her rebellious spirits. Like Don Quixote or Arabella in Charlotte Lennox's *The Female Quixote* (1752), Angelina believes everything she reads. On the road to meet her idol, Angelina repeatedly makes a spectacle of herself. She encourages a man with a harp to play for her, viewing him as a rustic figure from a bygone time; when she extravagantly rebukes him for playing a modern tune, he concludes from her excessive behavior that she must be mad. She tries to recite poetry in the evening air only to be accosted by a band of urchins who beg for money. At one point, when she attempts "to make a display of sensibility," "a fine theatrical scene" (165), she is openly mocked by an audience of lower-class spectators. Although the narrator reports her exploits in a light, ironic tone, the reader is privy to the shame of Angelina's exposure. Her folly leads her into situations that strain the comic effect, as when her feet bleed because she wears delicate slippers instead of walking shoes.

When Angelina finally reaches Araminta, truth and fiction violently collide. Not only is Araminta's real name less than romantic—Miss Hodges—but she lives in squalor and is physically unattractive. The narrator directs us to imagine "a woman, with a face and figure which seemed to have been intended for a man, with a voice and gesture capable of setting even man, 'imperial man' at defiance" (222). As in the case of Mrs. Freke, Miss Hodges's eccentricity originates from a masculine build. She even has "a voice more masculine than her looks" (223). In short, "Miss Hodges was not the sort of person our heroine expected to see."

In *Angelina*, Edgeworth employs the female grotesque for fairly conservative ends. Although she avoids censoring feminist ideas per se, she lampoons Anne's romanticism and Miss Hodges's feminism so thoroughly that one might think she opposed all feminist ends. But the moral of this story, which appears among Edgeworth's *Moral Tales for Young People,* is that young women should use good sense and judgment rather than trust in rhetoric and romance. Angelina's romantic posing has little to do with practical feminism; it has much more to do with egotism masquerading as sentiment. Edgeworth uses the female grotesque and the perils of female exposure as controlling devices in the tale: if women do not use sense and judgment, the story cautions, they risk making spectacles of themselves. Anne Warwick's final enlightenment drives the moral home by brutally contrasting truth and fiction, sentimental rhetoric and seedy reality: "The disorder, &c.—for the words must be said—slatternly dirty appearance of her Araminta's dress, and of every thing in her apartment, were such as would make a Hell of Heaven." Further, the thought of retreating to a cottage with Miss Hodges (and her lover) "overwhelmed our heroine with the double fear of wretchedness and ridicule" (330).

When we turn from Edgeworth's fiction for young people to her novels, we encounter more complex versions of the female grotesque and more sophisticated relations between the feminist and other women. In *Belinda,* Harriet Freke plays a trickster role in influencing the heroine to think for herself, but she also leads Lady Delacour into absurd and dangerous situations that reveal the depth of cultural hostility to women who step out of their feminine roles. In her own person, Lady Delacour embodies the basis of women's violent comedy: her marital life is a state of warfare, and her body is aging in a society that valorizes youth; yet, to exert a measure of control in the midst of harsh reality, she laughs and maintains a comic front. Lady Delacour's comments when narrating her story to Belinda shed further light on the workings of violent comedy: "Life is a tragicomedy! Though the critics will allow of no such thing in their books, it is a true representation of what passes in the world, and of all lives mine has been the most grotesque mixture, or alternation, I should say, of tragedy and comedy" (47).

A scene of comic transgression, orchestrated by Mrs. Freke, gives Lady Delacour a breast wound, which she strives to keep secret for most of the novel and which is described at one point as "a hideous spectacle" (24). Mrs. Freke, herself possessed of masculine strength (and "downright ugly" [34]), encourages Lady Delacour to fight a duel against Mrs. Luttridge—a gamester, politician, and excellent shot. Against her better judgment, Lady Delacour agrees to the duel and dons masculine attire; in her challenge she states that, although she has "the misfortune to be a woman," she will nonetheless fight like a man (45). The duel scene begins on a note both sombre and ludicrous, with Lady Delacour fearful, the prospect of injury great, and the combatants asserting their manliness. In the end, however, the duel is not fought. Lady Delacour sustains a wound in the breast when her pistol misfires, and the combatants become a spectacle for a mob. Here, the comedy changes from one of transgression to that of exposure: "I had scarcely discharged my pistol when we heard a loud shout on the other side of the barn, and a crowd of town's people, country people, and haymakers, came pouring down the lane towards us, with rakes and pitchforks in their hands. An English mob is really a formidable thing. . . . [T]he untutored sense of propriety amongst these rustics was so shocked at the idea of a duel fought by women in *men's clothes*, that I verily believe they would have thrown us into the river with all their hearts" (47). One conclusion that Lady Delacour draws from the mob's behavior is that "they would not have been half so much scandalized if we had boxed in petticoats," that is, if the women had been on display as conventional female bodies, a more legitimate form of spectacle. "The want of these petticoats," declares Lady Delacour, "had nearly proved our destruction, or at least our disgrace" (47).

When Lady Delacour and Mrs. Freke act in socially unacceptable ways, they are not only vulnerable to condemnation but also to malicious treatment. As a "female outlaw" (231), Mrs. Freke offers Lady Delacour a new perspective on women's status as outsiders. Lady Delacour pays a high price for this insight, but the novel provides other examples of female degradation that women experience as a part of life—a marriage market in which men dissect them into "eyes, nose, mouth . . . legs" (17) and alcoholic husbands (Lord Delacour and his comrades). The mob scene only emphasizes women's precarious position.

By allowing the female grotesque to have some legitimate influence in *Belinda*, Edgeworth paves the way for the recuperation of this character that will take place in *Helen*. Esther Clarendon begins the novel as an eccentric grotesque, but by the conclusion, she stands in high favor as a defender of women and a true friend in need. Grotesque not in her appearance—Helen describes her as "really handsome" (45)—but in her behavior, Miss Clarendon is an independent woman in every sense of the word. She lives in a remote castle, refuses to accept social hypocrisy, and, like Mrs. Freke, insists upon calling things by their right names. Although Helen initially finds her character unpleasant, she ends up accepting Miss Clarendon's offer of asylum when rumor and scandal tarnish her own reputation. Miss Clarendon describes herself to Helen with a deliberately indelicate metaphor: "We shall get on, I see, Miss Stanley, if you can get over the first bitter outside of me—a hard outside, difficult to crack—stains delicate fingers, may be, . . . in the opening, but a good walnut you will find it, taken with a grain of salt" (46).

Miss Clarendon's sturdy frame and robust health set her in contrast to the emerging Victorian heroine. The narrator describes her as "peculiarly constituted" (368), but in a novel that favors honesty over social lying, her peculiarity is a virtue. In one comic scene, Miss Clarendon seeks treatment from a male dentist, St. Leger Swift, whose ideas about female delicacy are ludicrously out of place in his professional capacity. This scene demonstrates through juxtaposition the healthy eccentricity of Miss Clarendon. As a dentist, this man ought to be able to view a patient's teeth in a professional manner, but instead he cannot properly evaluate Miss Clarendon's toothache because he feels compelled (and entitled) to comment on their aesthetic qualities.

> "Fine teeth, fine! Nothing to complain of here, surely," said St. Leger. "As fine a show of ivory as ever I beheld. 'Pon my reputation, I know many a fine lady who would give—all but her eyes for such a set."
> "I must have this tooth out," said Miss Clarendon, pointing to the offender. (368)

Although Miss Clarendon is utterly matter-of-fact about the process of having her tooth pulled, St. Leger refuses to see her as anything but a nervous young female: "Every lady's nervous nowadays, more or less" (369). When he does attempt a diagnosis, he looks at the wrong tooth (in spite of Miss Clarendon's having pointed out the one that was causing her pain) and asserts that there is nothing wrong with her.

Eventually Miss Clarendon grows exasperated with his incompetence and takes aggressive action:

> But here Mr. St. Leger Swift, starting suddenly, withdrawing his hand from Miss Clarendon's mouth, exclaimed,—
> "My finger, ma'am! but never mind, never mind, all in the day's work. Casualty—contingencies—no consequence." (370)

Miss Clarendon does what no eighteenth- or nineteenth-century heroine is able to do—she bites the hand that claims to serve her. In spite of her less-than-elegant gesture, St. Leger resorts again to gallant phrases: "I—always am for the young and fair, that's my foible." In the end, Miss Clarendon walks out, preferring to bear the toothache than to put up with any more of the dentist's non-sensical behavior. He calls after her and her aunt, "Young lady's nervous, said so from the first. Nerves! nerves! all—open the door there—Nerves all" (371). His inability to see past the stereotypes about female behavior and acknowledge Miss Clarendon's forth-right individuality—even aggression—make him the comic butt of this scene, not her.

Because Edgeworth redefines the female grotesque in the per-son of Miss Clarendon and makes her feminism and assertiveness virtues instead of character flaws, the comedy of exposure in this scene ultimately involves violence against the man. The scene with the dentist represents a successful skirmish against male power, one in which the woman begins as object, but exits with her sub-jectivity intact. Miss Clarendon is an exceptional character, a woman with "a house of [her] own" (386) who exerts a direct and salutary influence on the heroine. Under her care, Helen gains strength, and through her actions, the course of scandal against Helen is halted. Interestingly, Miss Clarendon nurses a private af-fection for Granville Beauclerc, Helen's suitor, but does not enter into competition with the other woman or behave jealously to-ward her. Miss Clarendon may make a spectacle of herself when she speaks her mind and upholds the truth in public, but she clearly has the author's endorsement.

Burney's fiction contains more violent comedy than either Aus-ten's or Edgeworth's and probably more than any other writer of her day. Unlike Austen, whose violent comedy virtually disap-pears in her later works, or Edgeworth, who uses it sparingly and with varying degrees of intensity, Burney includes scenes in every novel that continue to shock readers. Not all of Burney's violence is comic, as Julia Epstein's study *The Iron Pen* makes clear. Epstein connects Burney's "obsession with violence and hostility" to her position in a society that placed strict controls on women. Epstein argues, "Surface propriety was purchased at the price of internal rage," a rage which then erupts in Burney's fictional "scenes of assault and moments of disguised anger" (5). Keeping in mind that Burney used humor as a coping and survival strategy, we can see in her violent comedy a desire to communicate a sense of solidarity with other women.

Burney's violent comedy vibrates between two poles: the previously described comedy of exposure and the comedy of confinement, which is directly related to that of transgression. An entry from her early journal shows that even before her first novel, she was painfully aware of the restrictions placed upon women and that she could turn the tables somewhat by making these restrictions a subject for laughter. In this entry from 1774, Burney has made it known to an assembled group that she intends to write a conduct book of her own, so her friends eagerly interrogate her about it:

> "[I]t will contain all the *newest fashioned* regulations. In the first place, you are never again to cough."
>
> "Not to *cough?*," exclaimed every one at once; "but how are you to help it?"
>
> "As to *that*," answered I, "I am not clear about it myself, as I own I am guilty sometimes of doing it; but it is as much a mark of ill breeding, as it is to *laugh*; which is a thing that Lord Chesterfield has stigmatized." . . .
>
> "And pray," said Mr. Crisp, making a fine affected face, "may you *simper?*"
>
> "You may *smile* Sir," answered I; "but to *laugh* is quite abominable; though not quite so bad as *sneezing*, or *blowing the nose*." . . .
>
> "But pray, is it permitted," said Mr. Crisp, very drily, "to *breathe?*"
>
> "*That* is not yet, I believe, quite exploded," answered I; . . . "I shall only tell you in general that whatever is natural, plain, or easy, is entirely banished from polite circles." (*Early Diary* 325–26)

In Burney's conduct book run mad, all natural behavior is re-

stricted and frowned upon; the body becomes a thing to be controlled, and every gesture exposes one to censure or ridicule.

Eleven years later, when Burney returned to this theme,
shortly before her five-year confinement at court, she included
even more graphic elements of violent suppression. Here are her
"Directions for coughing, sneezing, or moving, before the King
and Queen":

> In the first place you must not cough. If you find
> a cough tickling in your throat, you must arrest it
> from making any sound; if you find yourself chok-
> ing with the forbearance, you must choke—but
> not cough. In the second place, you must not
> sneeze. If you have a vehement cold, you must
> take no notice of it; if your nose membranes feel
> a great irritation, you must hold your breath; if a
> sneeze still insists upon making its way, you must
> oppose it, by keeping your teeth grinding to-
> gether; if the violence of the repulse breaks some
> blood-vessel, you must break the blood vessel—
> but not sneeze. (*Diary and Letters* 227–28)

Violent image begets violent image as the directions continue.
Next, the author commands that if "a black pin runs into your
head," one must not move to take it out. Neither pain nor tears,
anguish nor streaming blood, should cause one to budge in the
presence of royalty.

Burney offers one ghastly consolation to the suffering aco-
lyte: "If, however, the agony is very great, you may, privately, bite
the inside of your cheek, or of your lips, for a little relief; taking
care, meanwhile, to do it so cautiously as to make no apparent dent
outwardly. And, with that precaution, if you even gnaw a piece
out, it will not be minded: only be sure either to swallow it or
commit it to a corner of the inside of your mouth till they are
gone—for you must not spit" (228). Although none of Burney's
conduct rules are gender specific, her early knowledge of restraint
almost certainly came from her training as a well-bred, middle-
class daughter. Ironically, her appointment to the queen's ser-

vice—conceived of as a reward for her novel-writing talents—almost resulted in her death. The seriousness of the stakes justifies the violence of her imagery. In this comedy of confinement, Burney indicates that the self can be tortured by decorum and that the restraints of service can lead to self-destruction.

If Burney was painfully aware of the dangers of confinement, she was even more terrified at the thought of exposure. She hid while members of her family read her work, became nearly hysterical when her father discovered a page of her diary, and shrank from the public gaze. To exorcize this fear, she wrote numerous comic scenes in which women become spectacles. The old women's footrace in *Evelina,* which afforded Burney's father much laughter, typifies the balance between horror and humor that Burney maintains in her violent comedy. Evelina feels pity at the sight of the "so weak, so infirm, so feeble" old women; by contrast, the other spectators find the women intrinsically funny: "for they no sooner came forward, than they were greeted with a laugh from every beholder" (311). In a society that glamorizes youthful beauty, aging women are reflexively viewed as female grotesques. Although Evelina describes this scene as "truly ridiculous," she takes the women's feelings into account. Her report of the first leg of the race indicates her deep ambivalence: "When the signal was given for them to set off, the poor creatures, feeble and frightened, ran against each other, and, neither of them able to support the shock, they both fell to the ground" (311–12). In fact, Evelina evinces so much sympathy for the old women that we might well ask whether this scene is supposed to be funny at all.

Rather than argue for one appropriate response to the old women's footrace, I would like to use it as a borderline case to discuss a broader point about our response to violent comedy. In order for violence involving people to seem comic, a certain objectification must take place. When someone falls down in front of us in the street, for example, we normally respond by rushing to his or her aid, not by laughing. In this instance, we immediately identify with the person. When it happens on television, however, we are just as likely to laugh as to feel philanthropic. Comic response can be impeded by what Wallace Stevens describes in *The Necessary Angel* as "the pressure of reality" (13). According to

Freud, one's degree of involvement in the painful aspects of an experience determines its comic potential:

> [T]he release of distressing affects is the greatest obstacle to the emergence of the comic. As soon as the aimless movement does damage, or the stupidity leads to mischief, or the disappointment causes pain, the possibility of comic effect is at an end. This is true, at all events, for a person who cannot ward off such unpleasure, who is himself its victim or is obliged to have a share in it; whereas a person who is not concerned shows by his demeanour that the situation involved contains everything that is required for a comic effect. (228)

On the one hand, the slapstick elements in the female footrace scene affect our visual, aesthetic imagination and our sense of propriety: the comic effects arise out of incongruity. Evelina's pity, on the other hand, and her description of the women as "poor creatures, feeble and frightened" impose their subjective reality on us and draw out our sympathy. Thus, Doody writes of the footrace, "The action spills over the boundary lines of comic acceptability" (56). In most violent comedy, the reality we suppress by laughing continues to reverberate under the surface.

Since Burney's fiction contains so much violence, we must frequently choose between laughter or sorrow. When Madame Duval is beaten, stripped, and left screaming in a ditch, can we find this humorous? Doody argues that Madame Duval's character "allowed Burney to express astonishment and anger at the violence with which women really are treated while apparently going along with a jest" (51). I would further suggest that Burney invites us to go along with the joke so that we may learn from our objectifying laughter. Burney takes the jokes against women out of the hands of misogynist satirists and robs them of their easy targets. Her violent comedy has a built-in feminist critique. If we find it painfully humorous, we are one step closer to understanding her anger at and defiance of the brutal treatment of women when we recognize our own complicity.

In a number of scenes in Burney's novels, female exposure leads to violent comedy. For example, in *Cecilia*, Mr. Monkton and Mr. Briggs accost and embarrass the heroine during a masquerade ball that ends with a comic destruction of the room in which the ball is held. In *Camilla*, lower-class people ridicule Eugenia's deformities when she and Camilla are trapped in Mr. Dubster's summerhouse. Also in *Camilla*, Mrs. Mittin and Camilla wander around the seaside town, get mistaken for robbers because of their eccentric behavior, and eventually find themselves cornered by a mob.

In *The Wanderer*, Burney introduces a feminist grotesque figure who embodies the situation of the female comic writer who produces violent comedy. Elinor Joddrell, like Juliet, must accept a diminished position as a result of social conventions. Elinor plays a double role: her impassioned speeches and suicide attempts should make her a tragic figure, but her delivery, her timing, and her overly dramatic staging and costuming all combine to reduce her to a figure of farce. Her character fits the comic mold—eccentric, grotesque—at the same time as her emotions and cleverness contribute "consequence" to an otherwise one-dimensional personage. Like Mrs. Freke, Elinor enjoys novelty; she admires the "freaks and vagaries that give zest to life" (20). But whereas Mrs. Freke appropriates the feminist role in order to gain social status as a new personality, Elinor sincerely values the "rights of woman" and plays out her eccentricities to an unsympathetic audience.

Elinor refuses to be silent and repeatedly makes a spectacle of herself. She obsessively discusses her life in terms of comedy and tragedy and views suicide as the necessary validation of her seriousness. Before her first attempt to take her life, she explains to Juliet that her "plot" is about to unfold, adding, "though I know not whether the catastrophe will be tragic or comic, I am prepared in my part for either" (144). At another point she puzzles over how to describe the drama of her life: "the comedy, tragedy, or farce, of my existence" (148). In a kind of gothic comedy, the suicide attempts become more absurd with repetition. After the first one, when Juliet distracts her from stabbing herself, Elinor exclaims, "What farce is this?" (169).

In the aftermath of her second suicide attempt, Elinor refers to her life as a "burlesque dumb show" and rejects its "farcical forms" (355). She laughs bitterly at the thought of what the world would say "to find that I still live, after the pompous funeral orations, declaimed by myself, upon my death." She addresses the world's laughter, claiming that only an adherence to conventions could save her from being an object of general mockery: "Well, ye that laugh, laugh on! for I, when not sick of myself, laugh too! But, to escape mockery, we must all be guided one by another; all do, and all say, the very same thing" (377). In spite of the embarrassment of her first two failures at suicide, Elinor makes yet another elaborately staged attempt. She lures both Juliet and Harleigh to a church at night where they discover her in a shroud, with an engraved tombstone and a coffin ready and waiting for her final act, but all to no avail. Once more, she refers to her life as a "tragi-comedy" and curses the length of the final act. Although Elinor ultimately survives, her life offers a tragicomic commentary on contemporary feminism. She describes herself as one who has "strayed from the beaten road" only "to discover that all others are pathless" (836). Death would be a path of sorts, but Elinor must continue to live out the bitter comedy of female existence.

Nonetheless, Elinor, as a rich, unmarried woman, can cast her reputation to the winds and claim a degree of independence that would have been unknown to most women. She can finance her eccentricities and stand at a distance from the ridicule of the world. Initially a caricatured feminist who mouths revolutionary statements to shock her audience, Elinor emerges as a latter-day Cassandra, whose message, though taken for madness, cannot be refuted.

I end my discussion of violent comedy with Burney's Elinor Joddrell not because this character is so funny—in fact, she and her creator may be those who could see the most humor in her situation—but because she testifies to the effort it takes to translate pain into comedy. Since Sandra Gilbert and Susan Gubar's landmark study, *The Madwoman in the Attic*, feminist critics have attributed signs of madness, debility, and disease in women's texts to the condition of women under patriarchy. Abandoned women, like Bertha Mason in *Jane Eyre*, have come to stand for the submerged anger of all women who are confined within a system that restricts their growth and limits their development.

Jane Eyre's description of Bertha Mason's laughter reveals a connection to the laughter of the female comic writer and suggests a possible response. Jane has just been discussing her solitary walks in which she contemplates the situation of women, concluding, "It is thoughtless to condemn them, or laugh at them, if they seek to do more or learn more than custom has pronounced necessary for their sex." Bertha Mason's laugh, which Jane mistakenly attributes to Grace Poole, reinforces the feminist message: "When thus alone, I not unfrequently heard Grace Poole's laugh: the same peal, the same low, slow, ha! ha! which, when first heard, had thrilled me" (141). Just as Bertha Mason's "goblin ha! ha!" defies all attempts to silence her (238), the violent comedy of Burney, Edgeworth, and Austen demands an audience.

Theirs is not a comedy of madness, however; it is a comedy of strength. Comic strategies freed these middle-class British writers to promote a feminist message in their works. My purpose throughout this study has been to put their comedy in its historical context so that its subversiveness can come to light. Like Jane Eyre, these eighteenth-century writers thrilled to the sound of strange laughter. "You only have to look at the Medusa straight on to see her," writes Hélène Cixous, "And she's not deadly. She's beautiful and she's laughing" (255). Burney, Edgeworth, and Austen shared in the laugh of the Medusa, a laughing feminism that has been overlooked for too long.

Notes

Preface

1. The admiration of the two younger authors for Burney is well documented. Edgeworth even wrote to Burney at one point, asking if she would be interested in corresponding with an isolated Irish writer, but received no reply. Austen listed only books by these two authors in her impassioned defense of the novel in *Northanger Abbey*.

2. See also Moira Ferguson's anthology, *First Feminists*.

3. Kelly connects Austen's brand of feminism to the political issues of the Romantic period and indicates that then, as now, it would have been better to speak of feminism in the plural than to think of it as a unified set of ideas that transcend historical and cultural specificity.

4. Comic theory has never enjoyed a precise vocabulary. Even the great eighteenth-century lexicographer Samuel Johnson balked at the prospect of defining "comedy," remarking at the outset of an essay on this topic that "definitions are hazardous" (*Rambler* No. 125).

5. See Claudia Johnson's *Equivocal Beings* and *Jane Austen*; Mary Poovey's *The Proper Lady and the Woman Writer*; Kristina Straub's *Divided Fictions*; Julia Epstein's *The Iron Pen*; and Beth Kowaleski-Wallace's *Their Fathers' Daughters*.

Chapter 1

1. Laughter's most adamant eighteenth-century opponent, Lord Chesterfield, condemned this form of behavior as vulgar and inconsistent with a gentleman's comportment: "In my mind, there is noth-

ing so illiberal, and so ill-bred, as audible laughter" (49). He particularly despised "the disagreeable noise that it makes, and the shocking distortions of the face that it occasions" (49). Chesterfield's disgust stemmed, in part, from his contempt for the lower classes: "Loud laughter is the mirth of the mob, who are only pleased with silly things" (78). He advised his son to distinguish himself from the "mob" by controlling his laughter: "I could heartily wish, that you may often be seen to smile, but never heard to laugh while you live" (49). His nervousness about the lower-class taint and physical exposure that laughter entailed resembles, as we shall see, the attitudes expressed toward women's laughter by eighteenth-century conduct-book writers.

2. In "An Essay on the Freedom of Wit and Humour," Shaftesbury qualifies his defense of laughter by setting up boundaries between laughing gentlemen and their potential targets: "I am writing . . . in defence only of the liberty of *the club*, and of that sort of freedom which is taken amongst gentlemen and friends who know one another perfectly well. . . . The public is not, on any account, to be laughed at to its face" (53).

3. For a discussion of how the new domestic woman polarized class interests, see Nancy Armstrong's *Desire and Domestic Fiction*.

4. In sentimental comedy, according to Goldsmith, characters are basically good and have an "abundance of sentiment and feeling." "If they happen to have Faults or Foibles," he tells us, "the Spectator is taught not only to pardon, but to applaud them, in consideration of the goodness of their hearts; so that Folly, instead of being ridiculed, is commended" (188). In other words, sentimental comedy deals in the laughter of the heart and precludes critical laughter by striking a bargain with the audience's affections.

5. Robert Hume argues that Goldsmith's essay was mainly a publicity stunt to get more people into the theaters by making them believe that comedy was dying. Hume surveys plays that were being presented in the last third of the eighteenth century and shows that comedy was, in fact, alive and well. Richard Bevis, in his more detailed study, *The Laughing Tradition*, comes to the same conclusion.

6. See Stuart Tave's discussion in *The Amiable Humorist* of these shifts in taste (106–77).

7. I adopt this somewhat awkward construction in order to avoid the

conceptually unwieldy "feminized humor," which implies, even as it strives to avoid, an essentialist basis. Since "amiable humor" (Stuart Tave's term) does not carry an inflection of gender traits (the new comedy did consist of what were thought of as "feminine" traits) and "domestic humor" merely suggests humor in a domestic setting, I employ the variant "domesticated" to indicate the pressure of the domestic ideal upon humor. This distinction is particularly important when discussing the works of writers such as Burney, Edgeworth, and Austen, who wrote social comedies with domestic settings but who did not necessarily write "domesticated" or "feminized" comedy.

8. Domesticated humor, however, was more an ideal than a reality. It was one thing to reject critical laughter; it was quite another to find satisfying but uncensorious comic writing. Theatergoers and readers responded to this dilemma by treating all comedy as if it were domesticated. They increasingly ignored the critical aspects of comedy and focused instead on the indulging of characters' foibles. Comedy that could not be pressed into the service of the domestic ideal came to be dismissed as vulgar or "low." For the most part, women writers could be easily accommodated to the domestic model since their subject matter always involved women's lives, which were, by definition, private lives. Because the actions of the novels involved women, many readers automatically considered the works "light" and were prepared to adopt an indulgent perspective toward them.

9. For more specific discussions of the evolution of the terms "wit" and "humor" during the seventeenth and eighteenth centuries, see Louis Cazamian's *The Development of English Humor* (387–413), Edward W. Tayler's introduction to *Literary Criticism of Seventeenth-Century England*, J. E. Spingarn's introduction to *Critical Essays of the Seventeenth Century*, Gerald Chapman's essay "On Wit and Humor," and Stuart Tave's *The Amiable Humorist*. Virtually all of these studies address the class interests involved in the opposition of the two qualities, but none suggests that there might be a gender issue operating as well.

10. In spite of his promotion of the "feminine" virtues of humor, however, Hunt includes no women humorists in his anthology; moreover, his examples frequently focus on women as targets of male humor. Hunt's examples not only contributed to a growing percep-

tion of women's humorlessness, they also promoted images of female inferiority. For instance, he cites essayist Richard Steele's satire on Mary Astell's proposal for a female academy (*Tatler* No. 32), Addison's mockery of women who engage in politics (*Spectator* No. 81), and Byron's lampooning of the learned Donna Inez in *Don Juan*. That Hunt classifies his samples according to comic techniques makes his antifeminist choices even more pernicious, since they thereby acquire an air of universality.

11. When novelist and essayist J. B. Priestley came to write about English humor in the twentieth century, he focused exclusively on the domesticated variety, citing the private nature of the national temperament as the source of a subtle but genial kind of humor: "English humour . . . is curiously private and domestic . . . it is part of the atmosphere of the place, a hazy light on things; it manifests itself in innumerable slow grins and chuckles" (5). He leaves no doubt that the proper site of English laughter is within the enclosed domestic space: "everything in England that is of any importance is private and personal, . . . even our jokes have walls and hedges around them" (4). In Priestley's view, hostile laughter has no place within those walls; at most, there may be some "tender mockery" among friends. True humor radiates from the family circle: "It is to be found, of course, in some of the world's greatest literature, but it is also to be found, bubbling away, round the nearest corner, wherever there is a happy family. Husbands and wives, fathers and children, if they happen to be affectionate, fairly shrewd, and laughter-loving, appear to one another as comic characters in the best tradition of humour. The literature of this kind only universalizes a domestic joke" (16). Priestley's focus on the happy family as the basic unit for English humor reveals some of the pressures that made the domestic ideal such an attractive model for late-eighteenth-century and nineteenth-century audiences. The ability to barricade one's family away from the damaging effects of the world of commerce and industry became a sign of prestige in the Victorian period. "Walls" and "hedges" blocked off the still more private "home."

12. On the evolution of the family in early modern England, see Lawrence Stone's seminal study, *The Family, Sex and Marriage in England 1500–1800*.

13. A host of twentieth-century articles grapple with the issue of female humorlessness; their titles testify to its persistence: "Women

Have No Sense of Humor" (Allen), "But They Don't Seem to Know It" (Thurber), "Why More Women Aren't Funny" (Beatts), "Have Women a Sense of Humor" (Burdette), "Can Women Be Funny?" (Eimerl), "We Witless Women" (Hugh-Jones), "Are Women Humorous?" (Newell).

14. Ellen Pollak analyzes the "myth of passive womanhood" in *The Poetics of Sexual Myth*.

15. For an excellent discussion of *The Witlings* and the family controversy it occasioned, see Margaret Doody's *Frances Burney* (66–98).

16. For more information on Austen's reception and on her fate with more recent critics who have defined her humor as a pathological response to spinsterhood, see Claudia Johnson's introduction to *Jane Austen*.

17. Julia Epstein reviews Burney's reception history in *The Iron Pen* (197–231). Marilyn Butler discusses Edgeworth's fate at the hands of her biographers in the introduction to *Maria Edgeworth*.

18. Numerous studies have examined British women's rise to prominence in the world of letters over the course of the eighteenth century. See for example Jane Spencer's *The Rise of the Woman Novelist from Aphra Behn to Jane Austen*, Janet Todd's *The Sign of Angellica*, Cheryl Turner's *Living by the Pen*, and Catherine Gallagher's *Nobody's Story*.

Chapter 2

1. While the reliance on reason has provided a platform for many reformist movements of the eighteenth through twentieth centuries, the rhetoric of Enlightenment has also undoubtedly contributed to discourses of imperialism and colonialism, as well as to totalitarian doctrines. Max Horkheimer and Theodor Adorno's *Dialectic of Enlightenment* offers a critique of Enlightenment rhetoric and its implication in oppressive politics. As critics of Enlightenment discourse make clear, the metaphors of light and dark, the polarities of rational versus irrational beings, can be deployed to ostracize and/or dominate classes of people who are identified as outsiders or "others."

2. For a discussion of the learned lady as comic target, see Myra Reynolds's *The Learned Lady in England: 1650–1760*.

3. Patricia Yaeger attempts to dispel both misconceptions in her study of emancipatory strategies in women's writing. She argues that, in order to understand the rebelliousness of early women writers, we need to develop a "feminist theory of play" (211): "When a description of women's writing as 'play' is left out of feminist theory, when we take the weight of patriarchy—its force and inevitability—too seriously, we miss a great deal of what goes on in women's texts" (227). In spite of her contributions to both textual analysis and feminist comic theory, Yaeger does not attempt to historicize her argument and thus misses out on the primary source of women's playfulness in eighteenth-century feminist texts—their playful rationality. Whereas Yaeger, in her discussion of Mary Wollstonecraft, sees rationality as being at odds with playfulness in *A Vindication*, I argue that Wollstonecraft is freed for feminist play precisely because of her insistent rationality. Because Yaeger regards this aspect of Wollstonecraft's writing as separate from her intentions, as irrational, she misjudges both Wollstonecraft's achievement and her place in the history of feminism.

4. The 1975 Brentham Press facsimile reprint of *Woman Not Inferior to Man* attributes its authorship to Lady Mary Wortley Montagu. Even though there are no clear grounds for this attribution, Montagu did share some of the sentiments of "Sophia" and expressed comparable views in the essays she wrote concerning the status of women in her periodical, *The Nonsense of Common Sense*.

5. On the use of laughter as a revolutionary weapon, James Feibleman articulates the historical connection between comedy and revolution: "The pursuit of comedy always flourishes during periods of excessive unrest and change, troublous times of wars and revolutions. For at such a time more than at any other is it possible to see and to point out the contradictions and disvalues of actuality. Then also is the opportunity for great hope in the future: that it will be moulded nearer to the ideal logical order" (30). Because of its ability to unmask ideological order and to posit an ideal logical order, comedy would seem to have obvious applications for feminist writers at the end of the eighteenth century. Even though several studies have elaborated on the influence of the French Revolution on the development of British feminism (see, for example, Alice Browne's *The Eighteenth Century Feminist Mind*, Jane Rendall's *The Origins of Modern Feminism*, and Katharine Rogers's *Feminism in Eighteenth-*

Century England), none has evaluated the role of humor in feminist writings of the period.

6. In utilizing metaphors of slavery, Wollstonecraft does not take into account British involvement in actual colonial slavery. Several recent works have situated eighteenth-century feminist discourse in relation to the colonialism and orientalism of the period: Moira Ferguson's *Subject to Others* and *Colonialism and Gender Relations from Mary Wollstonecraft to Jamaica Kincaid;* Joyce Zonana's "The Sultan and the Slave."

7. Bakhtin discusses the struggle for control of discourse as bound up with political change. He identifies parodic stylization as an important tool for overcoming the "persuasive discourse" of the dominant group: "This process—experimenting by turning persuasive discourse into speaking persons—becomes especially important in those cases where a struggle against such images has already begun, where someone is striving to liberate himself from the influence of such an image and its discourse by means of objectification, or is striving to expose the limitations of both image and discourse. The importance of struggling with another's discourse, its influence on the history of an individual's coming to ideological consciousness, is enormous. One's own discourse and one's own voice, although born of another or dynamically stimulated by another, will sooner or later begin to liberate themselves from the authority of the other's discourse" (348). In novels, the process Bakhtin describes can be carried out through characters' speeches that may be directly or implicitly satirized by the narrator, other characters, and the context. According to Bakhtin, the novel can be an important site for covert resistance to oppression. As a polemical text, *A Vindication of the Rights of Woman* openly ridicules patriarchal discourse by parodying its rhetoric.

8. Walpole flung this famous insult at Wollstonecraft in response to her attack on Marie Antoinette in her essay on the French Revolution, not in response to her feminist tract. As R. M. Janes points out, "Walpole's hostility was directed against the female republican writer, and not against the vindicator of the rights of woman" (299).

9. Although Little examines twentieth-century authors and views an awareness of women's oppression as more available to these later authors, she posits exceptional circumstances from which revolu-

tionary comedy could emerge: "We can expect . . . in a time of social change, that the work of writers who perceive themselves as 'outsiders,' as persons assigned to the threshold of a world that is not theirs, will manifest the distinctive features of inversion, mocked hierarchies, communal festivity, and redefinition of sex identity. If the work of such writers is comic, it will be comedy that mocks the norm radically, and perhaps generates hints and symbols of new myths" (*Comedy* 6). Most of Little's conditions fit the comic aspects of the *Vindication:* Wollstonecraft writes as an "outsider" at a time of social change; she mocks hierarchies and prophesies a future in which people will laugh at the bugbears of her age; above all, she demands a redefinition of sexual identity.

10. In this sense, her humor applies what Emily Toth calls "the humane humor rule." According to this rule, which Toth sees as a main feature of women's humor, humane writers "do not satirize what cannot be helped . . . they mock people for their choices" ("Laughter" 201). Although I take issue with Toth's assumption of women's innate benevolence, her rule holds true in Wollstonecraft's case.

11. As Kathleen Rowe points out, "When men make jokes about women, they assert their already-existing social power over them. When women make jokes about men, they invert—momentarily— the social hierarchy" (19).

Chapter 3

1. See Chapter 1 for a discussion of negative aspects of the sentimental family.

2. In her study of Burney's life and works, Katharine Rogers underscores the importance of a supportive family background to the woman writer's career: "Like the Austens and the Edgeworths, the Burneys formed an enthusiastic support group—an inestimable advantage for modest ladies in an age when women novelists might still be suspected as disreputable or egotistical" (*Frances Burney* 10).

3. In Freud's view, jokes require three people (either present or implied) to produce their yield of pleasure: a teller, an object of aggression, and, in the case of hostile jokes, a "passionless third person" who embodies conventional moral restrictions (103). In hostile jokes, the third person advocates the renunciation of hostile deeds,

so the teller uses a joke to win over the third person and take sides with him against the enemy: "By making our enemy small, inferior, despicable or comic, we achieve in a roundabout way the enjoyment of overcoming him—to which the third person, who has made no efforts, bears witness by his laughter" (103).

While I find Freud's theory of tendentious jokes to be a useful account of how aggression gets channeled into humorous outlets, I must point out that such jokes are in Freud's view the province of men, whom he believes to be naturally more aggressive than women. See Frances Gray's critique of Freud's comic theory in *Women and Laughter* (28–29).

4. In a similar vein, Susan Purdie argues that "joking paradigmatically involves a discursive exchange whose distinctive operation involves the *marked* transgression of the Symbolic Law and whose effect is thereby to constitute jokers as 'masters' of discourse: as those able to break and to keep the basic rule of language" (5).

5. Despite her use of therapeutic laughter, Burney suffered from weak health and bouts of extreme depression during her years at court. Nevertheless, the fact that she joined in fellowship and raillery at such a bleak point in her life harkens back to her early use of laughter as a conspiratorial tool and as a safety valve.

6. One could argue that, in mocking other women, such as her stepmother and Mrs. Schwellenberg, Burney was taking out her hostility on acceptable targets within the patriarchal system and possibly even engaging in self-hatred or misogyny. I take up some of these issues in Chapter 6 in my discussion of the risks and advantages of satirizing women, and, as I show in Chapter 5, Burney also made men the butts of her jokes.

7. See the preface to *Joseph Andrews* and my discussion of it in Chapter 1.

8. See Marilyn Butler's biography (45–48) for a more detailed account of Edgeworth's "naughtiness."

9. Edgeworth more directly contributed to the debate on women's rights with the partly satirical *Letters for Literary Ladies* (1795).

10. For more detailed discussions of *The Wanderer* and feminism, see Rose Marie Cutting's "A Wreath for Fanny Burney's Last Novel" and "Defiant Women."

11. Mr. Scope's fear of the contagion that will begin in a milliner's shop may be connected with contemporary fears about the effects of the novel on the lower classes. Joyce Tompkins identifies the milliner's apprentice as an emblem of the novel-buying lower orders (2). Nineteenth-century essayist William Hazlitt, for one, claimed that "only young ladies from the boarding-school or milliners' girls, read all the new novels that come out" (320).

Chapter 4

1. Hazlitt refers to Burney as Madame D'Arblay throughout his essay with this one exception, which occurs immediately after a full paragraph on women's nature. By returning her to the status of a "miss," he performs an act of belittlement that is mirrored by the message he conveys about women in general.

2. See Marlene LeGates's "The Cult of Womanhood in Eighteenth-Century Thought," Mary Poovey's *The Proper Lady and the Woman Writer*, Nancy Armstrong's *Desire and Domestic Fiction*, and Kathryn Shevelow's *Women and Print Culture* for analyses of the ideal domestic woman.

3. Although Burney was less than twenty years old when she penned her praise of Maria Allen, we can hear echoes of her youthful longing for a "new & Open path" forty years later in Elinor Joddrel's lament, "Alas! Alas! . . . must Elinor too—must even Elinor!—. . . find that she has strayed from the beaten road, only to discover that all others are pathless!" (*The Wanderer* 836).

4. Edgeworth undoubtedly modeled her piece on Jane Collier's 1753 *Essay on the Art of Ingeniously Tormenting*, which begins with an inversion of the Golden Rule, advising its readers to do unto others what they would *least* wish to have done unto them. Austen and Burney also seem to have enjoyed Collier's essay: Burney alludes to it in *The Wanderer* in her presentation of that consummate tormenter, Mrs. Ireton, and Austen's Mrs. Norris practices Collier's lessons on the hapless Fanny Price in *Mansfield Park*. I examine Collier's essay in greater length in Chapter 7 and discuss Burney's Mrs. Ireton and Austen's Mrs. Norris in Chapter 6.

5. Alison Sulloway develops a thesis that reinforces my own: "The

generic topics of eighteenth-century women satirists, such as Austen and her favorite fictional predecessors, Frances Burney and Maria Edgeworth, included not only the abusers of women and other underdogs but also the very patriarchal systems that granted men absolute legal and social power over them" (xvi).

6. Halifax devotes a large section of his *Advice to a Daughter* (1688) to detailing the varieties of ill temper that a husband may exhibit and to suggesting diplomatic strategies for the unfortunate wife. Lest we see Halifax's views as having become outdated by the end of the century, we should recall that Richard Steele found this section of Halifax's essay so compelling that he reprinted it in *The Ladies Library, Written by a Lady*, a work that was influential well into the nineteenth century.

7. Two particularly useful studies are Kenneth Moler's *Jane Austen's Art of Allusion*, which provides references to specific targets of Austen's literary satire, and Claudia Johnson's *Jane Austen*, which places the elements of literary parody in a political context.

8. Rose Marie Cutting discusses the feminist message of *The Wanderer* in "A Wreath for Fanny Burney's Last Novel."

9. Possibly a reference to Wollstonecraft's "horse-laugh" in *A Vindication* (see my discussion in Chapter 2 of Wollstonecraft's defiant laughter).

Chapter 5

1. The "sic" is Troide's interpolation (Burney, *Early Journals* 331).

2. Troide includes this letter in an appendix as Allen's "earliest surviving letter" to Burney (331).

3. See "A Laughter of Their Own" (201) and "Forbidden Jokes and Naughty Ladies" (11). Nancy Walker supports Toth's rule, arguing that women's laughter at males is based on specific examples, often stereotypes, of male foolishness and that women do not mock men in general (135–36). Judy Little makes a similar distinction between mocking individual norms and making fun of men ("Satirizing the Norm" 40).

4. Women laughing at men as a group or at the category of "man" has

political resonances that are different from men laughing at women as a group insofar as the power differential between men and women in male-dominated societies is slanted toward men. Of course, class and race differentials can exist within societies that place some women above some men; however, even when this is the case, "man" as a category tends to be accorded more power.

5. Mitchell has conducted several studies in which she argues that most anthropological accounts of humor have ignored gender differences in humor appreciation: "The Sexual Perspective in the Appreciation of Jokes" (1977), "Hostility and Aggression Toward Males in Female Joke Telling" (1977), and "Some Differences in Male and Female Joke-Telling" (1985). Female folklorists have an advantage over their male colleagues when it comes to researching women's oral humor—they can gain access to circles that would normally exclude men. For example, Rayna Green was able to collect specimens of Southern women's bawdy humor from the source; as she puts it, "the dirt stays in the kitchen" (30). Like Mitchell, Green found that men figure prominently in women's humor: "in general, men are more often the victims of women's jokes than not. Tit for tat, as we say. Usually the subject for laughter is men's boasts, failures, or inadequacies" (31).

6. David Monaghan, for instance, while acknowledging that Austen's "keen individual intelligence" conflicted with eighteenth-century conservative views of women, claims she nonetheless believed that women "have a crucial role to play in preserving the *status quo*" (110). Monaghan concludes his essay on "Jane Austen and the Position of Women" by emphasizing that her conformist stance prevents her from entertaining a feminist position unless everyone else goes along with it: "Only when the society changes does Jane Austen look for a change in the woman's area of activity" (121). For examinations of various aspects of Austen's relation to the feminism of her day, see Devoney Looser's recent collection, *Jane Austen and Discourses of Feminism*.

7. Austen probably had this passage in mind when she offers up Mr. Collins's reading of Fordyce's *Sermons* to Lydia Bennet's inattention (*Pride and Prejudice* 68).

8. Sylvana Tomaselli argues that the "conceptualisation of the condition of woman as one of slavery is so frequent as to be almost a common-place in the Enlightenment" (112). Tomaselli's "The En-

lightenment Debate on Women" uncovers a tradition which linked women "to culture and the process of its historical development" (101).

9. Allen's boldness in borrowing Featherstone's clothing contrasts sharply with Burney's stage fright during the actual theatrical performance. Burney compares her paralysis to her fear of a male authority figure: "I had lost all power of speaking steadily, & almost of being understood; & as to action, I had not the presence of mind to attempt it: surely, only Mr. Crisp could excite such terror in me!" (*Early Journals* 162).

10. As Alice Browne points out, "eighteenth-century writers were usually being ironic when they referred to men as the 'Lords of Creation,' and fictional women were allowed some spirited parodies of the rhetoric of male superiority" (25).

11. Lord Merton, in *Evelina*, indicates a similar desire to dominate his fiancée by wringing his whip as he pays her a compliment: "'You have been, as you always are,' said he twisting his whip with his fingers, 'all sweetness'" (280). In this gesture, Burney suggests that Lady Louisa's control of her suitor will be over once they cross the threshold of matrimony.

12. Burney calls Dubster's taste into question along with his ability to appraise women. In the chapter entitled "Specimens of Taste," Burney provides a detailed description of Dubster's humorously kitschy domestic nest: "on the first story, a little balcony, decorated in the middle and at each corner with leaden images of Cupids; and, in the attic story, a very small venetian window, partly formed with minute panes of glass, and partly with glazed tiles; representing, in blue and white, various devices of dogs and cats, mice and birds, rats and ferrets, as emblems of the conjugal state" (274). This insipid iconography relates Mr. Dubster's bad taste in architecture to his bad values concerning marriage and women. His poor-quality imitations of upper-class property (a hole in the ground for a grotto, a dirty pond with a mass of rubbish in the middle for a lake with an island, and a zigzag path through some low brushwood for a labyrinth) reveal the limitations of his imagination. Just as in his sexist statements, where he unjustly attacks women and unwittingly parodies male power, in his building practices he mindlessly imitates what he cannot comprehend.

13. Burney herself would have learned Latin had her father not feared the scorn that such knowledge might bring upon her. As Hester Thrale angrily reports, "Dr. Burney did not like his Daughter should learn Latin even of *Johnson* who offered to teach her for Friendship, because then She would have been as wise as himself forsooth, & Latin was too Masculine for Misses—a narrow Souled Goose-Cap the Man must be at last" (502).

14. Warren Roberts notes that Austen's family on both sides had ties to Oxford: an ancestor of her mother helped found St. John's College; and her grandfather, father, and two of her brothers were Oxford graduates (17).

15. Edgeworth does not seem to employ comic male authority figures in her fiction. She did, however, boast that "a female spirit of opposition" played a role in her relations with her own father (qtd. in Butler 288).

16. She also offers an example of Natalie Zemon Davis's idea of "woman on top," a form of carnivalesque behavior practiced during times of political unrest: "Play with the various images of woman on top . . . kept open an alternate way of conceiving family structure" (172). Davis explains that for a culture that found it difficult to see the family as an institution with a history that could change through time, "the ambiguous woman on top of the world of play made the unruly option a more conceivable one" (175).

17. In their mockery of patriarchal men, Burney, Edgeworth, and Austen identify the root of women's oppression. Dale Spender writes of exposing the myth of male supremacy as a project for the most radical feminism: "If and when sufficient members of society no longer give consensus to the myth of male superiority, if and when they no longer act in a manner which acquiesces in that superiority and permits it to go unchallenged, then, rather than being taken for granted, that power will need to be defended or transformed" (2). By disclosing that what men define as important might not be so valuable after all, these novelists demonstrate how a shift in perspective can challenge male superiority and go a long way toward undercutting patriarchal power.

18. Even the avowedly conservative Hannah More, who tentatively concedes that men's intellects are superior to women's, protests against universal male supremacy: "the weakest man instantly lays hold on

the concession; and, on the mere ground of sex, plumes himself on his own individual superiority; inferring, that the silliest man is superior to the first rate woman" (*Strictures* 2.27).

Chapter 6

1. As in most cases of feminist writing of the period, here issues of identification and difference are cast as having importance primarily within the scope of white, middle- or upper-class experience. For an exploration of early British women writers and race relations, see Moira Ferguson's *Subject to Others*.

2. For a more complete discussion of eighteenth-century misogynist satire, see Felicity Nussbaum's *The Brink of All We Hate*.

3. For example, though one might argue that Swift and Pope had reformist agendas in writing their satires against women (i.e., they wanted to discourage bad behavior and to encourage a higher standard for women), we cannot doubt the uses to which their satire was put during the century and beyond. Pope's phrase "Most women have no character at all" was frequently detached from its literary context, a context which might in some ways mitigate its misogynistic tone.

4. See Vincent Carretta's reprinting and discussion of both engravings in *Eighteenth-Century Life* 6.1 (1980) and 6.2–3 (1981).

5. The argument underlying Mrs. Arlbery's statements may be traced back to that of Mary Astell, who contends that women ought to give serious thought to the consequences of marrying, since in doing so they choose to give up their liberty.

6. I discuss Collier's *Art of Ingeniously Tormenting* in relation to violent comedy in Chapter 7. Both Mrs. Ireton and Austen's Mrs. Norris take their cues from Collier's model.

7. Betty Rizzo traces the biographical basis of Burney's concern for humble dependents in *Companions Without Vows*. She sees Mrs. Ireton as a satirical portrait of Mrs. Schwellenberg, the woman who tormented Burney during her service at court. As Rizzo argues, Mrs. Ireton and the two other older women who abuse the heroine—Mrs. Maple and Mrs. Howel—are "all the more terrifying because they have totally bought into the benefits of patriarchal privilege" (107).

Chapter 7

1. Breton's *Anthologie de l'humour noir* (1939), for instance, contains only male authors, as does Bruce Friedman's *Black Humor* (1965) and Douglas Davis's *The World of Black Humor* (1967). Friedman's anthology suggests in the cartoon on its cover that "black humor" is intrinsically misogynist and inaccessible to women. From out of a black box (with a pink bra caught in its lid) one caption reads, "Darling, how could you possibly laugh at a time like this (sob)? It's just so sick (groan!). What's that book called, any way?". The other caption responds, "BLACK HUMOR, my dear (ha! ha! ha!) BLACK HUMOR, my darling (evil snicker!)."

2. Lawrence Stone estimates that during this period roughly one-third of all infants died within fifteen days of birth and that between a quarter and a third of the children of peers and peasants died before the age of fifteen (68). Moreover, childbirth was as dangerous for the woman as it was for the infant. In difficult births, the baby might be pulled out in pieces with a hooked instrument, a practice that usually killed the mother as well; even in seemingly successful deliveries, as in the case of Mary Wollstonecraft, the onset of puerperal fever often ended the mother's life.

3. In Edgeworth's *Castle Rackrent* (1800), Sir Kit imprisons his wife for seven years because, as a Jew, she disliked having pork on their table. To justify the inclusion in her novel of a situation that her readers might consider extraordinary, Edgeworth cites a well-known contemporary case: "This part of the history of the Rackrent family can scarcely be thought credible; but in justice to honest Thady, it is hoped the reader will recollect the history of the celebrated Lady Cathcart's conjugal imprisonment" (29).

4. One comic theorist argues that such humor provides a key to the mental state of oppressed people: "Gallows humor is an unmistakable index of the morale and spirit of resistance of the oppressed, the absence of which reveals either resigned indifference or a serious breakdown in the will to resist tyrannization" (Boskin 49).

5. One eighteenth-century woman writes of the violent temperament of one husband in terms remarkably similar to Collier's: "He is thought to be one of the worst humoured men in the world. He says if his Lady be a good-natured woman he will break her heart, and if she be ill natured he will break her neck" (qtd. in Brophy 174).

6. Park Honan claims that Austen modeled Alice after herself to entertain her family with a comic account of her own red cheeks
   (71–72).

7. John Halperin, for example, denounces this section and the author
   who penned it: "only a woman deficient in feeling and, yes 'taste,'
   could have written it. . . . [Austen] stands revealed, personally, in
   the most unflattering light here" (305).

8. For example, Rousseau's ideal Sophie becomes beautiful when men
   look at her: "She is hardly pretty at first sight, but the more one sees
   her, the better she looks." Even as he claims to deny the importance
   of beauty, Rousseau rhapsodizes on Sophie's beautiful body: "no one
   could have a better figure, a more beautiful complexion, a whiter
   hand, a daintier foot" (393). Wordsworth's famous assertion "we
   murder to dissect" correctly describes the violence inherent in such
   objectification.

9. Paul McGhee explains how gender can influence humor reception:
   "The humor of any hostile joke depends on who tells the joke and
   under what circumstances. Thus, a female-disparaging joke will be
   funnier to women if it is told by another woman than if a man tells
   it" (208).

10. In *Tom Jones*, for example, Fielding includes not fewer than four
    scenes of female exposure that intermingle violence and grotesque
    images of women's bodies. Each scene is intended to be comic,
    and each reveals something about the position of women in mid-
    eighteenth-century England, but they all tend to reinforce the sta-
    tus quo in disturbing ways. They merit attention here in order to
    illustrate how they differ from a feminist comedy of exposure.
        The first scene of female exposure occurs when Mrs. Partridge
    attacks her husband because she believes him to be the father of
    Jenny Jones's child. Fielding prepares the reader for comedy by in-
    troducing Mrs. Partridge's wrath with an extended simile, likening
    her to a savage feline. And, indeed, she lashes out ferociously, but
    only to be subdued the more completely.

> Not with less fury [than a cat] did Mrs. Partridge
> fly on the poor pedagogue. Her tongue, teeth and
> hands, fell all upon him at once. His wig was in
> an instant torn from his head, his shirt from his
> back, and from his face descended five streams of

blood, denoting the number of claws with which nature had unhappily armed the enemy.

Mr. Partridge acted for some time on the defensive only; indeed he attempted only to guard his face with his hands; but as he found that his antagonist abated nothing of her rage, he thought he might, at least, endeavour to disarm her, or rather to confine her arms; in doing which, her cap fell off in the struggle, and her hair being too short to reach her shoulders, erected itself on her head; her stays likewise, which were laced through one single hole at the bottom, burst open, and her breasts, which were much more redundant than her hair, hung down below her middle; her face was likewise marked with the blood of her husband; her teeth gnashed with rage; and fire, such as sparkles from a smith's forge, darted from her eyes. So that altogether, this Amazonian heroine might have been an object of terror to a much bolder man than Mr. Partridge.

He had, at length, the good fortune, by getting possession of her arms, to render those weapons, which she wore at the ends of her fingers, useless; which she no sooner perceived, than the softness of her sex prevailed over her rage, and she presently dissolved in tears, which soon after concluded in a fit. (97)

This violently comic passage has the overall effect of taming the "Amazonian" woman by mocking her body: when Fielding exposes her spiky hair and sagging breasts, he converts her into a spectacle for the reader and effectively violates this character's independence of will. Partridge has only to grab her arms for her to be reduced to the blubbering female the reader has been led to expect.

Two of the other three scenes of female exposure in *Tom Jones* follow the same pattern. In the first of these, Molly Seagrim, another Amazon whose appearance is described as having "very little of feminine in it" (169), does battle with Goody Brown; after a violent skirmish, both are naked from the waist up. Fielding devotes a good deal of space to a discussion of their breasts by pointing out that women fighters like to hit each other's breasts as a particularly deadly tactic and then lingering over a description of Goody Brown's as "resembling an antient piece of parchment, upon which anyone might have drummed a considerable while, without doing her any great damage" (175). Not too subtly, Fielding equates a fierce spirit with masculinity and vulnerability with femininity through his denigration of these two female bodies.

In the last of the three bare-breasted scenes, Tom Jones discovers Mrs. Waters "stript half naked, under the hands of a ruffian, who had put his garter round her neck, and was endeavouring to draw her up to a tree" (440–41). After rescuing the apparent victim of an attempted rape, Tom has trouble taking his eyes away from her well-shaped breasts, a task not made easier by the woman, who refuses to accept his offer of a coat and chooses instead to walk bare-breasted behind him to the nearest town. Later, when Mrs. Waters falsely cries out "rape" to protect her reputation, the earlier situation seems to have been less like an attempted rape and more like an illicit sexual encounter with consensual elements of violence.

These scenes, in which minor women characters are stripped and exposed, are more graphic than the final scene that we will consider, but not any more disturbing. Fielding subjects even the fair Sophia to another's demeaning gaze. In a comic moment of failed gallantry, Sophia falls from her horse into the arms of a rescuing landlord, only to be dropped the next instant because he cannot bear her weight; during this fall she inadvertently exposes her private parts. When Sophia rises from the ground "an immoderate grin . . . rising from the bye-standers . . . made her suspect what had really happened." Although Fielding coyly withholds a description from "those readers who are capable of laughing at the offence given to a young lady's delicacy" (512), his underlying message seems to be that this demeaning type of exposure can happen to any woman who adopts male behavior or engages in rebellious activities, such as running away from home.

Fielding's female grotesques and female exposures highlight a male-centered perspective on unruly women. Their force must be checked, and even one who is praised for her submissiveness—as is Sophia—must have her power further curbed by an untimely fall. Although Fielding was not without some sympathy for women's rights (see Angela Smallwood's study of Fielding and early eighteenth-century feminism, *Fielding and the Woman Question*), he bares women's bodies with little regard for the antifeminist implications of his comedy.

Works Cited

Addison, Joseph, and Richard Steele. *The Spectator*. Ed. Donald Bond. 5 vols. Oxford: Clarendon P, 1965.

Alexander, William. *The History of Women, From the Earliest Antiquity to the Present Time*. Dublin, 1779.

Allen, Robert Thomas. "Women Have No Sense of Humor." *Maclean's* 64 (1 June 1951): 18+.

Armstrong, Nancy. *Desire and Domestic Fiction: A Political History of the Novel*. New York: Oxford UP, 1987.

Astell, Mary. *The First English Feminist: Reflections Upon Marriage and Other Writings by Mary Astell*. Ed. Bridget Hill. London: Gower, 1986.

———. *Some Reflections Upon Marriage*. 4th ed. 1730. New York: Source Book, 1970.

Austen, Henry. "Biographical Notice of the Author." Vol. 5 of *The Novels of Jane Austen*. 3d ed. Ed. R. W. Chapman. Oxford: Oxford UP, 1933.

Austen, Jane. *Emma*. 1816. Vol. 4 of *The Novels of Jane Austen*. 3d ed. Ed. R. W. Chapman. Oxford: Oxford UP, 1933.

———. *Jane Austen's Letters to Her Sister Cassandra and Others*. 2d ed. Ed. R. W. Chapman. London: Oxford UP, 1959.

———. *Mansfield Park*. 1814. Vol. 3 of *The Novels of Jane Austen*. 3d ed. Ed. R. W. Chapman. Oxford: Oxford UP, 1933.

———. *Minor Works*. Vol. 6 of *The Novels of Jane Austen*. 3d ed. Ed. R. W. Chapman. Oxford: Oxford UP, 1933.

———. *Northanger Abbey*. 1818. Vol. 5 of *The Novels of Jane Austen*. 3d ed. Ed. R. W. Chapman. Oxford: Oxford UP, 1933.

———. *Persuasion*. 1818. Vol. 5 of *The Novels of Jane Austen*. 3d ed. Ed. R. W. Chapman. Oxford: Oxford UP, 1933.

———. *Pride and Prejudice*. 1813. Vol. 2 of *The Novels of Jane Austen*. 3d ed. Ed. R. W. Chapman. Oxford: Oxford UP, 1933.

———. *Sense and Sensibility*. 1811. Vol. 1 of *The Novels of Jane Austen*. 3d ed. Ed. R. W. Chapman. Oxford: Oxford UP, 1933.

Bakhtin, Mikhail. "Discourse in the Novel." *The Dialogic Imagination*. Trans. Caryl Emerson and Michael Holquist. Ed. Michael Holquist. Austin: UP of Texas, 1981.

Barreca, Regina. Introduction. *Last Laughs: Perspectives on Women and Comedy*. New York: Gordon and Breach, 1988.

———. *They Used to Call Me Snow White . . . But I Drifted: Women's Strategic Use of Humor*. New York: Viking, 1991.

———. *Untamed and Unabashed: Essays on Women and Humor in British Literature*. Detroit: Wayne State UP, 1994.

Beatts, Anne. "Why More Women Aren't Funny." *New Woman* Mar./Apr. 1976: 22+.

Bennett, John. *Strictures on Female Education*. 1795. New York: Source Book, 1971.

Bergson, Henri. "Laughter." *Comedy*. Ed. Wylie Sypher. Baltimore: Johns Hopkins UP, 1956.

Bevis, Richard. *The Laughing Tradition: Stage Comedy in Garrick's Day*. Athens: UP of Georgia, 1980.

Boskin, Joseph. *Humor and Social Change in Twentieth-Century America*. Boston: Trustees of the Public Library, 1979.

Breton, André. *Anthologie de l'humour noir*. 1939. Paris: J. J. Pauvert, 1989.

Brontë, Charlotte. *Jane Eyre*. 1847. London: Penguin, 1987.

Brophy, Elizabeth Bergen. *Women's Lives and the Eighteenth-Century English Novel*. Tampa: U of South Florida P, 1991.

Brown, Martha. "Fanny Burney's 'Feminism': Gender or Genre?" *Fetter'd or Free?: British Women Novelists, 1670–1815*. Eds. Mary Anne Schofield and Cecilia Macheski. Athens: Ohio UP, 1986.

Browne, Alice. *The Eighteenth Century Feminist Mind*. Sussex: Harvester P, 1987.

Brownstein, Rachel. "Jane Austen: Irony and Authority." *Last Laughs: Perspectives on Women and Comedy*. Ed. Regina Barreca. New York: Gordon and Breach, 1988.

Burdette, Robert. "Have Women a Sense of Humor?" *Harper's Bazaar* 36 (July 1902): 597–98.

Burke, Edmund. "Reflections on the Revolution in France." 1790. *The Works of the Right Honourable Edmund Burke*. Ed. Henry Rogers. London, 1841.

Burney, Frances. *Camilla; or a Picture of Youth*. 1796. Ed. Edward A. Bloom and Lillian D. Bloom. New York: Oxford UP, 1983.

————. *Cecilia; or Memoirs of an Heiress.* 1782. New York: Penguin, 1986.

————. *Diary and Letters of Madame D'Arblay.* 7 vols. Ed. Charlotte Barrett. London: Henry Colburn, 1842.

————. *The Early Diary of Frances Burney, 1768–1778.* Ed. Annie Raine Ellis. London: George Bell and Sons, 1889.

————. *The Early Journals and Letters of Fanny Burney.* Vol. 1. Ed. Lars E. Troide. Oxford: Clarendon, 1988.

————. *Evelina; or the History of a Young Lady's Entrance into the World.* 1778. Oxford: Oxford UP, 1982.

————. *The Wanderer; or Female Difficulties.* 1814. New York: Pandora, 1988.

Butler, Marilyn. *Maria Edgeworth: A Literary Biography.* Oxford: Oxford UP, 1972.

Carretta, Vincent. "An Abridgment of Mr. Pope's Essay on Man: An Unrecorded Print in the Library of Congress Collection." *Eighteenth-Century Life* 6.1 (1980): 102–5.

————. "An Essay on Woman: Another Unrecorded Print in the Library of Congress Collection." *Eighteenth-Century Life* 6.2–3 (1981): 114–18.

Cazamian, Louis. *The Development of English Humor.* Durham: Duke UP, 1952.

Chapman, Gerald Wester. "On Wit and Humor." *Literary Criticism in England, 1660–1800.* New York: Knopf, 1966.

Chapone, Hester. *Letters on the Improvement of the Mind.* 1773. Boston: W. Wells, 1809.

Chesterfield, Earl of. *Letters to his Son and Others.* London and Melbourne: Dent, 1986.

Cixous, Hélène. "The Laugh of the Medusa." *New French Feminisms: An Anthology.* Eds. Elaine Marks and Isabelle de Courtivron. Trans. Keith Cohen and Paula Cohen. New York: Schocken, 1981.

Collier, Jane. *Essay on the Art of Ingeniously Tormenting; with Proper Rules for the Exercise of the Pleasant Art.* 1753. London, 1795.

Cutting, Rose Marie. "Defiant Women: The Growth of Feminism in Fanny Burney's Novels." *Studies in English Literature* 17 (1977): 519–30.

————. "A Wreath for Fanny Burney's Last Novel: *The Wanderer's* Contribution to Women's Studies." *Illinois Quarterly* 37.3 (1975): 45–64.

Davis, Douglas M., ed. *The World of Black Humor: An Introductory Anthology of Selections and Criticism.* New York: Dutton, 1967.

Davis, Natalie Zemon. "Women on Top: Symbolic Sexual Inversion and Political Disorder in Early Modern Europe." *The Reversible World: Symbolic Inversion in Art and Society.* Ed. Barbara A. Babcock. Ithaca: Cornell UP, 1978.

Donaldson, Ian. *The World Upside-Down: Comedy From Jonson to Fielding.* Oxford: Clarendon, 1970.

Doody, Margaret A. *Frances Burney: The Life in the Works.* New Brunswick, NJ: Rutgers UP, 1988.

Douglas, Mary. "Jokes." *Implicit Meanings: Essays in Anthropology.* Boston: Routledge and Kegan Paul, 1978.

Drake, Judith. *An Essay in Defence of the Female Sex.* 1696. New York: Source Book, 1970.

Dresner, Zita Zatkin. "The Housewife as Humorist." *Regionalism and the Female Imagination* 3.2/3 (1977/78): 29–38.

Duff, William. *Letters on the Intellectual and Moral Character of Women.* 1807. *The Feminist Controversy in England 1788–1810.* Ed. Gina Luria. New York: Garland, 1974.

Eagleton, Terry. *The Rape of Clarissa: Writing, Sexuality and Class Struggle in Samuel Richardson.* Oxford: Basil Blackwell, 1982.

Eco, Umberto. "The Frames of Comic 'Freedom.'" *Carnival!* Ed. Thomas A. Sabeok. New York: Mouton, 1984.

Edgeworth, Maria. *Angelina; or L'amie Inconnue.* Vol. 2 of *Moral Tales for Young People.* 1801. *The Feminist Controversy in England 1788–1810.* Ed. Gina Luria. New York: Garland, 1974.

———. *Belinda.* 1801. New York: Pandora, 1986.

———. *Castle Rackrent.* 1800. Oxford: Oxford UP, 1969.

———. *Essay on the Noble Science of Self-Justification. Letters for Literary Ladies.* 1795. *The Feminist Controversy in England 1788–1810.* Ed. Gina Luria. New York: Garland, 1974.

———. *Helen.* 1834. New York: Pandora P, 1987.

———. *Letters for Literary Ladies.* 1795. *The Feminist Controversy in England 1788–1810.* Ed. Gina Luria. New York: Garland, 1974.

———. *Manoeuvering.* 1809. London, 1857.

———. *Patronage.* 1814. New York: Pandora P, 1986.

Eimerl, Sarel. "Can Women Be Funny?" *Mademoiselle* 15 (Nov. 1962): 151+.

Epstein, Julia. *The Iron Pen: Frances Burney and the Politics of Women's Writing.* Madison: U of Wisconsin P, 1989.

Feibleman, James. *In Praise of Comedy: A Study in Its Theory and Practice.* New York: Russell and Russell, 1962.

"Feminine Humour." *Saturday Review* 15 July 1871: 75.

Ferguson, Moira. *Colonialism and Gender Relations from Mary Wollstone-craft to Jamaica Kincaid.* New York: Columbia UP, 1993.

———, ed. *First Feminists: British Women Writers 1578–1799.* Bloomington: Indiana UP, 1985.

———. *Subject to Others: British Women and Colonial Slavery 1670–1834.* New York: Routledge, 1992.

Fielding, Henry. *The History of Tom Jones.* 1749. London: Penguin, 1986.

———. *Joseph Andrews.* 1742. Ed. R. F. Brissenden. London: Penguin Books, 1983.

Fordyce, James. *Sermons to Young Women.* Dublin: J. Williams, 1767.

Freud, Sigmund. *Jokes and Their Relation to the Unconscious.* Trans. James Strachey. New York: Norton, 1963.

Friedman, Bruce, ed. *Black Humor.* New York: Bantam, 1965.

Gallagher, Catherine. *Nobody's Story: The Vanishing Acts of Women in the Marketplace 1670–1820.* Berkeley and Los Angeles: U of California P, 1994.

Gilbert, Sandra, and Susan Gubar. *The Madwoman in the Attic: The Woman Writer and the Nineteenth-Century Literary Imagination.* New Haven: Yale UP, 1979.

Gisborne, Thomas. *An Enquiry into the Duties of the Female Sex.* 1797. *The Feminist Controversy in England 1788–1810.* Ed. Gina Luria. New York: Garland, 1974.

Goldsmith, Oliver. "An Essay on the Theatre or A Comparison between Laughing and Sentimental Comedy." 1773. *The Idea of Comedy: Essays in Prose and Verse, Ben Johnson to George Meredith.* Ed. W. K. Wimsatt. Englewood Cliffs, NJ: Prentice-Hall, 1969.

Gray, Frances. *Women and Laughter.* Charlottesville: UP of Virginia, 1994.

Green, Rayna. "Magnolias Grow in Dirt: The Bawdy Lore of Southern Women." *Southern Exposure* 4 (1977): 29–32.

Gregory, John. *A Father's Legacy to His Daughters.* 1774. *The Feminist Controversy in England 1788–1810.* Ed. Gina Luria. New York: Garland, 1974.

Grotjahn, Martin. *Beyond Laughter.* New York: McGraw-Hill, 1957.

Halifax, George Saville, Marquis. *The Lady's New-year's Gift: or, Advice to a Daughter.* 1688. *The Works of George Saville, Marquis of Halifax.* Vol. 2. Ed. Mark N. Brown. Oxford: Clarendon P, 1989.

Halperin, John. *The Life of Jane Austen.* Baltimore: Johns Hopkins UP, 1984.

Harding, D. W. "Regulated Hatred: An Aspect of the Work of Jane Austen." *Scrutiny* 8.4 (1940): 346–62.

Hare, Augustus J. C. *The Life and Letters of Maria Edgeworth.* 2 vols. Boston: Houghton, Mifflin and Co., 1895.

Hays, Mary. *Appeal to the Men of Great Britain in Behalf of Women.* 1798. *The Feminist Controversy in England 1788–1810.* Ed. Gina Luria. New York: Garland, 1974.

———. *Letters and Essays, Moral and Miscellaneous.* 1793. *The Feminist Controversy in England 1788–1810.* Ed. Gina Luria. New York: Garland, 1974.

Hazlitt, William. *The English Comic Writers and Miscellaneous Essays.* 1819. Everyman's Library. Ed. Ernest Rhys. London: Dent, 1946.

Hemlow, Joyce. "Fanny Burney and the Courtesy Books." *PMLA* 65 (1950): 732–61.

———. *The History of Fanny Burney.* London: Oxford UP, 1958.

Honan, Park. *Jane Austen: Her Life.* New York: Fawcett Columbine, 1987.

Horkheimer, Max, and Theodor W. Adorno. *Dialectic of Enlightenment.* New York: Herder and Herder, 1972.

Hugh-Jones, Siriol. "We Witless Women." *Twentieth Century* July 1961: 16–25.

Hume, Robert D. "Goldsmith and Sheridan and the Supposed Revolution of 'Laughing' against 'Sentimental' Comedy." *Studies in Change and Revolution: Aspects of English Intellectual History 1640–1800.* Ed. Paul J. Korshin. Menston: Scolar P, 1972.

Hunt, Leigh. *Wit and Humour, Selected From the English Poets.* London: Smith, Elder and Co., 1846.

Hunt, Linda. "A Woman's Portion: Jane Austen and the Female Character." *Fetter'd or Free?: British Women Novelists, 1670–1815.* Eds. Mary Anne Schofield and Cecilia Macheski. Athens: Ohio UP, 1986.

Hutcheson, Francis. *Reflections Upon Laughter.* Glasgow, 1750.

Isaak, Jo Anna. *Feminism and Contemporary Art: The Revolutionary Power of Women's Laughter.* London and New York: Routledge, 1996.

James, Henry. "The Lesson of Balzac." 1905. *The House of Fiction.* Ed. Leon Edel. London, 1957.

Janes, R. M. "On the Reception of Mary Wollstonecraft's *A Vindication of the Rights of Woman.*" Mary Wollstonecraft. *A Vindication of the Rights of Woman.* Norton Critical Edition. 2d ed. Ed. Carol H. Poston. New York: Norton, 1988.

Johnson, Claudia L. *Equivocal Beings: Politics, Gender and Sentimentality in the 1790s: Wollstonecraft, Radcliffe, Burney, and Austen.* Chicago: U of Chicago P, 1995.

————. *Jane Austen: Women, Politics, and the Novel.* Chicago: U of Chicago P, 1988.

Kaufman, Gloria. "Feminist Humor as a Survival Device." *Regionalism and the Female Imagination.* 3.2/3 (1977/78): 86–93.

————. Introduction. *Pulling Our Own Strings: Feminist Humor and Satire.* Bloomington: Indiana UP, 1980.

Kelly, Gary. "Jane Austen, Romantic Feminism, and Civil Society." *Jane Austen and Discourses of Feminism.* Ed. Devoney Looser. New York: St. Martin's, 1995.

Kirkham, Margaret. *Jane Austen: Feminism and Fiction.* New York: Methuen, 1986.

Kowaleski-Wallace, Beth. *Their Father's Daughters: Hannah More, Maria Edgeworth, and Patriarchal Complicity.* New York and Oxford: Oxford UP, 1991.

LeGates, Marlene. "The Cult of Womanhood in Eighteenth-Century Thought." *Eighteenth Century Studies* 10 (1976): 21–39.

Levine, Lawrence. "The Meaning of Slave Tales." *Black Culture and Black Consciousness: Afro-American Folk Thought from Slavery to Freedom.* New York: Oxford UP, 1977.

Little, Judy. *Comedy and the Woman Writer: Woolf, Spark, and Feminism.* Lincoln: UP of Nebraska, 1983.

————. "Humoring the Sentence: Women's Dialogic Comedy." *Women's Comic Visions.* Ed. June Sochen. Detroit: Wayne State UP, 1991.

————. "Satirizing the Norm: Comedy in Women's Fiction." *Regionalism and the Female Imagination.* 3.2/3 (1977/78): 39–49.

Looser, Devoney, ed. *Jane Austen and Discourses of Feminism.* New York: St. Martin's, 1995.

Lorde, Audre. *Sister Outsider: Essays and Speeches by Audre Lorde. The Crossing Press Feminist Series.* Freedom, CA: Crossing, 1984.

Martin, Robert Bernard. *The Triumph of Wit: A Study of Victorian Comic Theory.* Oxford: Clarendon P, 1974.

McGhee, Paul. *Humor: Its Origin and Development.* San Francisco: W. H. Freeman, 1979.

Meredith, George. "An Essay on Comedy." *Comedy.* Ed. Wylie Sypher. Baltimore: Johns Hopkins UP, 1956.

Michie, Helena. *Sororophobia: Differences Among Women in Literature and Culture.* New York: Oxford UP, 1992.

Mitchell, Carol. "Hostility and Aggression Toward Males in Female Joke Telling." *Frontiers* 3.3 (1978): 19–23.

————. "The Sexual Perspective in the Appreciation of Jokes." *Western Folklore* 36 (1977): 303–29.

————. "Some Differences in Male and Female Joke-Telling." *Women's Folklore, Women's Culture*. Eds. Rosan A. Jordan and Susan J. Kalčik. Philadelphia: UP of Pennsylvania, 1985.

Moler, Kenneth. *Jane Austen's Art of Allusion*. Lincoln: UP of Nebraska, 1968.

Monaghan, David. "Jane Austen and the Position of Women." *Jane Austen in a Social Context*. Ed. David Monaghan. London: Macmillan, 1981.

More, Hannah. *Coelebs in Search of a Wife*. London, 1808.

————. *Strictures on the Modern System of Female Education*. 1799. 2 vols. *The Feminist Controversy in England 1788–1810*. Ed. Gina Luria. New York: Garland, 1974.

Newell, Margaretta. "Are Women Humorous?" *Outlook and Independent* 14 Oct. 1931: 206+.

Nussbaum, Felicity. *The Brink of All We Hate: English Satires on Women: 1660–1750*. Lexington: UP of Kentucky, 1984.

Okin, Susan Moller. "Women and the Making of the Sentimental Family." *Philosophy and Public Affairs* 11.1 (1981): 65–88.

Outram, Dorinda. *The Body and the French Revolution: Sex, Class, and Political Culture*. New Haven: Yale UP, 1989.

Paulson, Ronald. *Satire and the Novel in Eighteenth-Century England*. New Haven: Yale UP, 1967.

Pennington, Lady Sarah. *A Mother's Advice to Her Absent Daughters*. 1761. Ed. Randolph Trumbach. New York: Garland, 1986.

Perry, Ruth. *Women, Letters, and the Novel*. New York: Amis, 1980.

Pollak, Ellen. *The Poetics of Sexual Myth: Gender and Ideology in the Verses of Swift and Pope*. Chicago: UP of Chicago, 1985.

Poovey, Mary. *The Proper Lady and the Woman Writer: Ideology as Style in the Works of Mary Wollstonecraft, Mary Shelley, and Jane Austen*. Chicago: UP of Chicago, 1984.

Pope, Katherine V. "The Divided Lives of Women in Literature." *Representations: Social Constructions of Gender*. Ed. Rhoda K. Unger. Amityville, NY: Baywood, 1988.

Priestley, J. B. *English Humour*. London: Longmans, Green, and Co., 1929.

Purdie, Susan. *Comedy: The Mastery of Discourse*. Toronto: University of Toronto P, 1993.

Rendall, Jane. *The Origins of Modern Feminism: Women in Britain, France and the United States, 1780–1860*. London: Macmillan, 1985.

Reynolds, Myra. *The Learned Lady in England: 1650–1760*. Boston: Houghton Mifflin, 1920.

Richardson, Samuel. *Sir Charles Grandison*. 1753–54. Ed. Jocelyn Harris. Oxford: Oxford UP, 1986.

Rizzo, Betty. *Companions Without Vows: Relationships Among Eighteenth-Century British Women*. Athens: U of Georgia P, 1994.

Roberts, Warren. *Jane Austen and the French Revolution*. London: Macmillan, 1979.

Rogers, Katharine M. *Feminism in Eighteenth-Century England*. Urbana: UP of Illinois, 1982.

———. *Frances Burney: The World of "Female Difficulties."* New York: Harvester Wheatsheaf, 1990.

———. "Inhibitions on Eighteenth-Century Women Novelists: Elizabeth Inchbald and Charlotte Smith." *Eighteenth Century Studies* 11 (1977): 63–78.

Rogers, Kay. "Deflation of Male Pretensions in Fanny Burney's *Cecilia*." *Last Laughs: Perspectives on Women and Comedy*. Ed. Regina Barreca. New York: Gordon and Breach, 1988.

Rousseau, Jean-Jacques. *Émile, or On Education*. 1762. Trans. Allan Bloom. New York: Basic Books, 1979.

Rowe, Kathleen. *The Unruly Woman: Gender and the Genres of Laughter*. Austin: U of Texas P, 1995.

Russo, Mary. "Female Grotesques: Carnival and Theory." *Feminist Studies/Critical Studies*. Ed. Teresa de Lauretis. Bloomington: Indiana UP, 1986.

Sanborn, Kate. *The Wit of Women*. New York: Funk & Wagnalls, 1885.

Sanday, Peggy Reeves. *Female Power and Male Dominance: On the Origins of Sexual Inequality*. Cambridge: Cambridge UP, 1981.

Shaftesbury, Anthony, Earl of. "An Essay on the Freedom of Wit and Humour." *Characteristics of Men, Manners, Opinions and Times*. 1711. Ed. John M. Robertson. London, 1900.

Sheppard, Alice. "From Kate Sanborn to Feminist Psychology: The Social Context of Women's Humor, 1885–1985." *Psychology of Women Quarterly* 10 (1986): 155–70.

Shevelow, Kathryn. *Women and Print Culture: The Construction of Femininity in the Early Periodical*. London: Routledge, 1989.

Simon, Richard Keller. *The Labyrinth of the Comic: Theory and Practice from Fielding to Freud*. Tallahassee: Florida State UP, 1985.

Simons, Judy. *Fanny Burney*. London: Macmillan, 1987.

Smallwood, Angela. *Fielding and the Woman Question: The Novels of Henry Fielding and the Feminist Debate 1700–1750*. New York: St. Martin's, 1989.

Smith, Hilda L. *Reason's Disciples: Seventeenth-Century English Feminists.* Urbana: UP of Illinois, 1982.

"Sophia." *Woman Not Inferior to Man.* 1739. London: Brentham, 1975.

Southam, B. C., ed. *Jane Austen: The Critical Heritage.* Vol. 1. London: Routledge and Kegan Paul, 1968.

Spacks, Patricia Meyer. "Austen's Laughter." *Last Laughs: Perspectives on Women and Comedy.* Ed. Regina Barreca. New York: Gordon and Breach, 1988.

Spencer, Jane. *The Rise of the Woman Novelist from Aphra Behn to Jane Austen.* New York: Basil Blackwell, 1986.

Spender, Dale. *Man Made Language.* London: Routledge & Kegan Paul, 1980.

Spingarn, J. E. Introduction. *Critical Essays of the Seventeenth Century.* Bloomington: Indiana UP, 1957.

Stevens, Wallace. *The Necessary Angel: Essays on Reality and the Imagination.* New York: Vintage, 1951.

Stone, Lawrence. *The Family, Sex and Marriage in England 1500–1800.* London: Weidenfeld and Nicolson, 1977.

Straub, Kristina. *Divided Fictions: Fanny Burney and Feminine Strategy.* Lexington: UP of Kentucky, 1987.

Sulloway, Alison. *Jane Austen and the Province of Womanhood.* Philadelphia: U of Pennsylvania P, 1989.

Tave, Stuart M. *The Amiable Humorist: A Study in the Comic Theory and Criticism of the Eighteenth and Early Nineteenth Centuries.* Chicago: U of Chicago P, 1960.

Tayler, Edward W. Introduction. *Literary Criticism of Seventeenth-Century England.* New York: Knopf, 1967.

Thrale, Hester Lynch. *Thraliana: The Diary of Mrs. Hester Lynch Thrale.* Ed. Katharine C. Balderston. Oxford: Clarendon P, 1942.

Thurber, James. "But They Don't Seem to Know It." *Maclean's* 64 (1 June 1951): 19+.

Todd, Janet. Introduction. *Men by Women.* New York: Holmes and Meier, 1981.

———. *Sensibility: An Introduction.* New York: Methuen, 1986.

———. *The Sign of Angellica: Women, Writing and Fiction, 1660–1800.* London: Virago, 1989.

Tomaselli, Sylvana. "The Enlightenment Debate on Women." *History Workshop Journal* 20 (1985): 101–21.

Tompkins, Joyce. *The Popular Novel in England: 1770–1800.* Lincoln: UP of Nebraska, 1961.

Toth, Emily. "Forbidden Jokes and Naughty Ladies." *Studies in American Humor* 4 [New Series] 1/2 (Spring/Summer 1985): 7–17.

———. "A Laughter of Their Own: Women's Humor in the United States." *Critical Essays on American Humor*. Eds. William B. Clark and W. Craig Turner. Boston: G. K. Hall, 1984.

Turner, Cheryl. *Living by the Pen: Women Writers in the Eighteenth Century*. London and New York: Routledge, 1992.

Walker, Nancy. *A Very Serious Thing: Women's Humor and American Culture*. Minneapolis: UP of Minnesota, 1988.

Winston, Mathew. "Black Humor: To Weep with Laughing." *New York Literary Forum* 1 (1978): 31–43.

"Wit and Humour." *Westminster Review* 48 (1847): 13–31.

Wollstonecraft, Mary. *A Vindication of the Rights of Woman*. 1792. Norton Critical Edition. 2d ed. Ed. Carol H. Poston. New York: Norton, 1988.

Woolf, Virginia. "Jane Austen." *The Common Reader: First Series*. 1925. Ed. Andrew McNeillie. New York: Harcourt Brace Jovanovich, 1984.

———. "Professions for Women." *The Death of the Moth and Other Essays*. 1942. New York: Harcourt, Brace, 1942.

———. "Women Novelists." *Contemporary Writers*. 1965. New York: Harcourt Brace Jovanovich, 1976.

Yaeger, Patricia. *Honey-Mad Women: Emancipatory Strategies in Women's Writing*. New York: Columbia UP, 1988.

Young, Edward. *Love of Fame, The Universal Passion*. London, 1730.

Zonana, Joyce. "The Sultan and the Slave: Feminist Orientalism and the Structure of *Jane Eyre*." *Signs* 18.31 (1993): 592–617.

Index

Books in the HUMOR IN LIFE AND LETTERS SERIES